The Obstinate Questionings
of English Romanticism

The Obstinate Questionings
of English Romanticism

L. J. Swingle

Louisiana State University Press

Baton Rouge and London

Typeface: Linotron Aldus
Typesetter: G&S Typesetters, Inc.
Printer: Thomson-Shore, Inc.
Binder: John Dekker and Sons, Inc.

10 9 8 7 6 5 4 3 2 1

Chapters One and Two appeared, in somewhat different form, as "The Romantic Emergence: Multiplication of Alternatives and the Problem of Systematic Entrapment," *Modern Language Quarterly*, XXXIX (1978), 264–83, and "On Reading Romantic Poetry,"
Publications of the Modern Language Association, LXXXVI (1971), 974–81, respectively.
Chapter Four previously appeared, in somewhat different form, as "The Poets, the
Novelists, and the English Romantic Situation," *Wordsworth Circle*, X (1979), 218–28,
and is reprinted by permission.

Library of Congress Cataloging-in-Publication Data

Swingle, L. J., 1940–
    The obstinate questionings of English romanticism.
    Bibliography: p.
    Includes index.
    1. English literature—19th century—History and
criticism.   2. Romanticism—England.   3. Philosophy
in literature.   I. Title.
PR457.S9   1987   820'.9'145   87-3769
ISBN 0-8071-1353-0

For Nikki and Becca

But for those obstinate questionings
Of sense and outward things,
Fallings from us, vanishings;
Blank misgivings of a Creature
Moving about in worlds not realized . . .

WILLIAM WORDSWORTH
"Ode: Intimations of Immortality"

Contents

Acknowledgments

I am grateful to the American Philosophical Society for a grant that helped me considerably during an early stage in my research. My debt to Donald H. Reiman is incalculable, as this project was mostly his idea at its outset and he struggled with me on it through several stages and crises of its development. I also received aid beyond the call of custom from Stuart Curran, who pointed out to me some of the more silly errors and omissions in my thinking about the nineteenth century; from David S. Durant, who performed a like service in defense of the eighteenth century; and from Morse Peckham, who was most supportive of my good intentions and indulgent of my failure to live up to them. These good angels, of course, are not responsible for the deficiencies of the final product, since, like the Idiot Boy, I often persisted in hurly-burlying into the woods my own way. Karl Kroeber is the spirit in the woods.

Abbreviations Used in Notes

The Obstinate Questionings
of English Romanticism

Introduction

Thinking About Romanticism

T HE issue I am concerned with here is the relative prominence of questioning in relation to ideology in English Romantic writing. Were the Romantics fundamentally interested in articulating systems of belief—as, for example, a philosophy of organicism, a theory of the creative imagination, an epistemology grounded in the primacy of heart over head? Or were they, to the contrary, fundamentally dubious about such beliefs and interested, instead, in pursuing the questions that appear to militate against an ideological orientation of thought?

There has been considerable critical discussion of this issue in Romantic studies. For the first fifty years or so of the twentieth century the ideological position was generally dominant. Although there was some recognition of a skeptical streak running through Romantic writing—most clearly in the second-generation poets John Keats, Percy Bysshe Shelley, and George Gordon, Lord Byron—Romantic scholarship was usually preoccupied with the idea that Romanticism must be some sort of philosophical system, characterized by a fixed set of beliefs, discovery of which should allow the reader to make good sense of most of the important things going on in Romantic art.[1]

---

1 · Early studies of skeptical influences in Romanticism include: C. D. Thorpe, *The Mind of John Keats* (New York, 1926); D. G. James, *Scepticism and Poetry: An Essay on the Poetic*

1

Much conventional thinking today about what "Romantic" means traces back to this traditional critical approach to Romanticism. Articles in the more popular weekly magazines, for example, and class notes in our more conservative literary-survey courses are still apt to yield up such propositions as "Romantics love Nature" and "Romanticism celebrates the Individual over the General."

Stirring in the 1950s, however, and then growing into an increasingly prevalent critical orientation through the 1960s and the 1970s was an alternative approach that insisted upon the significance, and even primacy, of a probing, questioning impulse in Romantic thought. Morse Peckham, for example, noted the propensity of Romantic writers to view metaphysical activity "at right angles." Robert Langbaum, discussing Romanticism as a "modern tradition," emphasized the search undertaken by Romantic writers for an empiric ground for values, postulating that they discovered such a ground in the test of experience. Jack Stillinger showed that we readers are hoodwinking ourselves if we take Keats's "Eve of St. Agnes" to be a mere dreamlike Romantic expression of love's triumph over all obstacles. Earl R. Wasserman proposed that what unites Romantic writers is not their common beliefs but rather their common need to find a firm basis for belief. For this more recent direction in Romantic scholarship the key words for analysis of Romantic writing were not so much *philosophy* and *belief* but rather *skepticism* and *irony*.[2]

Imagination (London, 1937); E. W. Marjarum, *Byron as Skeptic and Believer* (New York, 1938); and, most influentially, C. E. Pulos, *The Deep Truth: A Study of Shelley's Skepticism* (Lincoln, Neb., 1954). The classic analysis of ideological Romantic theory is Morse Peckham's "Toward a Theory of Romanticism," *PMLA*, LXVI (1951), 5–23. Peckham later radically altered his approach to Romantic theory; see "On Romanticism: Introduction," *SIR*, IX (1970), 217–24. The most influential recent defenses of ideological Romantic theory are probably M. H. Abrams, *Natural Supernaturalism: Tradition and Revolution in Romantic Literature* (New York, 1971), and Jerome J. McGann, *The Romantic Ideology: A Critical Investigation* (Chicago, 1983).

2 · Morse Peckham, "The Place of Architecture in Nineteenth-Century Romantic Culture," in *The Triumph of Romanticism* (Columbia, S.C., 1970), 133; that essay originally appeared in 1956. Robert Langbaum, *The Poetry of Experience: The Dramatic Monologue in Modern Literary Tradition* (New York, 1957); "Romanticism as a Modern Tradition" is the title of the opening chapter. Jack Stillinger, "The Hoodwinking of Madeline: Scepticism in 'The Eve of

A still more recent entry to this field, contributing analyses that often ran parallel to explorations of Romantic skepticism and irony, was the critical movement loosely called Deconstruction. The combined, or sometimes entangled, influences of these various lines of reformation, as it were, in Romantic studies find dramatic expression in the discussions of Romanticism that now commonly inhabit scholarly books and journals and more advanced courses of university instruction. The reader who ventures any great distance into the labyrinth of Romantic scholarship today is likely to run upon such musings as: "The history of Romantic poetry and aesthetics can be seen as the gradual bringing to light of a counterplot within the apparently utopian narrative of Romantic desire, through the confrontation of recognitions initially hidden in the subtexts rather than the texts of works."[3] The drama of Romanticism here becomes one of tensions and undercuttings, wherein things hidden take things apparent by surprise, subtexts rising up to torpedo the assurances of texts.

If we turn our attention to Romantic writing itself, we can see pretty easily how the tension between the ideological and the anti-ideological orientation to Romanticism might have developed. The ideological position comes first, as it is the most obvious. When we look at Romantic poems, we find ourselves confronted with a lot of doctrinal propositions. William Blake's *The Marriage of Heaven and Hell* contains the assertion that "without Contraries is no progression" (Plate 3). William Wordsworth's "Tintern Abbey" gives us "Nature never did betray / The heart that loved her"

St. Agnes,'" *Studies in Philology*, LVIII (1961), 533–55; Earl R. Wasserman, "The English Romantics: The Grounds of Knowledge," *SIR*, IV (1964), 17–34. In more recent criticism important work bearing on the issue of Romantic skepticism includes Jerome J. McGann, *Fiery Dust: Byron's Poetic Development* (Chicago, 1968); Earl R. Wasserman, *Shelley: A Critical Reading* (Baltimore, 1971); Stuart Curran, *Shelley's Annus Mirabilis: The Maturing of an Epic Vision* (San Marino, Calif., 1975); Michael G. Cooke, *Acts of Inclusion: Studies Bearing on an Elementary Theory of Romanticism* (New Haven, 1979); John P. Farrell, *Revolution as Tragedy: The Dilemma of the Moderate from Scott to Arnold* (Ithaca, 1980); and Thomas McFarland, *Romanticism and the Forms of Ruin: Wordsworth, Coleridge, and the Modalities of Fragmentation* (Princeton, N.J., 1981). On Romantic irony, see esp. David Simpson, *Irony and Authority in Romantic Poetry* (Totowa, N.J., 1979), and Anne K. Mellor, *English Romantic Irony* (Cambridge, Mass., 1980).

3 · Tilottama Rajan, *Dark Interpreter: The Discourse of Romanticism* (Ithaca, 1980), 21.

(ll. 122–23), while Samuel Taylor Coleridge's "This Lime-Tree Bower My Prison" offers the alternative proposition that "Nature ne'er deserts the wise and pure" (l. 60). Keats's "Ode on a Grecian Urn" serves up the famous equation "Beauty is truth, truth beauty" (l. 49). The catalog could be extended indefinitely, providing such a wealth of propositions that the mind is teased into thoughts about how to order them all, how to find the common denominators that will make coherent sense of these apparent rallying cries of the Romantic "movement." This notion that Romanticism must indeed be a movement, some kind of forceful and positive assertion of beliefs, finds reinforcement in the apparent antipathy to doubt and questioning that occurs in some Romantic works. Blake's "Inspired Man" in *Milton* is moved to "cast off the idiot Questioner who is always questioning, / But never capable of answering" (Plate 41). Keats's sonnet "Why Did I Laugh Tonight?" laments the mind's experience of questioning.

> O mortal pain!
> O darkness! darkness! ever must I moan,
> To question heaven and hell and heart in vain!
> (ll. 6–8)

Shelley's "Alastor" commences with an appeal to the "Mother of this unfathomable world" that the unfathomable be made less so, as the poem's speaker seeks "to still these obstinate questionings / Of thee and thine" (ll. 26–27). Such passages make questioning seem a hindrance to the Romantic desire to gain or maintain ideological certainty.

However, the issue is not all that clear-cut. For example, when Shelley employs the phrase "obstinate questionings" in "Alastor," he is inviting us to recall the famous dramatic turn in Wordsworth's "Ode: Intimations of Immortality," in which questioning appears in a different light. The eighth stanza of Wordsworth's ode contains a lament for the "inevitable yoke" that time lays upon the growing child.

> Full soon thy Soul shall have her earthly freight,
> And custom lie upon thee with a weight,
> Heavy as frost, and deep almost as life!
> (ll. 128–30)

This darkest point of the ode sets up the dramatic reversal in the poem's ninth stanza, wherein Wordsworth offers his variation of the classic elegaic turn from the mind's brooding upon the frosty desolation of winter to its recognition of the warming consolations of spring: "O joy! that in our embers / Is something that doth live" (ll. 131–32). This "something" that is capable of rekindling our embers and thereby melting the encroaching frost of custom is the "thought of our past years." And the essence of this recollection of our past years, for which the poet now offers up his "song of thanks and praise," is the experience of questioning.

> But for those obstinate questionings
> Of sense and outward things,
> Fallings from us, vanishings.
> ("Intimations of Immortality," ll. 142–44)

These obstinate questionings that may have caused us such anguish and bewilderment in our youth, when we experienced them so powerfully, are now recognized to be, once we have in age nearly lost them, the warmth of life itself. They are by no means something to be dispelled; rather they must be recovered if we are to ward off a deadly winter.

This imagery of opposition between the frosty yoke of custom and the fiery embers of recollected questioning links Wordsworth's celebration of the questioning impulse to the myth of the fire-giving Prometheus, who plays such an important role in Romantic thought generally. Like Promethean fire, questioning is a flame that seems to produce both pain and delight. On the one hand, it is a light that burns, destroying all apparent havens of stable certainty and thus leaving the mind to torture itself in darkness, as in Keats's aforementioned sonnet. But, on the other hand, the destruction of those havens of stable certainty might be experienced, alternately, as a movement toward freedom. The flame melts the ice of winter, burning away the heavy yoke of customary belief. This highly charged tension is marked most dramatically in Blake's "Tyger," a poem composed entirely of a series of unanswered questions. Like this questioning, the beast of Blake's poem burns; but that burning is bright. The beast is fearful, but it is also "symmetrical." The implied promise of the Tyger's presence in the

Songs of Innocence and of Experience is that its flames may be capable of melting the snows of an imprisoning winter that Experience finds itself confronting: "A little black thing among the snow: / Crying weep, weep, in notes of woe!" ("The Chimney Sweeper," ll. 1–2). In Blake, Wordsworth's inevitable yoke of custom is called "mind-forg'd manacles" ("London," l. 8). In both Blake and Wordsworth, questioning is a flame whose burning offers the possibility of escape from chains.

This more affirmative view of the questioning impulse tends to find manifestation even in those Romantic poems that seem at first glance inimical to questioning. Although the youthful narrator of Shelley's "Alastor" yearns, so he thinks, to "still these obstinate questionings," he proceeds to tell the tale of a poet who is the most persistent of questioners.

> Does the dark gate of death
> Conduct to thy mysterious paradise,
> O Sleep?
>
> (ll. 211–13)

We follow the Poet's wanderings in pursuit of this question, wanderings described significantly in the imagery of heat and cold.

> When early youth had past, he left
> His cold fireside and alienated home
> To seek strange truths in undiscovered lands.
>
> (ll. 75–77)

These truths are never found, and we are left to contemplate only the Poet's death, wherein cold finally triumphs.

> —till the minutest ray
> Was quenched, the pulse yet lingered in his heart.
> It paused—it fluttered. But when heaven remained
> Utterly black, the murky shades involved
> An image, silent, cold, and motionless,
> As their own voiceless earth and vacant air.
>
> (ll. 657–62)

As "voiceless earth" and "vacant air" imply, the Poet's search for answers is fruitless. There are no voices or presences in the world outside the human questioner that can offer response. Yet the pervasive imagery of the poem—again that of a Promethean fire in contest with the cold—invites us to perceive the fruitless questing of the Poet as not foolish and misguided but profound. The questioning Poet is the fiery principle—"Obedient to the light / That shone within his soul" (ll. 492–93)—roaming through a cold, deadly darkness of "murky shades," until his "minutest ray" is finally quenched. The narrator's lament for the dead underscores the dramatic tension upon which Shelley is building his poem.

> But thou art fled
> Like some frail exhalation; which the dawn
> Robes in its golden beams.
> (ll. 686–88)

The fire burns and makes one yearn to avoid its painful presence. This burning also can finally kill. If the obstinate questioning cannot be stilled, it threatens to drive the questioner to an early death. But this fire is also what wards off the encroaching cold of the outer world. Without it we are left with only an "image, silent, cold, and motionless." As with Blake and Wordsworth, then, the deadly fire begins to look like the principle of life.

Keats's "Why Did I Laugh Tonight?" presents a mirror image of this twist of thought. In the midsection of the sonnet the tortuous questioning of heaven, hell, and heart is characterized as a "mortal pain," an anguish that kills. But then Keats executes a shifty maneuver as he moves to the poem's conclusion.

> Yet could I on this very midnight cease,
> And the world's gaudy ensigns see in shreds.
> Verse, fame, and beauty are intense indeed,
> But death intenser—death is life's high meed.
> (ll. 11–14)

The mortal pain of questioning metamorphoses into a death that is the "high meed" of life, the reward for living or perhaps the liquor of life itself.

The sense to be made of this turn is hinted at by the value terms *intense* and *intenser*. If the more intense is posited to be the more life rewarding or fulfilling, then the highest intensity of life experience must surely be a mortal pain. The experience of dying offers the most eloquent testimony to the existence and preciousness of the life that is being consumed. In Keats's poem, then, as in Shelley's, the apparent negative is transvalued. Obstinate questioning becomes associated with a heightened sense of life.

These evidences of the significant role played by questioning in Romantic writing suggest that the anti-ideological position in Romantic studies is probably correct. Romantic writing contains considerable ideology, but one has to consider its function. It generally appears in some sort of dramatic context that requires us to think about artistic ends that extend beyond or militate against dogmatic expression. When Wordsworth writes in "Tintern Abbey," "We see into the life of things" (l. 49), he immediately turns our attention from dogma to inquiry by adding in the next phrase of the poem, "If this / Be but a vain belief" (ll. 49–50). Accurate thinking about the nature of Romanticism would appear to demand investigation of the implications of this odd artistic maneuver: what does it mean for a writer to assert and undercut assertion in the same breath? Contemporary work on Romantic irony—most particularly Anne Mellor's *English Romantic Irony* and David Simpson's *Irony and Authority in Romantic Poetry*—has been fruitfully pursuing this line of inquiry.

There remains, though, considerable suspicion in some scholarly circles concerning the validity of the anti-ideological position. Several studies published in the 1980s seem bent upon reinstituting the proposition that systems of belief are the fundamental, defining factors in Romantic writing.[4]

---

4 · In "The Rise of Modern Science and the Genesis of Romanticism," *PMLA*, XCVII (1982), 8–30, Hans Eichner argues in terms of "Romantic systems" and "Romantic philosophy," assuming that one can refer sensibly to such quantities (14, 15). In *Romanticism and Ideology: Studies in English Writing, 1765–1830* (London, 1981), David Aers, Jonathan Cook, and David Punter are only slightly more cautious, dividing Romantic systems up into "different positions within a spectrum from revolt to counter-revolutionary affirmation of dominant ideologies and the 'status quo'" (3). In *English Romanticism: The Grounds of Belief* (De Kalb, Ill., 1983), John Clubbe and Ernest J. Lovell, Jr., propose that there is "a fundamental coherence in the beliefs" of the Romantic poets and that in the poets' "maturity" these beliefs "reveal a remarkable consistency" (1).

The most self-consciously theoretical of these counterreformation studies is Jerome J. McGann's *Romantic Ideology: A Critical Investigation.* Arguing that, just as most people once supposed, there is indeed a clear, definable "ideology of the Romantic tradition" in early-nineteenth-century English literature, McGann offers an interesting explanation for the movement of recent Romantic scholarship away from this perception. According to Mc-Gann, scholars who fail or refuse to recognize the ideological basis of Romantic writing thereby reveal themselves to be the victims of a Romantic ideology that pretends to distrust ideology.[5]

This incipient swerve back in the direction of Romanticism as ideology seems to me erroneous. But the motivation that appears to lie behind it is interesting and worth thinking about, because it brings into sharp relief some difficulties in the questioning orientation to Romanticism that need to be addressed. Part of the impetus behind revival of the ideological argument seems traceable to scholarly distaste for the excesses of Deconstruction. So, for example, one of the recent ideological Romantic studies contains wry references to "the mandarin prose and convoluted argument of some recent practitioners of Romantic criticism," who turn out to be "the Yale school or their epigones" and "the Structuralists and the Deconstructionists."[6] This suggests, I suspect, that one reason the more conservative party in Romantic scholarship clings so stoutly to its ideological convictions is that it views Romantic questioning as mostly the dubious brew of a passing scholarly fad. It is hard not to feel a touch of sympathy for this attitude. When a movement in scholarly inquiry begins looking increasingly fey, it is tempting to ignore it and scurry back to older pastoral sanities. And there is no doubt that sane analysis of the questioning impulse in Romantic literature has sometimes become tangled up in odd critical fancies.[7] But the fact that the Mad Hatter and March Hare throw tea parties does not mean it is a mistake to drink tea. The fact that some question-oriented criticism of Romantic writing seems to have been bent mostly on vindicating commitment to exotic theories of

5 · I should probably note that McGann perceives me as an exemplary member of this befuddled scholarly group. See McGann, *Romantic Ideology,* 59–76.
6 · Clubbe and Lovell, *English Romanticism,* 10, 163n30.
7 · A sensible critique of the deconstructive method is offered by Frank Lentricchia in *After the New Criticism* (Chicago, 1980).

value or language, or on exhibiting the antic intellect of the critic, does not imply that the basic direction of criticism that investigates Romantic questioning is misguided. It does, however, suggest that argument for Romantic questioning that is colored by appeals to the prophetic utterances of Friedrich Nietzsche, Jacques Derrida, and the like is not so generally persuasive as one might wish. So it ought to be avoided. Reasonable analysis of Romantic questioning is probably better served by employing a more familiar historical approach that pays attention to such contemporaries of the phenomenon as Thomas Paine and William Godwin, and that seeks a style of analysis that would be amenable to Samuel Johnson's common reader.

The need for a more fully articulated historical approach in analysis of Romantic questioning extends beyond these issues of points of reference and argumentative style. The older ideological orientation to Romantic scholarship was grounded in much supporting historical analysis that appears to render comprehensible why a distinctive Romantic ideology developed from factors operative in the eighteenth century, how that ideology molded the careers of the writers who were attracted to it, and what eventually happened to Romantic ideology during the later course of the nineteenth century. This texture of supporting historical analysis has great persuasive impact. By comparison, Romantic questioning enjoys a much less extensive and firmly grounded historical analysis.[8] We have considerable "new critical" analysis of questioning in particular Romantic texts. But this alone is not always entirely convincing, except perhaps to the critic doing the analysis. In the absence of a sufficiently powerful analysis of the historical context that can explain the presence of this perceived questioning in Romantic texts, the scholar who supposes he already possesses a satisfactory explanation of Romantic ideology may remain understandably suspicious

---

8 · Probably Shelley's skepticism has attracted the most substantial amount of historical analysis; see Pulos, *Deep Truth*, and Wasserman, *Shelley*. In *English Romantic Irony* Mellor sketches an eighteenth-century context for her concept of Romantic irony, and she devotes considerable attention to Friedrich Schlegel, whose writings on irony she employs as a "paradigmatic model" to explain English ironic impulses (6). I think the rigidity of this model creates some difficulties; see my review of Mellor's book in *MLQ*, XLII (1981), 99–104. Simpson in *Irony and Authority* acknowledges the need to ground Romantic irony in a historical context, and regrets that he lacks space in his study to address that issue (xi–xii).

about a radically competing reading of the Romantic texts that asks him to discover questions where he had always perceived answers. Something very like this situation is what one encounters with McGann's *Romantic Ideology*. McGann appears to believe that scholars who doubt the ideological reading of Romantic texts must be deluded because he simply cannot understand how such doubt is rationally possible. Thus, for example, when he states that the "doctrinal structures which writers like Blake, Wordsworth, and Coleridge developed . . . are well known and need not be rehearsed again," or that "informed persons *do* generally agree on what is comprised under the terms Romantic and Romantic Movement," he is not arguing a case but simply insisting with a touch of exasperation upon what he firmly believes "informed persons" would have to believe.[9] The hard problem, I suspect, for scholarship that sees Romanticism as fundamentally a questioning rather than ideological phenomenon is to come to terms with this notion of what informed persons must believe, which McGann's study so forcefully articulates.

In the following chapters I have tried to address this problem by focusing upon a number of issues that are critical in the disagreement between the position that holds Romanticism to be an ideology and the one that views Romanticism as a questioning phenomenon. The most basic of these issues concerns the eighteenth-century context of the Romantic emergence. I seek, first, to show how variations of ideological thinking about Romanticism are grounded in a faulty conception of this eighteenth-century context and how a more accurate conception of the pressures that developed during the eighteenth century accounts for the questioning impulse that characterizes the Romantic emergence. One way to produce this case would be to emphasize the skeptical thrust of the eighteenth and early-nineteenth-century philosophical tradition. Key figures might be David Hume, William Drummond, and, perhaps, Friedrich Schlegel.[10] I am not convinced, however, that this tells us quite as much about the mental life of the literary tradition as we sometimes like to believe. I have tried, therefore, to build up a somewhat less formal, more literary model of the intellectual situation that induces

9 · McGann, *Romantic Ideology*, 67, 18.
10 · So suggest Pulos, *Deep Truth*, and Mellor, *English Romantic Irony*.

Romantic questioning in literary minds. Next, I inquire into the effects produced by this Romantic questioning. How does the questioning impulse manifest itself in the characteristic strategies of Romantic literary art? And how does this questioning, which begins as a problem for Romanticism, develop into a Romantic celebration? In discussing these questions I give attention to all the major Romantic poets, but I devote particular, extended attention to Wordsworth. Shelley and, perhaps, Keats would have been the obvious candidates for such special treatment, but for precisely that reason they are probably not the best test of the argument. Wordsworth, on the other hand, is a good test, because he is usually the Romantic poet most forcefully invoked in support of the opposing, ideological position.[11] It is especially important, therefore, to recognize that Wordsworth is actually at the very heart of the questioning phenomenon in Romanticism. And it is also important to recognize that this questioning is not merely a peculiarly poetic issue in the Romantic period. Why, if it is such a vital factor in the intellectual life of the time, should it exert such a powerful influence on someone writing a poem in the Romantic period and not on someone writing a novel as well? Therefore, to complete my inquiry into the pressures of questioning upon Romantic writing, I address the issue of relations between the period's novelists and poets, seeking to show that the question-induced characteristics of Romantic poetry make their significant appearance in the novels of the age also. Finally, in my concluding chapter I return to the broad issue of historical context. As I begin with the attempt to trace the rise of Romantic questioning in the eighteenth-century context, I close by attempting to show the transformations it undergoes in its Victorian phase.

11 · Classic studies that have established and maintained the identification of Wordsworth with Romantic ideology include: Arthur Beatty, *William Wordsworth: His Doctrine and Art in Their Historical Relations* (Madison, Wis., 1922; rev. ed. 1927); N. P. Stallknecht, *Strange Seas of Thought* (Durham, N.C., 1945); Melvin M. Rader, *Wordsworth: A Philosophical Approach* (Oxford, U.K., 1967); and Abrams, *Natural Supernaturalism*. The force of this view of Wordsworth remains disturbingly impressive, as suggested, for example, by the fact that in *English Romantic Irony* Mellor exempts Wordsworth from her argument, contra Abrams, that the Romantic poets exhibit behavior more ironic than ideological.

· One ·

The Romantic Situation

The Ground of Romantic Questioning

THE way we read Romantic literary works depends a good deal upon the notions we have about the Romantic situation. If we believe the Romantic situation was fundamentally characterized by revolutionary fervor, for example, with Romantic-inclining minds caught up in a "movement" that aimed to replace an old, error-ridden manner of thinking with a new, vibrant perception of truths, then we will tend to scan Romantic writing for the ideological matter it may contain. If we believe, further, that this new Romantic ideology is particularly concerned with love of nature, for example, or with celebration of imagination, then we will tend to isolate the nature factors in a Romantic work as most worthy of attention or we will believe we perceive imagination operating significantly in the Romantic work, whether it contains any apparent reference to imagination or not. We commonly find in Romantic writing the things our presuppositions about the Romantic situation tell us should be there. Our problem, therefore, must be to inquire into why we may hold the presuppositions we do. The solution, I suspect, has mostly to do with the theory of Romanticism we have absorbed, often semiconsciously, into our thinking.

As theories of Romanticism exert powerful influence upon readings of Romantic writing, so assumptions about the character of the pre–Romantic eighteenth century strongly influence those theories of Romanticism. One type of Romantic theory—what Morse Peckham has termed the "attributional construction of Romantic theory"—involves seeing the eighteenth century as an age dominated by a relatively stable ideology.[1] Romanticism, then, when it is viewed as a "movement" in revolt against eighteenth-century thinking, seems a competing ideology. Hence we arrive at a Romantic philosophy set off against an Augustan or Neoclassical philosophy. Building upon this basis of assumptions, attributional Romantic theory proceeds to construct a list of distinctively Romantic ideological attributes that is antithetical to a list of eighteenth-century attributes. Thus Romantic individuality is a revolt against eighteenth-century commitment to the general; Romantic organicism is a revolt against eighteenth-century mechanism; Romantic revolt itself is a revolt against an eighteenth-century belief in stability.

It is some version of this basic direction in critical thinking that usually underlies the doctrine-oriented readings of Romantic literature so prevalent in an earlier generation of Romantic scholarship. One would have tended to read Wordsworth's "Tintern Abbey," for example, as a celebration of Wordsworth's doctrine of nature, accentuating the lines "Nature never did betray / The heart that loved her" (ll. 122–23) because one supposed this to accord with a key attribute of Romanticism: Romantic love of nature grounded in the revolt of Romanticism against an eighteenth-century preference for city over country. Such attributional thinking may sound slightly crude today, but strains of it remain with us. It seems likely, for example, that continuing identification of the creative imagination as somehow the very essence of Romanticism owes much of its surprising staying power to echoes of the old idea that the pre–Romantic eighteenth century was an age that frowned sternly (rationally?) on imaginative activity. This yoking of

1 · Peckham, "On Romanticism," 218.

the Romantic age with imagination and of the preceding age with an anti-imaginative bias flies in the face of considerable scholarly evidence. Many years ago, W. J. Bate showed that notions about the unifying activity of imagination, popularly associated with Romantic thought, actually can be traced to "one of the offshoots of the doctrine of *coalescence* which was developed by some of the eighteenth-century associationalists." And, more recently, James Engell has demonstrated with overwhelming thoroughness that a great many eighteenth-century minds indulged in theorizing about the power of imagination. One might, in fact, almost argue that it is the Romantic age that becomes particularly doubtful about imaginative power— "Adieu! the fancy cannot cheat so well / As she is fam'd to do."[2]

An alternative construction of Romantic theory, more prevalent in influential work on Romanticism during the past quarter of a century, posits that Romanticism should be identified not with a list of attributes but rather with a problem to be solved. As Morse Peckham argued the case for problematic theory in 1970, the "problem of understanding Romanticism is the problem of locating with accuracy its problem."[3] In problematic Romantic theory the eighteenth century plays a different role. Instead of furnishing Romanticism with an ideology to revolt against, it bestows upon Romanticism the crisis that creates the Romantic problem. Prior to 1970, studies that moved in the direction of problematic theory tended to discover some type of disintegrating process in the eighteenth century. Romanticism, accordingly, was thought to have inherited the problem of unification or restructuring. R. A. Foakes gave succinct expression to the basic concept: "Order out of Chaos: The Task of the Romantic Poet."[4]

---

2 · W. J. Bate, *From Classic to Romantic: Premises of Taste in Eighteenth-Century England* (Cambridge, Mass., 1946), 118; James Engell, *The Creative Imagination: Enlightenment to Romanticism* (Cambridge, Mass., 1981); John Keats, "Ode to a Nightingale," ll. 73–74.

3 · Peckham, "On Romanticism," 217. See also Marshall Brown, *The Shape of German Romanticism* (Ithaca, 1979), wherein Brown argues that in German studies Romanticism has generally been described in terms of systems of belief and "content-oriented categories like the infinite, nature, music" that are reductive (13). Brown holds for the German Romantics a view that applies equally well to the English Romantics: "It is unhelpful to look for fixed groupings where individual authors are ceaselessly experimenting and where no single author can be held to a fixed position" (14).

4 · This is the title of the third chapter of R. A. Foakes's book *The Romantic Assertion: A Study in the Language of Nineteenth-Century Poetry* (New Haven, 1958).

Hypotheses describing the precise nature of this eighteenth-century drift toward chaos and of the Romantic struggle to reassert order varied. Earl R. Wasserman posited the gradual breakdown of a traditional "cosmic syntax" in the eighteenth century, from which followed the Romantic task of formulating a "subtler language"; and then, in a subsequent essay, he suggested that the "impotence of later eighteenth-century poetic epistemology" left the Romantics with the problem of reestablishing a "significant relationship between the subjective and objective worlds." Peckham argued, alternately, that what happened in the eighteenth century was exhaustion of the "logical possibilities of identifying Nature with order and value," from which followed a Romantic problem of "reconstituting value."[5] In either case the eighteenth century was thought to have left Romanticism with a loss or void, imposing upon Romantic writers the anguishing task of somehow replenishing the void with a new system of belief or value. This basic paradigm continues to exert influence on contemporary Romantic scholarship. In *English Romantic Irony*, for example, Anne K. Mellor argues that "Romantic irony is both a philosophical conception of the universe and an artistic program" that emerges from the "background of political revolution and post–Enlightenment distrust of the capacity of human reason to ascertain the laws of nature, or, indeed, any absolute truths concerning the ways of the world." This association of the revolution with distrust involves positing a breakdown of belief in the eighteenth century—from which follows, in turn, the natural conclusion that the Romantics must have been seeking recovery of belief (in Mellor's terms a "philosophical conception" and a "program").[6]

Problematic Romantic theory offers advantages over the relatively inflexible attributional theory. It invites one to think more about the intellectual tensions and nervous energy in Romantic thought. It prepares one to

5 · Respectively: Earl R. Wasserman, *The Subtler Language* (Baltimore, 1959), and "English Romantics," 20, 33; Morse Peckham, "Toward a Theory of Romanticism: II. Reconsiderations," *SIR*, I (1961), 4–5. See also Peckham's *Triumph of Romanticism*, 132–33 *et passim*.
6 · Mellor, *English Romantic Irony*, 4. See also Michael G. Cooke, *The Romantic Will* (New Haven, 1976), wherein Cooke's distinction between Neoclassical and Romantic conceptions of the self reflects a similar set of assumptions. With the Neoclassical self, as Cooke sees it, "No man is an island; and it is therefore necessary to look at the self in the light of the system"; but in the Romantic period, conversely, "the self is seen rather in search of a system" (58).

anticipate (rather than to devalue or ignore) diversity among the several Romantic writers, and even diversity in the individual Romantic at different stages in his career. If the Romantics share a problem rather than some fixed set of doctrines, then one would expect their behavior to be fluid, even erratic, as their understanding of and responses to the problem changed. Significant consequences follow for reading Romantic literature. One begins to look a lot more closely for the tensions that may be operating in the literary text. The struggle to solve a problem may be expected to create frustration, answers that perhaps do not actually answer, patterns of psychological self-deception or ambivalence. Problematic Romantic theory begins to nudge the reader away from a doctrine-oriented approach to Romantic literature and toward Romantic questioning, often with the accent falling on a psychological explanation of literary tensions and ambiguities. When the Romantic text appears to be advancing some system of belief and yet also undercutting it or advancing doubt—"If this / Be but a vain belief," writes Wordsworth in "Tintern Abbey" (ll. 49–50)—this might be taken to reflect the writer's failure to solve the Romantic problem, a failure that traces perhaps to complex pressures in the writer's psychological makeup.

The order-chaos version of problematic Romantic theory, however, has its own problems. If attributional theory tends to reduce the eighteenth century to a caricature of cold reptilian Reason for the sake of a warm apotheosis of Romantic Feeling and Imagination, then the order-chaos formulation of problematic theory tends to make the eighteenth century play dying animal for the sake of a heroic Romantic rebirth. But eighteenth-century scholars have been striving patiently for many years to combat the wildly simple notion that their era exhibits merely the decline and fall of an aged Neo-classicism and the eager stirrings of a young and vibrant Romanticism to come. If we grant even a modicum of validity to the argument that an "age of sensibility" arises during the eighteenth century, for example, then it is not easy to reconcile this process of development with the view that the century is marked by some process of increasing exhaustion, disintegration, or impotence.[7] Nor are such supposed eighteenth-century dissolutions easily

7 · See, especially, Northrop Frye, "Towards Defining an Age of Sensibility," *ELH*, XXIII (1956), 144–52. See also George Dekker, *Coleridge and the Literature of Sensibility* (New York, 1978).

reconciled with the revolutionary ambience that grows stronger with the progress of the century. What are we to make of the outbursts of energy, confidence, and unhesitating insistence that Answers Are at Hand that characterize the revolutionary "spirit of the age" in the later decades of the eighteenth century?[8] Clear, considerable data exist to support the proposition that the environment in which Romanticism emerges is characterized more by big bangs of energy and assertion than by whimpers of exhaustion and perplexity.

These difficulties on the eighteenth-century side of the order-chaos theory are matched by difficulties on the Romantic side. Much Romantic literature seems concerned with situations of overabundance rather than with the signs of lack or void produced by a problem of dissolution or exhaustion. Instead of disintegration of systems of value and belief, we seem to encounter in many Romantic texts dramatizations of systematic overload. Wordsworth's "Tables Turned," for example, presents a debate between persons who already have systems, ideologies, conceptions of order. Their problem seems to be merely that each stubbornly insists on clinging to his own ideas and ignoring the other's. Turn this Romantic table, in other words, and you find, not a void, but only a differing table. Blake's famous proposal that "Opposition is true Friendship" similarly seems to imply Romantic preoccupation less with the ruins of systems and more with a situation of multiple and dynamic systematic oppositions (*The Marriage of Heaven and Hell*, Plate 20).

Byron offers an interesting observation about systems of ideology in *Don Juan.*

> One system eats another up, and this
> Much as old Saturn ate his progeny;
> For when his pious consort gave him stones
> In lieu of sons, of these he made no bones.

8 · See M. H. Abrams, "English Romanticism: The Spirit of the Age," in Northrop Frye (ed.), *Romanticism Reconsidered* (New York, 1963), wherein we are reminded that the "formative age of Romantic poetry was clearly one of apocalyptic expectations, or at least apocalyptic imaginings" (37).

> But System doth reverse the Titan's breakfast,
> And eats her parents, albeit the digestion
> Is difficult. Pray tell me, can you make fast,
> After due search, your faith to any question?
> (Canto 14, ll. 1–2)

Systems of ideology, like Frankenstein's creation, threaten to destroy their creators. The "parents" of a given system, apparently, tend to become caught up in their construct, forgetting to undertake the "due search" that would save them from having absolute faith in their answer to any question. This view of systems as potential devourers clearly appears to militate against the notion that the Romantics were looking for some sort of order to shore up against encroaching chaos. Order, in this view, looks to be at least as dangerous as chaos.

A drowning man, one supposes, would clutch frantically at things that might save him—without being overly particular about the nature of those things, especially if not many things are available for clutching. But the Romantics seem to have been extremely particular, exhibiting a tentative, suspicious approach toward the systems of thought and value they touched.[9]

9 · Romantic writing reflects great ambivalence about the value of "system." In his fragmentary essay "On Life," Shelley recommends Drummond's *Academical Questions* as "perhaps the most clear and vigorous statement of the intellectual system" (Donald H. Reiman and Sharon B. Powers [eds.], *Shelley's Poetry and Prose* [New York, 1980], 476). In Volume 3, Essay 5, of *The Friend* Coleridge announces that the quest to find *"a ground that is unconditional and absolute, and thereby to reduce the aggregate of human knowledge to a system"* constitutes the "grand problem, the solution of which forms, according to Plato, the final object and distinctive character of philosophy" (Barbara E. Rooke [ed.], *The Collected Works of Samuel Taylor Coleridge: No. 4; The Friend* [2 vols.; Princeton, N.J., 1969], I, 361). Keats proposes a "faint sketch of a system of Salvation" in his letter on "Soul-making" to George and Georgiana Keats, February 14 to May 3, 1819, in Hyder Edward Rollins (ed.), *The Letters of John Keats* (2 vols.; Cambridge, Mass., 1958), II, 10. But Keats's hesitant phrase "a faint sketch" points toward the recurring Romantic dis-ease about system and recalls Charles Lamb's sympathetic description of minds that are "rather suggestive than comprehensive": "Hints and glimpses, germs and crude essays at a system, is the utmost they pretend to" ("Imperfect Sympathies," in E. V. Lucas [ed.], *The Works of Charles and Mary Lamb* [6 vols.; London, 1912–13], II, 68). In *Coleridge and the Pantheist Tradition* (Oxford, U.K. 1969), Thomas McFarland nicely qualifies the drive toward system in the Romantic who was

This seems to imply either that the Romantics did not sense themselves to be floundering in a void or else that they saw a great many things around them that offered live options for clutching. If either of these conclusions is true, then something is wrong with the hypothesis that Romanticism inherited a problem of chaos, disintegration, or vacancy from the eighteenth century.

During the past decade or so a quite different, almost diametrically opposed direction in Romantic theory has been developing. Perhaps the Romantics are confronted, not with a void to be filled, but rather with some sort of burden of presences—structures or pressures that loom over them, hindering free movement and hedging them in. The Romantic problem, then, would be less the need to find or construct, and more the need to escape. Variations of this hypothesis underlie work proceeding along a number of different lines in recent Romantic studies, ranging from Walter Jackson Bate's historically grounded examination of the "burden of the past" upon the Romantic poets to Harold Bloom's more abstract and gnostic speculations about the poets' oppression by the "anxiety of influence." [10] A common ground underlying differences among such studies is reversal of critical thinking about the supposed Romantic passion for order. Now order itself is recognized to be problematic for the Romantics, and Romantic activity is recognized to have more to do with strategies of evasion than with plans for construction. This turn in the direction of Romantic theory leads to analysis of Romantic writing that emphasizes the questions the writing provokes and

probably most infatuated with that narcotic: "Coleridge's endeavour was always toward system. But this orientation was first of all the need to connect rather than the need to complete" (110).

10 · W. J. Bate, *The Burden of the Past and the English Poet* (Cambridge, Mass., 1970); Harold Bloom, *The Anxiety of Influence: A Theory of Poetry* (New York, 1973). Thomas Weiskel, in *The Romantic Sublime: Studies in the Structure and Psychology of Transcendence* (Baltimore, 1976), seeks to analyze "a moment—call it the sublime or original moment—in which a burden of the past, but not exclusively) is lifted and there is an influx of power" (11). In *Romantic Origins* (Ithaca, 1978), Leslie Brisman characterizes the Romantics in terms of their various attempts to escape the burden of entrapment within merely natural origins, which seems to threaten loss of freedom through submission to natural law. In *Irony and Authority*, David Simpson proposes that the Romantic struggle against the burden of authority produces a poetry designed to "make us confront the question of authority" (xi).

that views these questions as a factor in self-conscious Romantic strategy rather than as indications of psychic conflict.

INSTEAD of passing on to the Romantics a landscape of mental ruins, the eighteenth century actually confronts the Romantics with a situation of extreme fertility. Proliferation of ideological systems in the eighteenth century leaves Romanticism confronted with a wealth of seemingly viable but conflicting alternatives. This means we should probably think of Romanticism in terms of a situation rather than of a problem. To the extent that this eighteenth-century fertility offers the Romantics the excitement of expanding possibilities, the Romantic experience is not a problem but a joy. From one perspective the Romantic situation involves the mind's eager recognition that there are alternative options for thought, new and different possibilities on the intellectual horizon, teasing the mind toward optimistic exertions of its power. However, this same situation can create hard problems also: the very existence of those new and contrary possibilities casts a shadow of doubt upon the adequacy of any given orientation of thought and value that the mind is tempted to organize into a rigorous ideology.

In either case, though, the eighteenth century is best understood by thinking of multiple processes of development rather than of decay. The ever-accelerating breakdown of confidence in medieval and Renaissance verities actually serves to encourage growth: it offers a hospitable environment for the burgeoning of diverse systems of thought and value. Old systems continue to command the allegiance of some people, but also new systems (and new variations of still older systems) emerge and find space to flourish. Today eighteenth-century scholars are by no means agreed upon exactly what takes place during the course of the eighteenth century. But at the least their arguments reveal that the eighteenth century does not exhibit single-minded devotion to any one principle (such as reason or Newtonianism); nor does it exhibit an orderly evolution from one dominant ideology to another; nor does it exhibit simple decline from one dominant ideological system to a state of enervation and decay.[11] The eighteenth cen-

11 · On the erratic fortunes of Newtonianism in the eighteenth century, see Margaret C. Jacob, "Newtonianism and the Origins of the Enlightenment: A Reassessment," *ECS*, XI

tury is, after all, that period when in France both Jean Jacques Rousseau and Voltaire could cultivate their considerable gardens—and yet the gardens of Versailles could manage to retain a considerable amount of cultivation as well. In England it is the period in which the supposed eighteenth-century progress from city to country runs up against such resistant facts as Alexander Pope's affection for rural retirement and the later Samuel Johnson's affection for life in London. It would be convenient for popular stereotypes to find that some late-eighteenth-century poet, perhaps William Cowper, wrote the following lines: "You, who the sweets of rural life have known, / Despise th' ungrateful hurry of the town." But in fact those lines introduce a poem of 1713 by John Gay, titled "Rural Sports." Such stubborn facts should help to remind us that the early eighteenth century has its own internal variations and hints of divisionary possibilities. The later eighteenth century, stimulated by a profusion of ideas particularly active in the context of the American and French revolutions, offers a proliferation of these possibilities, not a dwindling down or movement of closure.[12]

During the course of the eighteenth century, many of the knavish or foolish systems that the company of Pope and Jonathan Swift consigned fondly to realms of darkness manage either to find their own spots in the sun or, more cleverly, to render darkness a desirable habitation. The man of

(1977), 1–25. On tensions between science and emerging preoccupations with imagination, see G. S. Rousseau, "Science and the Discovery of the Imagination in Enlightened England," ECS, III (1969), 108–35. On the issue of simple notions about the nature of the eighteenth century generally, see Donald Greene, "Augustinianism and Empiricism: A Note on Eighteenth-Century Intellectual History," ECS, I (1967), 33–68, and the subsequent exchange between Greene and Vivian de S. Pinto, "Augustan or Augustinian? More Demythologizing Needed?" ECS, II (1969), 286–300.

12 · In The Ordering of the Arts in Eighteenth-Century England (Princeton, N.J., 1970), Lawrence Lipking discusses a later-eighteenth-century movement to set the arts in order by trying to develop systematic principles determining hierarchies of taste, poetic eminence, and so forth—a phenomenon that would appear to suggest that systems are waxing rather than decaying in that period. Marilyn Butler has recently published a series of studies that give their reader a fine sense of the complexity of intellectual crosscurrents that characterize the late eighteenth and early nineteenth centuries: Jane Austen and the War of Ideas (Oxford, U.K., 1975), Peacock Displayed: A Satirist in His Context (London, 1979), and Romantics, Rebels, and Reactionaries (Oxford, U.K., 1981).

feeling as well as the man of reason, good sense and sensibility, the call of the wild and the civil conversation of the coffeehouse all manage to gain or to maintain eager (or decorous) followings during the century. The plain dealer could get his satisfaction from Richard Brinsley Sheridan's *The School for Scandal*, wherein investigation of surfaces leads to the triumph of Charles over his sentiment-strewing brother, Joseph. One who thought—or, rather, *felt*—less harshly about the flowers of sentimental rhetoric could find satisfaction in turning to Henry Mackenzie's *The Man of Feeling*. The devotee of imagination might be displeased by Johnson's warning concerning its dangerous prevalence in *Rasselas*, but he could take satisfaction from closing Johnson and opening Mark Akenside or William Collins. The admirer of Pope might lament the fortunes of the couplet while skimming Edward Young's poems or Thomas Percy's *Reliques;* but he could recover some faith in the proper order of things by turning to the poetry of Johnson or George Crabbe. Alternately, for one whose notion of the proper order of things made it appear that both Young and Johnson were snatching an art beyond the reach of grace, there were the pleasures of Christopher Smart's later poems or of Cowper's *Olney Hymns*, depending on one's taste in grace. Such familiar, varied examples of eighteenth-century literary production only begin to mark the great range of differing intellectual orientations that became available to the mind, not simply as some shadowy undercurrent but as live possibility, during the course of the period. It is with this atmosphere of multiplying intellectual alternatives that we should associate the eighteenth-century background to the Romantic emergence.

If, taking a distanced view, we observe that the eighteenth century begins to a large extent in satire and ends in revolution, we might be tempted to conclude that this progress implies a disintegration of order. But more careful thought suggests that this argument betrays a limited, party viewpoint. A closer view would reveal in that progress a proliferation of seriously competing systems of order. For Alexander Pope, the pen can be mightier than the sword because those Tibbalds who know not their own point are piddling. A revolutionary "spirit of the age" develops when the Tibbalds have managed to gain sufficient influence and, at the same time, the Popes have managed to retain sufficient influence for a state of highly charged indeterminacy to develop. Revolutions do not emerge simply within an atmosphere of disintegration produced by the decay of some once predominant system. To the contrary, revolutionary atmospheres develop in a cauldron of multiple-party expansion and maturation, wherein it has become increasingly uncertain which party is the piddler. Revolutionary atmospheres produce energetic expressions of confidence, belief, and exertion in behalf of order—when different parties have developed conflicting and yet comparably potent conceptions of what that order is or should be. William Godwin, breathing the revolutionary atmosphere of his own time, knew this: "Revolutions are a struggle between two parties, each persuaded of the justice of its cause, a struggle, not decided by compromise or patient expostulation, but by force only. Such a decision can scarcely be expected to put an end to the mutual animosity and variance."[13]

The key term in Godwin's observation is *persuaded*. The fundamental characteristic of a revolutionary atmosphere is that the involved parties are experiencing no confusions about order. Each party already has its cause, and is already so persuaded of the justice of its cause that exertions of force seem inevitable and yet incapable of resolving the conflict of persuasions. To a mind that is observing such a revolutionary atmosphere from a safe distance, it may appear that order has disintegrated and left a ruinous void. But to a mind confronting that revolutionary atmosphere close up, to a mind living within its turmoils, order is more likely to appear a demanding, even oppressive factor of existence, as opposing parties press in upon the mind with the competing ideologies of their rigid systems. That the eighteenth century takes on a revolutionary atmosphere should serve to remind us that mentalities of the period were experiencing the processes and effects of proliferation, more than the disintegration that we today may be tempted to read into the evolution.

This proliferation exerts significant pressures upon the mind; and it is with the nature of these pressures that we must particularly concern ourselves in thinking about the emergence of Romanticism. From such dogmatic formulas as Pope's "One truth is clear, 'Whatever *Is*, is *Right*,'"

13 · William Godwin, *Enquiry Concerning Political Justice and Its Influence on Morals and Happiness*, ed. F. E. L. Priestley (facsimile ed., 3 vols.; Toronto, 1946), I, 271.

eighteenth-century thought evolves in the direction of such revolutionary formulas as "We hold these truths to be self-evident." What has developed here is awareness of the possibility that alternative systems of truth might be seriously entertained by thought. In Pope's intellectual environment, the only real matter at issue was a distinction between clear and muddled thought. Clear thought leads to "one truth," and muddled thought to error; and what "we" hold (as opposed to what some "they" may hold) is not a factor in intellectual calculation because seriously viable alternative systems are not granted the possibility of existence. But in the revolutionary formula, the differing persuasions of competing ideologies begin to exert telling pressure on the mind's formulation of its truths. Thus, while we are holding *these* truths to be self-evident, there is by implication some "they" busily holding other truths that seem to them equally self-evident. This means that clarity of thought alone is no longer a sufficient basis upon which commitment to one system or the other may be established. Both parties may think with apparent clarity without ever reconciling their systems or exposing the error of one or the other, because their thought is operating within the confines of different geometries, as it were, or of different languages. Argument now is over the fundamental axioms, the principles held true, prior to the generation of differing systems of theorems or sentences.

In *The Rights of Man*, Thomas Paine sets out in argumentative pursuit of his opponent, Edmund Burke: "As Mr. Burke occasionally applies the poison drawn from his horrid principles, not only to the English nation, but to the French Revolution and the National Assembly . . . I shall, *sans ceremonie*, place another system of principles in opposition to his."[14] Paine obviously would like to be able to claim that Burke has no principles and that his conservative position is a mere welter of muddled thinking. Paine, like Pope before him, wants to believe, "One truth is clear." But the intellectual situation has changed, and Paine is acutely sensitive to the pressures of his time. Burke, like Paine, is doing geometry. Burke has his principles, however "horrid"; and his propositions, "poison" as they may be, are drawn

14 · Thomas Paine, *The Rights of Man: Part I*, in Moncure Daniel Conway, II (ed.), *The Writings of Thomas Paine* (4 vols.; New York, 1902–1908; rpr. 1969), II, 277.

from these principles. Burke appears to think clearly enough, that is, within the bounds of his own system. Paine's argument, therefore, shifts ground from an attack upon the quality of thought to an attack upon the axioms from which the thought derives its origin. Paine will give us another geometry, the *right* geometry: he will offer "another system of principles" in opposition to Burke's system. *We* hold *these* truths. The perceived terms of the intellectual conflict have shifted from order versus chaos to order versus order, as different systems of principles line up in competition with one another.

What particularly complicates this situation for a late-eighteenth-century person is the fact that the manner of thinking associated with the development of non-Euclidean geometries was at this time only a faint tremor on the horizon.[15] To most minds of the period, there could be ultimately only one valid logic or system of thought—as there was only one geometry, the Euclidean, drawn from the basis of a few self-evident principles. Accordingly, if two different systems of principles competed with each other, one or the other of them must of necessity be wrong. Contrary principles could not both be self-evident; nor could principles truly self-evident produce contrary geometries. Probing for self-evident principles, therefore, and developing the series of propositions that necessarily follow from them, one ought to be able—so it was fondly believed—to arrive at systems of demonstration commanding as much assent as Euclid. Thus William Godwin invokes the "truths of geometry" in his *Enquiry Concerning Political Justice*: we must learn, he urges, to "reflect upon the moral concerns of mankind with the same clearness of perception, the same firmness of judgment, and the same constancy of temper, as we are accustomed to do upon the truths of geometry." Thus too Thomas Paine, generally contemptuous of ancient authorities, celebrates Euclid in his *Age of Reason*: "I know, however, but of one ancient book that authoritatively challenges universal con-

15 · So Voltaire observes in the *Dictionnaire Philosophique*: "There is only one morality . . . just as there is only one geometry"; quoted from Eichner, "Rise of Modern Science," 17. See also Richard Olson, "Scottish Philosophy and Mathematics, 1750–1830," *Journal of the History of Ideas*, XXXII (1971), 29–44, esp. 35; more generally see Ettore Carruccio, *Mathematics and Logic in History and Contemporary Thought*, trans. Isabel Quigly (Chicago, 1965), 254–73.

sent and belief, and that is *Euclid's Elements of Geometry*; and the reason is, because it is a book of self-evident demonstration, entirely independent of its author, and of every thing relating to time, place, and circumstance." Underlying the period's preoccupation with first principles and self-evident truths is an ambition to achieve this Euclidean power of demonstration in issues of morals, religion, politics—perhaps life in general. In his *Dissertation on First Principles of Government*, Paine insists that "there is not a problem in Euclid more mathematically true, than that hereditary government has not a right to exist."[16]

What happens, however, when other minds nonetheless insist upon holding other truths? If we look forward into the nineteenth century, we can see minds beginning to accommodate themselves to such a situation. There is, for example, an interesting passage in Sir Humphry Davy's *Consolations in Travel; or, The Last Days of a Philosopher* (published posthumously in 1831), wherein Davy has one speaker in a philosophical dialogue reply to the argument of another: "Ambrosio speaks of the reasonableness of his own opinions; of course his notions of reason must be different from mine, or we have adopted different forms of logic."[17] In this notion that there may be different forms of logic, and that the mind can adopt one or another, we have faint stirrings of the concept that there may be multiple geometries available to the mind, geometries non-Euclidean as well as Euclidean, and that one develops propositions about truth and value only within the terms of the particular system one has first chosen, consciously or unconsciously, to adopt. Priority of obligation begins dissolving into priority of choice, as what follows necessarily in a logical demonstration depends, first, on the particular system of logic one chooses to work within.

This fundamental idea that the first principle in human concerns may be an act of *choosing* first principles from a pool of alternative possibilities exerts an influence even in later writings of William Godwin, as in the following passage from *Thoughts on Man*, published in 1831.

16 · Godwin, *Enquiry Concerning Political Justice* (Priestley, ed.), I, 396; Paine, *The Age of Reason*, in *Writings of Thomas Paine*, IV, 91, and *Dissertation on First Principles of Government*, in *Writings of Thomas Paine*, III, 258.

17 · Sir Humphry Davy, *Consolations in Travel; or, The Last Days of a Philosopher* (London, 1831), 81.

> In the boundless variety of the acts, passions and pursuits of human beings, it is absurd on the face of it to say that we are all governed by one motive, and that, however dissimilar are the ends we pursue, all this dissimilarity is the fruit of a single cause.
>
> One man chooses travelling, another ambition, a third study, a fourth voluptuousness and a mistress. Why do these men take so different courses?
>
> Because one is partial to new scenes, new buildings. . . . Because a second is attracted by the contemplation of wealth and power. Because a third feels a decided preference for the works of Homer, or Shakespear, or Bacon, or Euclid. . . .
>
> Each of these finds the qualities he likes, intrinsically in the thing he chooses.[18]

The Godwin of the later eighteenth century who had sought to unite us all in contemplation of the truths of geometry has lived through the Romantic period, and his mentality has shifted ground. One man chooses Euclid—but another chooses a mistress. The "self-evident" truths one begins with depend on the propensities of the self in question. We hover here on the verge of Victorian preoccupation with crises of choice, as in the monologue of Robert Browning's pope in *The Ring and the Book:* "Life's business being just the terrible choice" (X, l. 1232). Or one thinks of Alice and the Cheshire cat: "Would you tell me, please, which way I ought to go from here?" asks Alice. " 'That depends a good deal on where you want to get to,' said the Cat" (Chap. 6).

For most people in the late eighteenth century, however, "where you want to get to" still seemed to be dependent on where you "ought to go." Looking back upon Thomas Paine from a Victorian perspective, Leslie Stephen would remark in the *Dictionary of National Biography,* "Paine's bigotry was of the logical kind which can see only one side of a question, and imagines that all political and religious questions are as simple as the first

18 · William Godwin, "Of Self-Love and Benevolence," in *Thoughts on Man: His Nature, Products and Discoveries* (London, 1831), quoted from the Economics Classics rpr. (New York, 1969), 212–13.

propositions of Euclid."[19] Stephen's comment, as is common among the judgments that one intellectual age makes upon another, exhibits a sort of unconscious bigotry of its own. For Stephen, living in a nineteenth-century world that has long been familiarizing itself with the notion of different forms of logic, multiple geometries, and issues of choice, it seems obvious that questions have more than one "side"—which manner of visualizing questions implies the existence of multiple perspectives surrounding any given question. But for a late-eighteenth-century mind such as Paine's that would be an odd way of visualizing a question. Questions do not have different sides, like the faces of Janus; instead, they have factors, which can be reduced by the mind to principles, which can be shown to accord or not to accord with a few self-evident truths. If different minds disagree, therefore, one of them must be poisonous. In the late eighteenth century, accordingly, one system tended to war against another system in competition, as it were, for the mind's soul—somewhat as in the old play *Everyman*, except that in this case each system supposes the other to be hell.

In this situation, a crucial division begins to emerge between two fundamentally different orientations of mind. For warring bands of ideologues already engaged in conflict, "each persuaded of the justice of its cause," as Godwin had stated, the situation no doubt appears relatively clear and straightforward. Since each party "knows" its own system of principles is grounded in self-evidence, it also "knows" that anyone who might happen to hold contrary principles self-evident must be honestly mistaken or willfully corrupt—or, an extreme possibility, perhaps mentally diseased or unnatural. There is only one geometry; and therefore, since ours is right, theirs is not. But then there can also be a quite different orientation of mind: people who are not persuaded (or not fully persuaded) of the justice of either cause will be experiencing the situation in another manner. One system may look poisonous to a mind that already holds some alternative system; but upon what ground, prior to commitment, is the disinterested mind to determine which system, if either, is to be considered poisonous?

19 · *Dictionary of National Biography,* XV, 78.

THINKING people in the Romantic period did not suddenly become "Romantics," striking out against a dominant intellectual thrust of the eighteenth century. It is more accurate to conceive of Romanticism as a minority phenomenon arising in response to pressures within the Romantic period itself. Most people who thought seriously in the Romantic period where busily carrying on the eighteenth-century's devotion to systems and system building.[20] For most minds, the French Revolution did not fundamentally alter conviction. Writing in 1789, Edmund Burke had compared the commencement of the Revolution to a "wild *gas*" that had broken loose, and he opted for suspension of judgment about it "until the first effervescence is a little subsided, till the liquor is cleared, and until we see something deeper than the agitation of a troubled and frothy surface."[21] But when the surface cleared, much was left unchanged intellectually. Instead of settling basic questions and compelling men's minds to think differently from how they had before, the course of the Revolution actually helped accentuate the strain that had developed between opposed ideologies earlier in the eighteenth century. People who had been committed to ideologies grounded in the premise that traditional hierarchical constructions of society are most proper could discover in the revolutionary bloodbath confirmation of their principles: Observe how humanity set free is a beast unchained! But people committed to the alternate premise that it is this very hierarchical construction of society that renders humanity bestial also could discover in the bloodbath confirmation of their opposite principles: Observe how the people have been corrupted by generations of oppression under god, priest, and king! For most minds, the foundations of ideological thought were not severely shaken. When a dogmatic mind looked deeper than the "agitation of a troubled and frothy surface," it saw in the depths whatever it happened to believe it would see.

20 · This occasionally overlooked fact is mirrored by the similarly neglected fact that many people in the eighteenth century were engaged in behavior popularly supposed to be "Romantic." See W. J. Bate's argument in *Burden of the Past* that the "essence of the eighteenth century is the creation of the 'Romantic' and, in a variety of ways, the modern" (viii–ix). Richard E. Brantley, *Locke, Wesley, and the Method of English Romanticism* (Gainesville, Fla., 1984), argues similarly for clear principles of continuity, rather than contrariety, between main currents of eighteenth-century thought and Romantic thought.

21 · Edmund Burke, *Reflections on the Revolution in France*, in *The Works of the Right Honourable Edmund Burke* (6 vols.; London, 1906–1907), IV, 8.

w minds of the Romantic period, however, behaved differently. In
805 *Prelude*, Wordsworth recalls his attempt to anatomize the failure
is revolutionary commitments. In the process he gradually lost

> All feeling of conviction, and, in fine,
> Sick, wearied out with contrarieties,
> Yielded up moral questions in despair,
> And for my future studies, as the sole
> Employment of the inquiring faculty,
> Turned towards mathematics, and their clear
> And solid evidence.
>
> (X, ll. 899–905)

In this relatively rare but significant case, fundamental moral questions and
the mathematical model for attaining certainty part company. Wordsworth
turned to mathematics, not to resolve the questions that were troubling
him, but rather to escape from them. He decided that the realms of mathematics and moral questions were quite different from each other: in the former one could encounter "clear / And solid evidence"; but in the latter the
mind seemed to lose itself in a labyrinth of "contrarieties." It is this encounter with contrarieties that marks the mind's shift in the direction of Romantic thought.

The heartland of English Romantic territory is to be found in the space
that opens out between the claims of competing systems of thought. Between the inducements of the We and the They that are so vigorously holding their contrary truths to be self-evident, there is a middle ground or
border territory (consider Wordsworth's early drama *The Borderers*, for example, and Walter Scott's *Waverley* novels, which reflect a preoccupation
with life on the border). Here we encounter the Romantic mind, asking,
What truths, if any, are to be held when the pressure of contrarieties begins
to appear equal? A mind is not Romantic because it either loves or fears
nature, because it either trusts the people or fears the mob, because it either
embraces the saving guidance of influence or struggles against the anxiety of
influence. Romantic thought is characterized, not so much by the particular
propositions the mind is willing (or unwilling) to entertain, but rather by

the manner in which it tends to deal with propositions generally. Near its periphery, Romantic thought has to do with the uneasy suspicion that one might well (or perhaps better) be journeying back rather than forth—leaning toward a line of assertion, belief, or value alternative to, or even directly opposite from, the one being entertained at the present moment. Keats dramatizes such a crucial mental state in *Lamia*.

> For the first time, since first he harbour'd in
> That purple-lined palace of sweet sin,
> His spirit pass'd beyond its golden bourn
> Into the noisy world almost forsworn.
>
> (II, ll. 30–33)

Lycius suddenly finds himself wavering between contrarieties: on one side, the realm of Lamia into which he has journeyed; and on the other side, the noisy world almost—but, significantly, not quite—forsworn that lies behind him. As in Keats's more famous "half in love with easeful Death" ("Ode to a Nightingale," l. 52), the presence of the qualifier draws the mind back from absolute commitment, tempting it to turn in the direction from which it has come. The Romantic heartland is a state characterized by hovering near the middle, a condition in which the mind is conscious of being surrounded by the potent claims of many candidates for ideological commitment, each seemingly valid in its own terms—were one willing to hold its "truths" rather than those of its competitors self-evident. Dorothy Wordsworth is close to the Romantic center when she responds to a question concerning the Wordsworths' "system" for educating young Basil Montagu: "You ask to be informed of our system respecting Basil; it is a very simple one, so simple that *in this age of systems* you will hardly be likely to follow it. We teach him nothing at present but what he learns from the evidence of his senses."[22]

At first glance, Dorothy's response seems reminiscent of an early-

---

22 · Dorothy Wordsworth to Mrs. John Marshall, March 19, [1797,] in Ernest De Selincourt (ed.), *The Letters of William and Dorothy Wordsworth: The Early Years* (Oxford, U.K., 1967), 180.

eighteenth-century tendency of thought. It calls to mind the streak of scornful anti-intellectualism in Pope, for example, or Jonathan Swift's satiric campaigns against the various system-mongers of his time—the aspect of the Augustan period that led Duncan Forbes, arguing for Scott's affinity with the eighteenth century, to remark that the "distrust of systems and system-building" in Scott "was typical of the eighteenth century." [23] There are important differences, however. Pope and Swift tended to see themselves as living in an age of would-be builders of systems, when flocks of not-so-modest proposers were threatening to overwhelm civilization in darkness, obscuring the light of a few clear truths that were already known and that had to be defended. One's duty, therefore, was to strike out in support of light, denouncing the piddling Tibbalds from the stronghold of the common sense of mankind. But the Wordsworths, living later, perceive a different situation. They are living in an "age of systems"—which phrase implies that the system builders have had their way by this time and that they represent, not some eccentric new enthusiasm, but rather the established, respectable norm. It is because system building is so characteristic of the dominant spirit of the present age that one would "hardly be likely to follow" a program so simple as that which the Wordsworths are following. Dorothy Wordsworth's remark represents, not a Swiftian attack from perceived strength, but rather a defensive maneuver: a defense against a multitude of systematic encroachments that involves drawing back toward a system that is as minimally systematic as possible. Dorothy is seeking to escape a trap, not expose an obvious absurdity.

What greatly complicates this Romantic inclination of thought, however, is its instability. The trap has enticements, even for the mind that would escape it. In "this age of systems," it is hard not to listen to the spirit of the age. One thinks of Keats's mental struggle: "I have never yet been able to perceive how any thing can be known for truth by consequitive reasoning—and yet it must be—Can it be that even the greatest Philosopher ever [when] arrived at his goal without putting aside numerous objections." [24] Keats's wavering "and yet it must be—Can it be" underscores the instabil-

23 · Duncan Forbes, "The Rationalism of Sir Walter Scott," *Cambridge Journal*, VII (1953), 23.
24 · John Keats to Benjamin Bailey, November 22, 1817, in *Letters of John Keats*, I, 185.

ity of the Romantic state of mind, its tendency to submit even its own doubts to question. How can a systematic thinker develop some line of consecutive reasoning—does he simply ignore the numerous objections that arise from contrary lines of thought? For every Burke, there would seem to be a Paine. It must be the case that valid consecutive reasoning is possible. And yet, how? The Romantic is like a geometrician of traditional inclination who seeks to do *the* geometry, while at the same time his mind keeps confronting him with what seem to be multiple geometries and with the apparent fact that he might work with equal validity within each.

A large percentage of the problems that recur in Romantic scholarship derive from the error of supposing Romanticism to be a more solid, stable quantity than it really is. We often categorize individual writers of the Romantic period simply as "Romantics," forgetting that this label is at best a sort of critical shorthand that requires considerable qualification when we begin thinking carefully. The Romantic state of mind is experienced with varying degrees of intensity and persistence by different individuals during the Romantic period, and none of the people we call "Romantic" seem to exhibit it consistently or exclusively throughout their entire careers. Some of the Romantic writers finally made havens for themselves in the frameworks of established political and religious institutions. Many flirted in their early years with the attractive dogmatisms of revolutionary or semirevolutionary systems of thought. Young Wordsworth composed (though he did not publish) a letter to the Bishop of Llandaff; Shelley advocated the necessity of atheism and flung down pamphlets from his balcony in front of the Dublin citizenry; Blake warmed himself for a short time in the fiery rhetoric of Orc. Throughout their careers the Romantic writers lived with the temptation to fall into line with one or another of the systems of ideology so readily available to them during the Romantic period, and as one would expect, they occasionally fell. But the many dogmas that momentarily attracted them at various points in their lives—one thinks of Coleridge naming his male children Hartley, Berkeley, and then, curiously, Derwent—should not in themselves be thought of as intimately related to Romanticism. Romanticism has more to do with the state of mind that drives the Romantic writer from one momentary infatuation toward another and that prevents him from committing himself completely to some particular ideology.

The one system, if it can sensibly be called that, which the Romantics do tend to pursue with more than passing fervor involves striving for "acts of inclusion," as Michael G. Cooke has recently termed the phenomenon.[25] When so many competing systems are available that commitment to any one of them begins to look like a trap, then perhaps safety (and even truth?) lies in maintaining some sort of commitment to all the possibilities. Instead of employing the principle of exclusion, therefore, the mind turns toward a principle of inclusion: it strives to think in terms of "both/and" rather than of the more familiar "either/or."[26] Would it not be possible to discover a system of systems, one that reconciles all opposites? Or, at the least, perhaps there exists a manner of thinking that respects the sense, if not of reconciliation, then of wholeness. The mind almost experiences such wholeness in sublime moments of vision on Mount Snowdon, or even, more humbly, in the vale of Grasmere.[27] But on the other hand—and this "other hand" is nearly always forthcoming in Romantic thought—is it not possible that a principle of exclusion is operating even here, creeping into thought as the mind is pursuing "both/and" *rather than* "either/or"? Thus we often find the Romantic mind turning away from the whole and anxiously clinging to or seeking after experience that the principle of inclusion (sly dogmatic system in itself) threatens to exclude: "But there's a Tree, of many, one, / A single Field which I have looked upon" (Wordsworth's "Intimations of Immortality," ll. 51−52). The urge to wholeness may itself be a subtle trap, blinding us to the possibility that there may be a single ideology, a party program, a remote isle in "the deep wide sea of Misery" that is indeed The Way (Shelley's "Lines Written Among the Euganean Hills," l. 2). Most thinking people seem to believe they know, or that they are on the path toward knowing, The Way. Perhaps skepticism is only another entrapping system: We murder to dissect.

This Romantic uneasiness concerning even its own skeptical tendencies

25 · Michael G. Cooke, *Acts of Inclusion: Studies Bearing on an Elementary Theory of Romanticism* (New Haven, 1979).

26 · See E. D. Hirsch's chapter "Both-And Logic in the Immortality Ode" in his book *Wordsworth and Schelling: A Typological Study of Romanticism* (New Haven, 1960).

27 · See Karl Kroeber, "'Home at Grasmere': Ecological Holiness," *PMLA*, LXXXIX (1974), 132−41.

accounts for the almost baroque mixture of questioning and assertion that one finds in the writings of Romantic thinkers. This mixture makes it difficult, of course, to develop powerful generalizations about the Romantics as a group—and even about the individual Romantic writer. As soon as one begins generalizing, contrary evidences start plucking at one's sleeve. We encounter this difficulty as scholars and critics because the Romantics themselves encountered the same difficulty in their own mental experience. It does seem possible, however, to discern certain patterns or tendencies of intellectual and literary behavior among the Romantics that may help us comprehend the situation they faced and that permit us to begin tracing some of their inclinations in responding to it.

ROMANTIC thought tends to be preoccupied with competing voices, values, systems of belief. When we encounter a voice proclaiming alpha on Romantic ground, we are most likely to encounter close by some contrary voice aggressively defending (or sometimes subtly murmuring) omega. In Wordsworth's "We Are Seven," the little cottage girl has her own mathematical tale to tell, and it refuses to accommodate itself to the contrary tale of her adult inquisitor. For Keats's Apollonius, the metamorphosis of Lamia is mere accident rather than a fundamental change of essence, and so he persists in pronouncing her a serpent; but for Lycius and for the dramatic narrator of the poem, Lamia's appearance is her essence: "Ha, the serpent! certes, she / Was none" (*Lamia*, II, ll. 80–81). Coleridge invites us in "The Nightingale" to recall the Miltonic vision of that creature: "And hark! the Nightingale begins its song, / 'Most musical, most melancholy' bird!'" (ll. 12–13). But this Miltonic vision provokes in turn a contrary vision, the "different lore" that the poet and his party proclaim: "'Tis the merry Nightingale" (ll. 41–43). Romantic poetry is almost obsessively concerned with different lore and, consequently, with stubborn oppositions of thought and value. Proverbs of hell are opposed to the commandments of heaven, an ideology of Prometheus is organized in opposition to an ideology of Jupiter, and the tender idealisms of a young Don Juan are set off against the maxims of connoisseurship propounded by a Byronic narrator.

This literary phenomenon is by no means confined to the poetry of the Romantic period. In William Godwin's *Caleb Williams*, the aristocratic Mr.

Falkland plays heaven to the lowly Caleb's hell: "Why do you trifle with me? You little suspect the extent of my power," Falkland tells Caleb. "You might as well think of escaping from the power of the omnipresent God, as from mine!" (p. 144). In the *Frankenstein* of Godwin's daughter Mary, Frankenstein and his creature take turns accusing each other of radical acts of sin. In the works of Thomas Love Peacock, this drama of stark contrariety—which lends itself so readily to metaphysical expansions by way of such imagery as heaven and hell—explodes into a comic madhouse of multiplying systematizers, each scurrying about single-mindedly through the conversational landscapes of Peacock's novels, armed with his own intellectual orientation, his own system of logic, and his own peculiar vocabulary of definitions. For example, in *Nightmare Abbey*, published in 1818, Mr. Flosky addresses the assembled company: "I must do you, myself, and our mutual friends, the justice to observe, that let society only give fair play at one and the same time, as I flatter myself it is inclined to do, to your system of morals, and my system of metaphysics, and Scythrop's system of politics, and Mr. Listless's system of manners, and Mr. Toobad's system of religion, and the result will be as fine a mental chaos as even the immortal Kant could ever have hoped to see; in the prospect of which I rejoice" (Chap. 11).

This prospect of mental chaos, one notes, is associated not with disappearance of system but rather with a plethora of systems. The problem is that the mind is confronted with too many voices, each earnestly propounding its own peculiar conception of things. These differing conceptions are by no means fragmentary or dying. Instead, they are burgeoning and so enthralling that their proponents cannot admit the possibility of alternative thinking. This is particularly the theme of Peacock's earlier novel *Headlong Hall*, published in 1816, the instructive epigraph to which reads:

> All philosophers, who find
> Some favorite system to their mind,
> In every point to make it fit,
> Will force all nature to submit.

Accordingly, in *Headlong Hall* we encounter such conversations as the following:

"I am really astonished, gentlemen, at the very heterodox opinions I have heard you deliver: since nothing can be more obvious than that all animals were created solely and exclusively for the use of man."

"Even the tiger that devours him?" said Mr. Escot.

"Certainly," said Doctor Gaster.

"How do you prove it?" said Mr. Escot.

"It requires no proof," said Doctor Gaster: "it is a point of doctrine. It is written, therefore it is so."

"Nothing can be more logical," said Mr. Jenkison.

(Chap. 2)

The question becomes whether one can speak, as one used to think possible, of some universal truth that can be commonly determined by reference to a commonly apprehended "nature of things." This question itself becomes an object of debate in *Headlong Hall.*

MR. JENKISON. Good and evil exist only as they are perceived. I cannot therefore understand, how that which a man perceives to be good can be in reality an evil to him: indeed, the word *reality* only signifies *strong belief.*

MR. ESCOT. The views of such a man I contend are false. If he could be made to see the truth—

MR. JENKISON. He sees his own truth. Truth is that which a man *troweth.* Where there is no man there is no truth. Thus the truth of one is not the truth of another.

MR. ESCOT. I am aware of the etymology; but I contend that there is an universal and immutable truth, deducible from the nature of things.

MR. JENKISON. By whom deducible? Philosophers have investigated the nature of things for centuries, yet no two of them will agree in *trowing* the same conclusion.

(Chap. 7)

In Peacock, to be sure, dramatization of such questions produces largely comic effects. But there is a serious undercurrent to the comedy. This becomes increasingly apparent in Peacock's later novel *Crotchet Castle*, published in 1831. There, to take a single example, Squire Crotchet interrupts a debate over whether there is only one true logic to exclaim with a shade of pathos: "The sentimental against the rational, the intuitive against the inductive, the ornamental against the useful, the intense against the tranquil, the romantic against the classical; these are great and interesting controversies, which I should like, before I die, to see satisfactorily settled" (Chap. 2). But how can controversies be settled when "one nose points always east, and another always west, and each is ready to swear that it points due north" (*Crotchet Castle*, Chap. 4)?[28]

It is especially significant that even such seemingly conservative novelists of the Romantic period as Walter Scott and Jane Austen are also preoccupied with the hardening of thought into systems of fundamental opposition. In Scott's fiction, for example, tension between east and west, heaven and hell, turns into opposition between Whig and Tory, or supporters of the King and supporters of the Covenant. In Austen the historical metamorphoses into the domestic and we find households, or even members of the same household, set off against each other. In *Emma*, for example, Austen portrays the bewilderment of Mr. Woodhouse as he confronts what seems to him the chaos that reigns in his son-in-law's household. But she then makes Emma remark tellingly to her father: "That is the case with us all, papa. One half of the world cannot understand the pleasures of the other" (p. 81).

Austen touches on the heart of the Romantic matter in this speech of Emma's to her father. Romanticism is hardly alone in cleaving experience into such contrarieties as heaven and hell, spirit and body, king and people, reason and imagination. But what is particularly Romantic is the propensity to see these polarities as differing so fundamentally at the axiomatic level that each becomes not merely a viable system unto itself but also a nearly unsolvable mystery to systems beyond itself. William Shakespeare, for example, sets Antony off against Brutus, disturbing our minds for a time with dramatization of seemingly equally cogent arguments in justification of

---

28 · My thinking about Peacock's relationship to Romanticism has been strongly influenced by William Walling's fine essay " 'On Fishing Up the Moon': In Search of Thomas Love Peacock," in Donald H. Reiman *et al.* (eds.), *The Evidence of the Imagination* (New York, 1978), 334–53.

each of these warring parties. But this Shakespearean disturbance does not quite reach down to the axiomatic level. Shakespeare shows us Portia approaching Brutus to ask, "Is Brutus sick?"

> No, my Brutus;
> You have some sick offence within your mind,
> Which, by the right and virtue of my place,
> I ought to know of.
> (*Julius Caesar*, II, i, 261, 267–70)

He offers both Brutus and us the opportunity to recognize that Brutus' side of the question is in some basic way diseased.[29] But when such polarities are no longer viewed in terms of the struggle between health and disease, righteousness and perversity, clear and erroneous thought—when the opposition begins to be viewed, instead, as one that involves each side's radical inability to understand the other ("One half of the world cannot understand the pleasures of the other")—then we arrive at the intellectual situation provocative of Romantic thought. In Romanticism the voice of hell does not oppose that of heaven with the slogan, "Evil, be thou my Good." To the contrary, both hell and heaven are stoutly defending the good against the onslaughts of evil. They simply hold different axioms about what defines good and evil.

From a distanced or uncommitted perspective, contemplation of this situation tends to provoke uneasy awareness that any given conception of light, for example, could become, to another mind that happens to think differently, a conception of darkness. This provokes suspicion in Romantic thought about the sufficiency of systems of thought generally. Hence a kind of paradox: awareness of the rich multiplicity of intellectual possibilities engenders anxiety in particular situations that the mind might be failing to recognize some alternative of thought. If thought is allowed to pursue any

---

29 · For a useful discussion of how the Romantic period tended to bend Shakespeare toward conformity with its own preoccupations with multiple perspectives, see Joseph W. Donohue, Jr., *Dramatic Character in the English Romantic Age* (Princeton, N.J., 1970). See also the fifth chapter of Langbaum, *Poetry of Experience*.

given ideology any distance, is it not drifting into a trap of blind fanaticism, ignoring the possibility of some contrary pursuit of thought? William Godwin's odyssey toward Romanticism during the 1790s provides a revealing illustration. In 1797, four years after the appearance of *Enquiry Concerning Political Justice*, Godwin published a book titled *The Enquirer*. It is a collection of essays, which, as Godwin himself announces in his preface, is intended to present a "construction totally different" from that of the earlier *Enquiry*. There are, he explains, two basically different methods by which truth may be investigated. The first involves "laying down one or two simple principles, which seem scarcely to be exposed to the hazard of refutation; and then developing them." From this method, "we are led to hope" for two things: first, "that there will result a system consentaneous to itself"; and second, "that, if all the parts shall thus be brought into agreement with a few principles, and if those principles be themselves true, the whole will be found conformable to truth." This, he remarks, was the method he had attempted in the famous *Enquiry*.

Godwin then goes on to reveal the doubts he now has about that systematic method. Although an "enquiry thus pursued is undoubtedly in the highest style of man," it now appears to him "liable to many disadvantages," and "though there be nothing that it involves too high for our pride, it is perhaps a method of investigation incommensurate to our powers." One problem with the systematic method is that a "mistake in the commencement is fatal." Similarly, an "error in almost any part of the process is attended with extensive injury; where every thing is connected, as it were, in an indissoluble chain, and an oversight in one step vitiates all that are to follow." The reason Godwin is now so worried about such problems is that he has begun to see system itself as a sort of mental trap: "We proceed most safely, when we enter upon each portion of our process, as it were, *de novo* . . . there is danger, if we are too exclusively anxious about consistency of system, that we may forget the perpetual attention we owe to experience, the pole-star of truth." For this reason, Godwin has turned in *The Enquirer* toward the second method of investigating truth, which involves "incessant recurrence to experiment and actual observation." Now he "has attempted only a short excursion at a time; and then, dismissing that, has set out afresh upon a new pursuit." Godwin goes so far in this antisystematic direction as to assert that he "has not been severely anxious relative to inconsistencies that may be discovered, between the speculations of one Essay and the speculations of another." He presents his speculations "to the contemplative reader, not as *dicta*, but as the materials of thinking." The one-time systematizer has become a speculator, so anxious to avoid the "cold vanity of systems" that he is willing to entertain those inconsistencies that break system down.[30]

Godwin's address to his reader in the preface to *The Enquirer* calls to mind Wordsworth's later preface to *The Excursion:* "It is not the Author's intention formally to announce a system: it was more animating to him to proceed in a different course; and if he shall succeed in conveying to the mind clear thoughts, lively images, and strong feelings, the Reader will have no difficulty in extracting the system for himself."[31] Like Godwin, Wordsworth is giving the reader "materials of thinking." He offers the process of an excursion, a journey out from familiar, stable ground, as Godwin offers the activity of an enquirer rather than the end product of an enquiry. Wordsworth's remark that his reader should have no difficulty "in extracting the system for himself" needs to be considered in light of an important passage in *The Excursion* itself, wherein the Wanderer announces:

> If tired with systems, each in its degree
> Substantial, and all crumbling in their turn,
> Let him build systems of his own, and smile
> At the fond work, demolished with a touch.
> (IV, ll. 603–606)

We human beings of course discover in ourselves a propensity to build systems from experience (just as a shepherd builds a sheepfold, or a child a

30 · William Godwin, *The Enquirer* (London, 1797), v–viii. The last quotation is from Shelley, writing to Charles Ollier that Keats "has a fine imagination and ought to become something excellent; but he is at present entangled in the cold vanity of systems" (Letter of August 16, 1818 [Letter 476], in Frederick L. Jones [ed.], *The Letters of Percy Bysshe Shelley* [2 vols.; Oxford, U.K., 1964] II, 31). A favored entertainment among the Romantics was the practice of accusing one another of being trapped in systems and system building.
31 · Wordsworth, Preface to *The Excursion*, in Ernest De Selincourt and Helen Darbishire (eds.), *The Poetical Works of William Wordsworth* (5 vols.; Oxford, U.K., 1940–49), V, 2.

game from a deck of cards). But we should learn to stand back from our own propensity and smile at our "fond" work because, though we may love our constructs, they are foolhardy, "demolished with a touch."

Underlying this suspicion of system in both Godwin and Wordsworth is the Romantic question I raised earlier. If thought begins to proceed in any given direction, does this not mean that it has turned away from, that it is blinding itself to, the cogent claims of some other possible direction of thought? Any act of mental commitment, then, is in principle suspect and subject to a sudden shift of valuation: a given act can look for a moment heroic, or stabilizing; but then, contrarily, it can appear to be entangling the mind within boundaries of some particular vocabulary of thought, thereby rendering the mind incapable of understanding that "one half of the world" lying outside those boundaries. Among the Romantic poets, Blake seems to have been most sensitive to the fundamental dynamics of this issue. In *The [First] Book of Urizen*, the primal Fall is precipitated by emergence of a distinctive voice.[32]

> I have sought for a joy without pain,
> For a solid without fluctuation
> Why will you die O Eternals?
> Why live in unquenchable burnings?
>
> (Plate 4)

This Urizenic voice casts a "shadow of horror" in eternity, not because it promulgates the particular system it does, but because it promulgates system as such (Plate 3). Prior to Urizen's emergence:

> Earth was not: nor globes of attraction
> The will of the Immortal expanded
> Or contracted his all flexible senses.
> Death was not, but eternal life sprung.
>
> (Plate 3)

---

32 · In "Most Holy Forms of Thought: Some Observations on Blake and Language," *ELH*, XLI (1974), 555–77, Robert F. Gleckner argues that Blake, "as well as, of course, the other

Urizen seeks to establish (or, perhaps closer to Blake's notion of states, Urizen *is* the attempt to establish) meaning, The Meaning of this eternal activity—the original assertion of principles of value distinction and of a goal to be gained. But in so acting, Urizen gives rise to "globes of attraction": postulation of a quest also generates a quantity or context distinguished from and antithetical to the object of that quest, as postulation of *A* involves generation of *Not-A*. The Urizenic globe of attraction—a system of thought wherein expansion means ill rather than good, and "all-flexible" means "fluctuation" and "death" rather than a process of fertility—produces, first, an act of isolation, and second, a contrary globe of attraction wherein Urizenic ill becomes Orcean good. Thus of course the original expansion and contraction of the Immortal persists (like Pope's earlier Great Chain of Being, it cannot be fundamentally disrupted); but now the will of the Immortal has fragmented along lines of contrary party allegiances, the one party gathering under the banner of contraction and the other under the banner of expansion. Translated into less mythic terms, the mind divides against itself. Recall Goethe's *Faust:* "Zwei Seelen wohnen, ach! in meiner Brust, / Die eine will sich von der andern trennen" (Part I, ll. 1112–13).

Since the publication of Robert Langbaum's influential study *The Poetry of Experience* in 1957, it has been popular to propose that Romanticism invokes tests of experience as a means of resolving questions of truth and value. Godwin, in a previously quoted passage from *The Enquirer*, reminds us of "the perpetual attention we owe to experience, the pole-star of truth." But this appeal is much more a carry-over from the eighteenth century than it is a particularly Romantic phenomenon.[33] Experience may be confidently invoked to persuade us that cultivation of one's garden yields more pistachio nuts than does argument over whether this be the best or the worst of possible worlds, and experience may serve to reveal that Tom Jones is a better

---

Romantic poets," sought to create artistic forms that "invite us to imaginatively perceive their own self-destructiveness" (563).

33 · See Ernest Tuveson, "*An Essay on Man* and 'The Way of Ideas': Some Further Remarks," *Philological Quarterly*, XL (1961), 262–69, in which Tuveson discusses the eighteenth century's obsession with finding out experientially "what man really is, not what authority has said, or what philosophers have dreamed" (264).

fellow than his rival Blifil. But in Romanticism, while experience is still often invoked, it has itself become a problematic issue. Experience, for example, does not manage to demonstrate either that Frankenstein's creature is the good-natured being he claims to be or that he is the foul fiend Frankenstein claims him to be.[34]

The dilemma traces to Romantic suspicion that the basic premises of our thought mold our perception of experience, rather than the other way around. Thus the crucial line with which Blake marks our introduction to the world of his *Songs of Innocence and of Experience* is "And I stain'd the water clear" (Introduction to *Songs of Innocence*, l. 18). This line reads in contrary ways, depending on our mental predisposition of the moment: clear water is being stained dark; or, alternately, dark water is being stained clear. Blake's fundamental point is that the very act of writing, or of *composing* experience into any formulation, involves coloring (or bleaching) a precompositional nature of things.

As with the later singer at Key West in Wallace Stevens' poem, the song the mind sings composes the "reality" it believes it perceives—from which follows the view that the mind's singing of its particular song tends to inhibit it from hearing other songs, from perceiving other understandings of the world. Thus Blake's *Songs of Innocence and of Experience:* in the language of Innocence, for example, the act of guarding someone is perceived as protecting him from harm; but in the language of Experience, contrarily, that same activity implies confinement, as in a prison. For Innocence, "white as snow" means purity; but for Experience it means lack of life-giving warmth, absence of color, sterility, and stasis. Instead of appearing to be the humble handmaiden mediating between the mind and experience, therefore, the vocabulary of thought begins to look like a jealous master. This very mastery may be understood in contrary ways, depending upon whether the mind is singing a song of Innocence or one of Experience. For the mind singing within an Innocent vocabulary of thought, "a tender voice, / Making all the vales rejoice," is a lovely expression of the proper,

---

34 · I argue this thesis in "Frankenstein's Monster and Its Romantic Relatives: Problems of Knowledge in English Romanticism," *Texas Studies in Literature and Language*, XV (1973), 51–65.

desirable impulse to order, the power of the word gathering up life's divisions into a union of celebration ("The Lamb," ll. 7–8). But for a mind tuned to the vocabulary of Experience, sensitive to Tygers and to the biting chords of "mind-forged manacles," the word *Making* in "The Lamb" sounds like the clenching of a kid-gloved fist, and *tender* has a nasty, gastronomic ring.

Romantic preoccupation with competition among alternative systems, then, prompts meditation upon how a given vocabulary of thought may exert dominion over the mind, and this leads, in turn, toward meditations on both the weakness and the power of language.[35] In *Julian and Maddalo*, Shelley lets Julian receive the following reply to his impassioned argument:

> "My dear friend,"
> Said Maddalo, "my judgement will not bend
> To your opinion, though I think you might
> Make such a system refutation-tight
> *As far as words go.*"
>
> (ll. 191–95, italics mine)

To a mind looking in upon a systematic construction from beyond its boundaries, the words composing it seem not to go far at all. Words appear weak, because this distanced mind is aware of alternative languages, competing for recognition. Shelley laments in the "Hymn to Intellectual Beauty":

> No voice from some sublimer world hath ever
> To sage or poet these responses given—
> Therefore the name of God and ghosts and Heaven,
> Remain the records of their vain endeavour,
> Frail spells.
>
> (ll. 25–29)

The potency of language appears to exhaust itself in competition. Words begin to seem mere incantation, ignorant armies of names clashing by

35 · Simpson, *Irony and Authority*, discusses the Romantic search for a language that might prove resistant to the tyranny of "any system of institutional presuppositions" (68).

night. Hence the darkness of Keats's sonnet "Why Did I Laugh Tonight?": "O darkness!" darkness! ever must I moan, / To question heaven and hell and heart in vain!" (ll. 7–8). Once the mind becomes acutely conscious of the contention of voices, it runs the danger of falling into total disenchantment. As new Presbyter looks like Old Priest writ large, so heaven, hell, and heart begin to seem aspirants of the same dubious value.

This situation can generate a number of different responses. One of these, curiously enough, is a kind of awe or fascination. Once the mind experiences disenchantment, it may look back upon moments of linguistic involvement and commitment, and recognize in them an enchantment it had not perceived before; and this recognition can produce a sense of magic— hence, for example, Keats's reference to "the fine spell of words" in *The Fall of Hyperion* (l. 9). The situation can produce a quest for some new or unknown language, which casts a spell so powerful or so different that (for the moment at least) it transcends linguistic competition and wards off disenchantment. Alternately, a sense of linguistic frailty may lead to emphasis on the primacy of shape rather than concept: "O Attic shape! Fair attitude!"; "A speck, a mist, a shape, I wist!"; "And those foul shapes, abhorred by God and man— / Which under many a name and many a form"; "A dancing Shape, an Image gay, / To haunt, to startle, and way-lay."[36] Pressed to an extreme, this leads to Romantic interest in nonlinguistic arts: perhaps music, painting, or sculpture can express a tale more sweetly than rhyme. A sense of linguistic frailty leads also to the more fundamental inclination of the Romantic poet to favor in art the act of dramatization or the telling of a tale. When the adequacy of language becomes suspect, then the mind's impulse may be to fall back in the direction of the most primitive forms of attempted communication—showing something by acting out, or relating a bare sequence of events.

But Romantic literary art cannot, of course, completely free itself from the bonds of language. When Wordsworth writes, "Imagination—here the Power so called / Through sad incompetence of human speech," he expresses a Romantic literary predicament: human speech may be sadly incompe-

36 · Respectively, Keats, "Ode on a Grecian Urn," l. 41; Coleridge, "The Rime of the Ancient Mariner," l. 153; Shelley, *Prometheus Unbound*, 3, iv, ll. 180–81; Wordsworth, "She Was a Phantom of Delight," ll. 9–10.

tent, but some word must be employed to address that power that rises from the mind's abyss (1850 *Prelude*, VI, ll. 592–93). Faced, therefore, with the necessity of operating within linguistic confines, literary Romanticism confronts the dangerous potency inherent in whatever language the mind is forced, finally, to employ. Names may be frail spells, but to the mind engaged in wielding those spells they threaten to become extremely strong. A fundamental problem attendant upon Romanticism, then, is how to weave the spells of language without becoming helplessly caught up in the spell making—how to work competently with the sad incompetence of human speech. Wordsworth notes in his third "Essay upon Epitaphs" that "words are too awful an instrument for good and evil to be trifled with: they hold above all other external powers a dominion over thoughts."[37] The problem for the Romantics, if that dominion be inescapable, is to find means of breaking free from tyrannical despotism and of turning the potency of language to advantage. The problem for the critic treating the Romantics is to recognize the means that the Romantics employed, and to avoid falling into a linguistic despotism against which the Romantics themselves were struggling.

IN the penultimate line of Blake's "The Sick Rose," a lamenting singer of Experience refers with bitter irony to the "dark secret love" with which an invading worm seeks to "destroy" the life of a rose. But *destroy* here refers not to the reality of the situation but rather to how a mind of Experience perceives reality. What for the speaker is irony, therefore, functions to direct the reader's attention to a nonironic way of thinking about this "love"

37 · Wordsworth, "Essay upon Epitaphs," in W. J. B. Owen and Jane Worthington Smyser (eds.), *The Prose Works of William Wordsworth* (3 vols.; Oxford, U.K., 1974), II, 84. In *Wordsworth: Language as Counter-Spirit* (New Haven, 1977), Frances Ferguson "attempts to trace the winding course of the relationship between language and consciousness in Wordsworth's poetry" (xvii). In a notebook entry Coleridge observes that "it is the instinct of the Letter to bring into subjection to itself the Spirit" (Kathleen Coburn [ed.], *The Notebooks of Samuel Taylor Coleridge* [3 vols. to date; New York, 1957, 1961; Princeton, N.J., 1973], III, No. 4350. For a general overview of the development of Romantic ideas about language, see Chap. 2 in Gerald R. Bruns, *Modern Poetry and the Idea of Language: A Critical and Historical Study* (New Haven, 1974).

of the worm for the rose that is radically opposed to the way the speaker is thinking. The speaker (a lamenting gardener, father, worshipper, or would-be lover—or all combined) sees in the situation the devastation of his beloved rose's purity. But one might see it, just as well, as an act of fulfillment, quite literally an act of love between male and female elements of nature that insures the ongoing process of life. From this viewpoint, the speaker of Experience seeks not to preserve life but to arrest it and render it sterile.

In Keats's "La Belle Dame sans Merci" an enamored knight-at-arms says of the "fairy's child" he has encountered in the meads, "She look'd at me *as* she did love, / And made sweet *moan*," and then later, "And *sure in language strange* she said— / I love thee true" (ll. 19–20, 27–28, italics mine). As in the Blake lyric, Keats's employment of these phrases serves to alert the observing mind to a manner of thinking that is at odds with the one being expressed by the dramatic voice addressing us in the poem. Could this fairy child's "language strange" be understood, it *might* convey to us a much less lovable vision of her encounter with the forceful, single-minded knight.

Once the mind begins pondering the possibility that one half of the world cannot understand the pleasures of the other half, literary effects like those in Keats and Blake begin to follow: perhaps what looks like joy to the world's knights may look like rapine to the world's fairy children; what looks like rapine to the world's gardeners may look like love to the worms and roses of the world. The specter of enthrallment to single-minded perception haunts Romantic literary art. It fascinates the Romantic artist, and he is fond of exploring it in dramatic representations. However, it also threatens him, inasmuch as he himself is in danger of becoming enthralled. Hence Romantic concern for cultivating awareness that there either are or may be significant alternatives to any given manner of thinking about an issue or a phenomenon. One product of this concern is Romantic interest in seeking or simply positing the existence of some "language strange," a new, unapprehended alternative that might wrench the mind free of blind submission to whatever familiar language is commonly employed and trusted without question. Thus Shelley argues in *A Defence of Poetry* that new poets must always be arising in order to "create afresh the associations" of a poetic language that needs to be *"vitally metaphorical."*[38]

Perhaps the quest demands a new poet—but, alternately, perhaps the old poet can make himself new by turning from old methods of composition. In his preface to *Laon and Cythna*, Shelley announces that his poem "occupied little more than six months in the composition"; and he then defends this apparent haste with the argument that had he followed the more conventional method of "long labour and revision," he might have lost "much of the newness and energy of imagery and language as it flowed afresh from my mind."[39] We are encouraged to listen to the mind in new ways or, another alternative, to try to listen to new voices beyond the mind. "With what strange utterance did the loud dry wind / Blow through my ears!" exclaims Wordsworth in *The Prelude* of 1805 (I, ll. 348–49). The Romantic mind strives to tune the ear to "strange utterance." It listens to the confessions of opium eaters. It tries to hear the "ghostly language of the ancient earth" (1805 *Prelude*, II, l. 328). It entertains speculations about learning "the language of another world" (Byron, *Manfred*, III, iv, l. 7), and strains after "the language of the dead" (Shelley, *Prometheus Unbound*, I, l. 138).[40] It makes us attend to the voice of the Idiot Boy: "The cocks did crow to-whoo, to-whoo, / And the sun did shine so cold!" (Wordsworth, "The Idiot Boy," ll. 450–51). It teases the mind out of human thought and into perplexing confrontation with the tautological utterance of a Grecian urn.

But the primary purpose of such Romantic strains is not, as some older lines in Romantic criticism held, to lead the mind into uncommon revelation by pursuing "superior forms of consciousness and perception."[41] The purpose, instead, is to deliver the mind from its manacles by recalling thought to the prima facie possibility of basic alternatives: one *can* think differently. Thus, for example, in his much misunderstood poem *The Excursion*, Words-

38 · Shelley, *A Defence of Poetry*, in *Shelley's Poetry and Prose*, 482, italics mine.
39 · Shelley, Preface to *Laon and Cyntha*, in Roger Ingpen and Walter E. Peck (eds.), *The Complete Works of Percy Bysshe Shelley* (10 vols.; London, 1924–30), I, 246.
40 · Concerning the latter, see Norman Thurston, "The Second Language of *Prometheus Unbound*," *Philological Quarterly*, LV (1976), 126–33.
41 · The phrase is Northrop Frye's, from his *Study of English Romanticism* (New York, 1968), 29.

worth weaves an extremely complex drama from confrontation between the "bitter language of the heart" and the consolatory language of a distanced, reasoning intellectual perspective (III, l. 462). As recent criticism has begun to recognize, however, the poem's conflict does not resolve itself so readily as was once supposed into distinctions between error and right reason.[42] Instead, *The Excursion* is a dramatic meditation concerned with the persistence of irresolution; it has closer affinities with Johnson's "Conclusion, in Which Nothing Is Concluded" than with Pope's "One truth is clear." The bitter language of the heart is not silenced in *The Excursion;* nor is the voice of consolation delivered over to despondency. Thus, for example, in a crucial passage from Book III, the Solitary responds to one of the Wanderer's many consolatory effusions:

> Forgive me, if I say
> That an appearance which hath raised your minds
> To an exalted pitch (the self-same cause
> Different effect producing) is for me
> Fraught rather with depression than delight.
> (ll. 152–56)

As this passage suggests, Wordsworth's Solitary and Wanderer are antagonists in a recurring Romantic drama. Objective experience has metamorphosed into an "appearance," as the Solitary calls it, suggestive of the proliferation of competing perspectives that have emerged in the Romantic situation. And like Blake's singer of Innocence and singer of Experience, like Scott's Claverhouse and Burley, like Shelley's Julian and Maddalo, Wordsworth's Solitary and Wanderer are representations of the mind's tendency to become enthralled by the mental manacles of one exclusive perspective— color the world light or color it dark, proclaim it fire or proclaim it ice—from which it is not to be moved.

It is not so much the dramatic characters but rather the readers who are the primary object of artistic manipulation in such Romantic works. The

---

42 · See A. H. Gomme, "Some Wordsworthian Transparencies," *Modern Language Review,* LXVIII (1973), 507–20, esp. 519–20.

literary artifact is designed to move the reader, in company with the artist, toward a free mental space beyond or between enthrallments through simultaneous invocation of competing enthrallments. When the tyranny of words is pitted against itself, in that space where both Innocence and Experience, for example, are played off against each other before the mind's eye, consciousness carves out a space for itself in which it can evade the mind's natural tendency toward blind submission. William Hazlitt suggests in his essay "Logic," published in 1829, that the mind "has a natural bias to wrap up its conclusions (of whatever kind or degree) in regular forms of words, and to deposit them in an imposing framework of demonstration; it prefers the shadow of certainty to the substance of truth and candour; and will not, if it can help it, leave a single loop-hole for doubt to creep in at. Hence the tribe of logicians, dogmatists, and verbal pretenders of all sorts."[43]

It is not the Romantic ambition to merely engage in more of the same such tribal activity, nor is it even to bring all the differing tribes into union, pursuing the reconciliation of opposites that is sometimes thought to constitute the fixed idea of Romanticism. The Romantic ambition is to raise us above our "natural bias," to let us learn to control rather than to be controlled by the tribal impulse. One obvious way of beginning to do so is to become the distanced observer of different tribal behaviors. In *The Fortunes of Nigel*, Scott remarks of his hero that he "was somewhat immured within the Bastile of his rank." Nigel had not yet grasped "the important lesson, that amusement, and, what is of more consequence, that information and increase of knowledge, are to be derived from the conversation of every individual whatsoever, with whom he is thrown into a natural train of communication" (Chap. 27). It is important to escape from the "Bastile"—to listen to the voices of "every individual whatsoever," to free the mind by hearing songs other than the ones we normally sing.

When Blake, in a famous passage, makes Los proclaim, "I must Create a System, or be enslav'd by another Mans," it is tempting to posit that Blake's own goal is the establishment of system (*Jerusalem*, Plate 10). Generalizing from this, we might suppose that a like goal occupies the artistic energies of

---

43 · William Hazlitt, "Logic," in P. P. Howe (ed.), *The Complete Works of William Hazlitt* (21 vols; London, 1930–34), XX, 230.

the other Romantics as well. But this popular view overlooks two things. First, Los (and perhaps Blake behind Los?) proposes creation of a system, not as a goal desirable in itself, but rather as a technique for freeing the mind from the encroachments of extant systems. The program is one of Blake's several variations on the Romantic design discussed above, whereby the tyranny of words is to be pitted against itself. Second, as the following line in the Blake passage makes clear, Blake's primary emphasis is on the activity rather than on the product: "I will not Reason & Compare: my business is to Create" (Plate 10).[44] The construction of an order is significant, not for the sake of the particular order that is constructed, but for the constructive activity that frees the mind from submission to encroaching extant dogmatisms.

Blake's onetime patron William Hayley offers a more conventional mind's celebration of such creative activity in his glorification of the epic poet Ariosto: "Born every law of System to disown, / And rule by Fancy's boundless power alone" (*Essay on Epic Poetry*, III, ll. 155–56).[45] The quest is not to discover some system that is "true" and "real," the emanation of the *Ding an sich*; it is rather to escape "every law of System," to escape mere submission or blind acceptance, and instead to "rule." The quest is to gain control over the products of the mind's ordering impulse by rediscovering access to the activities of that impulse itself—to seek in the mind for that "boundless power" that makes the boundaries that we experience. We may combat submission to power by discovering the seeds of power within ourselves; and thus perhaps in ourselves we may find free space, interstices between systematic constructions.

It is this kind of thinking that underlies the creation of such curious literary phenomena as Byron's *Don Juan*, wherein the emphasis falls upon the

---

44 · In *Romantic Will* Cooke struggles with the paradox of Blake pitting system against system, and decides that Blake was not trying to "institute a state of atomic incoherence," but only trying to break down traditional notions of system in order to develop a new definition (123–24). Inclining toward the opposite view is Jerome J. McGann in "The Aim of Blake's Prophesies and the Uses of Blake Criticism," in Stuart Curran and Joseph Anthony Wittreich, Jr. (eds.), *Blake's Sublime Allegory* (Madison, Wis., 1973), 3–21. Robert F. Gleckner expands discussion of the issue to the Romantics generally in "Romanticism and the Self-Annihilation of Language," *Criticism*, XVIII (1976), 173–89.

45 · William Hayley, *Poems and Plays* (3 vols.; London, 1788), III, 54.

creative activity itself. One recalls Byron's response to his publisher John Murray's inquiry about that poem: "You ask me for the plan of Donny Johnny—I *have* no plan—I *had* no plan—but I had or have materials. . . . Why Man the Soul of such writing is it's licence?—at least the *liberty* of that *licence* if one likes." [46] It is significant that Byron's language here veers slightly in the direction of religious rhetoric. The "soul" of such writing as *Don Juan* does have, for a Romantic mind, something to do with the soul. Although the soul may be burdened by her earthly freight, she rediscovers something of her liberty and freedom of choice in the creative activity of *Don Juan.*[47]

46 · Byron to John Murray, August 12, 1819, in Leslie A. Marchand (ed.), *Byron's Letters and Journals* (12 vols.; Cambridge, Mass., 1973–82), VI, 207–208.

47 · In *Shelley's Annus Mirabilis,* Stuart Curran analyzes the close relationship between Romantic preoccupation with freedom and the skeptical impulse; see esp. his discussion of the "imperative" of a skeptical poet "to learn to live in that fluid realm between certainties" and his observation that "the point of skepticism is to free one from those external forms that settle questions by tyrannizing the mind" (155, 205).

· *Two* ·

Romantic Poetic Strategy

The Means and Ends of Questioning

U NTIL recently it was not gener-
ally supposed that Romantic poetry contained much strategy. Even the New
Critics, aficionados of intricate poetic maneuvering, tended to misjudge the
Romantics on this matter. William Empson, for example, looked for "doctrines" in Wordsworth's "Tintern Abbey": "Wordsworth seems to have
believed in his own doctrines and wanted his readers to know what they
were. It seems reasonable, then, to try to extract . . . definite opinions on
the relations of God, man, and nature, and on the means by which such
relations can be known."[1] Empson, a clear-minded reader of poetry, could
see that these postulated doctrines were not to be extracted from Wordsworth's poem. However, instead of deciding, therefore, that the postulate
must be wrong, Empson decided there must be some failing in Wordsworth.
That it did not occur to Empson to wonder if Wordsworth was pursuing
some strategy involving ideological questioning can be traced back to the
pressures of attributional Romantic theory discussed in the previous chap-

1 · William Empson, *Seven Types of Ambiguity*, (3rd ed. rev.; London, 1953), 151–52.

ter. Romantic poems, it used to be commonly assumed, were written to convey the dogmas of a Romantic ideology. This same doubtful direction in critical thinking about Romanticism was influential in perpetuating critical devaluation of Byron early in the twentieth century. Byron seems to play with ideologies. If Romanticism is an ideology, then Byron must not be a very substantial Romantic poet.

The order-chaos version of problematic Romantic theory works better. It redirects emphasis from ideology (order) in the poetry toward the difficult activity of doctrinal construction: the poet is now viewed as struggling to build or to maintain some solid ground in the midst of threatening chaos. For this type of theory one can see not arriving at doctrinal clarity as a sort of success. To fail in a heroic quest can appear heroic. Byron starts looking better: "When Byron 'contradicts' himself, he is not changing his mind but revealing its ability to see an idea or event in several different ways at nearly the same time." Perhaps Byron, like Hamlet, simply thinks too well. Coleridge also profits from this association of failure with heroic endeavor: "In the Conversation Poems, extensions of his development as poet and thinker, we find a struggle between the unifying imagination and the analytic, abstract force of speculative reason. . . . The surface play of scenery and friendly dialogue is a mask for the poet's inner struggle to organize the ideas about God and Nature which influenced his early life."[2]

However, this direction in critical thinking also gives little attention to matters of poetic strategy. When an ideology does not emerge clearly from the poetic construct, it is still assumed that one was intended to do so. The poet, so it is thought, must have been struggling to accomplish something that for some reason the poem does not succeed in producing. So, for example, in *Romantic Will* Michael G. Cooke argues of Keats's "Ode to a Nightingale" that, though "wishing to be a poem of consummations," it "remains a poem of problematical beginnings." And Earl R. Wasserman in *Shelley: A Critical Reading* argues in a similarly curious way about

---

2 · Jerome J. McGann, *"Don Juan" in Context* (Chicago, 1976), 104; James D. Boulger, "Imagination and Speculation in Coleridge's Conversation Poems," *JEGP*, LXIV (1965), 692–93. See also McFarland's argument in *Coleridge and the Pantheist Tradition* that for Coleridge, as for Hamlet, a "seeming indecision before conflicting claims is a true emblem of his integrity" (107).

Shelley's "Mont Blanc": "The assertion Shelley would like to make is evident, just as it is clear he wishes he could assert more than his 'modest creed' in the 'Conclusion' of 'The Sensitive Plant'; but the skeptical grounds of the poem will not sustain it."[3] Such critical thinking does not consider the possibility that the poet may be doing exactly what he intended in the poem and that the poem's ideological instability is part of a complex poetic strategy. Is it not perhaps most sensible to pursue this possibility that poets know what they are doing when they write as they do? A number of recent studies have moved in this direction.[4] The exploration leads us into the realm of Romantic questioning.

IN an essay titled "On Belief," published in the latter days of the Romantic period, William Godwin proposes that

> the mind of man is of a peculiar nature. It has been disputed whether we can entertain more than one idea at a time. But certain it is, that the views of the mind at any one time are considerably narrowed. The mind is like the slate of a schoolboy, which can contain only a certain number of characters of a given size. . . . Many things are therefore almost inevitably shut out, which, had it not been so, might have essentially changed the view of the case, and have taught me that it was a very different conclusion at which I ought to have arrived.[5]

This idea that holding one idea can militate against entertaining an alternative idea, since the mind's "views" at any given time are "considerably

---

3 · Cooke, *Romantic Will*, 169; Wasserman, *Shelley*, 238.
4 · See D. F. Rauber, "The Fragment as Romantic Form," *MLQ*, XXX (1969), 212–21, who argues for seeing the fragment as the highest embodiment of "romantic ideals and aims" (212). See A. Harris Fairbanks, "The Form of Coleridge's Dejection Ode," *PMLA*, XC (1975), who argues that ambiguity is "inherent in the form of the Romantic ode" (881). In *The Lyrics of Shelley* (Cleveland, 1972), Judith Chernaik proposes that Shelley's poems move "toward possibility, toward questions, rather than demonstrating or reaffirming doctrine" (62). Jerome J. McGann has argued that Byron's tales and metaphysical dramas served as a means of "exploring the intellectual questions which never ceased to bother him" (*"Don Juan" in Context* [26]); see, however, McGann's more recent thoughts about questioning in *The Romantic Ideology*.
5 · Godwin, *Thoughts on Man*, 254.

narrowed," recalls some of William Blake's key preoccupations, expressed early in the Romantic period: "For man has closed himself up, till he sees all things thro' narrow chinks of his cavern" (*The Marriage of Heaven and Hell*, Plate 14). Because of the character of the Romantic situation, discussed in the previous chapter, issues of mental freedom and entrapment figure most importantly in Romantic thought and literary art. Particular vocabularies of expression look suspect to a Romantic mind. Secure mental convictions look suspiciously like dogmatic imprisonments that narrow the mind's views, as Godwin says, and "inevitably shut out" alternative possibilities. For this reason the Romantic writer is inclined to entertain questions as a positive value. A question forces open doors that are closing and introduces rather than shuts out possibilities. Questioning prevents free inquiry from freezing into conviction.

Canto IV of *Childe Harold's Pilgrimage* opens with the famous lines, "I stood in Venice, on the Bridge of Sighs; / A palace and a prison on each hand." For the reader familiar with the geographical location Byron refers to, this seems at first an odd, even factually erroneous statement. The Bridge of Sighs actually lies between the Ducal palace on the one side and the Venetian state prisons on the other, whereas Byron's phrase "on each hand" seems to assert that a prison and a palace lie on both ends of the bridge on which his hero stands. But a moment's reflection clarifies Byron's design. Byron is placing himself (and us) carefully in the middle. To an unreflective mind the Bridge of Sighs would be something, not to take a stand upon, but to travel over—and the desirable direction of travel would appear obvious: better to move, if possible, from the prison side to the palace side. But Byron's phrasing functions to cast such clear, simple thinking into question by implying that there is really no difference between the two sides of the bridge. The palace itself is simply a disguised prison. What one really faces, then, is only a choice between imprisonments. We are invited, therefore, to stand with the hero in the middle, on the bridge, and to adopt a perspective that maintains its distance from the traps that lie at either end. We may profitably keep this Byronic maneuver in mind when reading Romantic poetry generally. It is usually a mistake to suppose that the Romantic poet must be eager to exchange his "Sighs" for the seemingly comfortable haven of some palatial dogmatic certainty. The Romantics were actually inclined to see prisons behind the palaces that loom up so temptingly at the end of the bridge. Hence the exploratory pattern of most Romantic poetry: a dynamic process that involves attraction and withdrawal, movement in some given direction balanced by movement or at least feints in alternative or even directly contradictory directions, questions that do not quite resolve themselves into sufficient answers, apparent answers that serve merely to raise more basic questions.[6]

That such maneuverings in Romantic poetry are either unconscious or accidental is extremely doubtful. When Keats exhibits his mind bidding adieu to the nightingale, for example, he marks the significance of that turn in "Ode to a Nightingale" with great care. This suggests that Keats has not been frustrated in his quest after the nightingale. To the contrary, he has been writing a poem that dramatizes such aspiration, explores its implications, and finally draws back from the prison that the exploration has revealed. The nightingale represents one of those many seeming palaces that the Romantic poets recognize to be attractive, offering the mind an apparent refuge from its Bridge of Sighs: "Here, where men sit and hear each other groan" (l. 24). But this refuge is only a temptation, a feathery version of the old Bower of Bliss. When Keats represents the mind drawing back from the nightingale with the words, "Forlorn! the very word is like a bell / To toll me back from thee to my sole self," there is a significant play on the word *sole.*[7] The famous analogue to this mind is Faust, whose soul is rescued from the cup of poison by the sound of bells, choirs, and a chorus of angels singing, "Christ is arisen!" When the nightingale disappears, it is said to be *"buried deep* / In the next valley-glades" (ll. 77–78, italics mine). The "sole

6 · Stuart M. Sperry's exploratory essay "Toward a Definition of Romantic Irony in English Literature," in Goerge Bornstein (ed.), *Romantic and Modern: Revaluations of Literary Tradition* (Pittsburgh, 1977), proposes that "indeterminacy" is a special "quality of awareness" that recurs in Byron, Shelley, and Keats (4–5). See also Donald H. Reiman, "Coleridge and the Art of Equivocation," *SIR,* XXV (1986), 325–50, for a fine analysis of how Coleridge employs "equivocation" in *Biographia Literaria* to establish claims without quite having to commit himself to them.

7 · Many readers sense either tragedy or loss in the return to self that occurs at the conclusion of Keats's nightingale ode. So, for example, Morris Dickstein, in *Keats and His Poetry: A Study in Development* (Chicago, 1971), sees the poem as charting "a circuitous but definitive course through visionary and naturalistic aspiration to tragic self-definition and self-knowledge" (xiv–xv). Recovery of the soul, however, is not tragic. (Keats is fond of the *sole/*

self," in contrast, has resisted temptation to seek a like burial. In thus delivering the soul from the nightingale, Keats executes a strategy that is emblematic of the characteristic Romantic ambition: to explore yet also to rise above enticing convictions that imprison.

U P to a point, reading Romantic poetry is much like reading René Descartes' famous *Meditations*. Descartes also leads us toward rather than away from questioning. Descartes' quest was for some proposition not open to doubt; and this quest was part of a program to deliver the mind from the possibility of error. Descartes' procedure was to adopt the tool of radical skepticism, submitting all beliefs to question, exposing them to the test of doubt and breaking them down when they proved doubtable. He moved metaphorically downward in the attempt to uncover the generally hidden or unconsidered assumptions that support belief. Ultimately, beneath those assumptions, he hoped to find a solid ground.

The Romantic poets, like Descartes, are questioners who invoke or subtly hint at negative examples, and explore the possibility that one might think quite differently from the way one happens to be thinking at the moment. They are wont to view experience in terms of veils or surfaces that cover important, unapprehended things. Hence Coleridge's preoccupation with sources "far inward"; Keats's ambition to "think *into* the human heart"; Wordsworth's concern to reveal the *"naked* dignity of man."[8] The movement in Romantic poems, as with Descartes, tends to be downward. One thinks, for example, of the journey in Blake's *Marriage of Heaven and Hell*: "So he took me thro' a stable & thro' a church & down into the church vault at the end of which was a mill: thro' the mill we went, and came to a cave. Down the winding cavern we groped" (Plate 17). Another familiar case in point would be the commencement of the Mariner's journey in Coleridge's "Rime of the Ancient Mariner."

---

soul pun. He uses it again when marking a crucial turn in "The Eve of St. Agnes": "These let us wish away, / And turn, sole-thoughted, to one Lady there" [ll. 41–42].)

8 · Samuel Taylor Coleridge, *Biographia Literaria*, ed. J. Shawcross (2 vols.; London, 1907), I, 66; Keats to John Hamilton Reynolds, May 3, 1816, in *Letters of John Keats*, I, 282; Wordsworth, Preface to *Lyrical Ballads*, in *Prose Works*, I, 140. Italics in the quotations are mine.

> The ship was cheered, the harbour cleared,
> Merrily did we drop
> Below the kirk, below the hill,
> Below the lighthouse top.
>
> (ll. 21–24)

Not *to* the lighthouse, as in the later design of Virginia Woolf, but rather *below* it: the concern is not to mark the beacons that guide us through the night but rather to investigate what ground, if any, those beacons rest upon. On one level, the Mariner's journey down, like that of Blake's persona and angel in *The Marriage of Heaven and Hell,* becomes the journey of skeptical inquiry, modeled upon the methods of logic and geometric thought. Upon what foundations do we build up our structures of belief and value; upon what unacknowledged axioms rest the "truths" we so confidently trust in living our lives? The mariner goes down merrily, unsuspectingly, but when he rises to the surface again, precisely reversing the downward sequence of "kirk," "hill," and "lighthouse," the once familiar world seems a dream.

> Oh! dream of joy! is this indeed
> The light-house top I see?
> Is this the hill? is this the kirk?
> Is this mine own countree?
>
> (ll. 464–67)

The motif of a downward journey has of course a long, venerable tradition. Homer and Virgil give us descents into the underworld; Pope depicts a mock-heroic journey down to the Cave of Spleen. But what is particularly Romantic in the Romantic poets' versions of the motif is the product of the journey. As we see in Coleridge's poem, the Mariner rises to the surface not with answers but with a flurry of questions. The downward journey in Romanticism tends to disrupt rather than to confirm or clarify.

In his *Meditations* Descartes asks, "How do I know that I am not myself deceived every time I add 2 and 3, or count the sides of a square, or judge of things yet simpler, if anything simpler can be suggested?"[9] Blake asks in *The Marriage of Heaven and Hell*: "How do you know but ev'ry Bird that cuts the airy way, / Is an immense world of delight, clos'd by your senses five?" (Plate 7). How do you know? The seemingly substantial world of beliefs, values, and conceptions of proper order loses its stability under the pressure of the Romantic question. The reader is forced backward or downward toward encounter with his presuppositions and then, beyond this, toward confrontation with whatever may account for his holding of those presuppositions.

In *The Marriage of Heaven and Hell* Blake announces his program of "printing in the infernal method, by corrosives, which in Hell are salutary and medicinal, melting apparent surfaces away, and displaying the infinite which was hid" (Plate 14). This has particular reference to Blake's peculiar process of illuminated printing, but it also helps to illuminate a common characteristic of Romantic poetry generally. The poetry of the Romantics employs the "infernal method": it melts apparent surfaces away by subjecting to scrutiny the sufficiency of established (heavenly) conceptions of things. Among its corrosive techniques, the most obvious is that of the direct question. Blake's "Tyger," a poem composed exclusively of questions, is an extreme example. One thinks too of such poems as Wordsworth's "Matthew," Keats's "Ode to a Nightingale," and Shelley's "Mont Blanc." These poems are structured so as to hold their question back until the end, letting it burst upon the reader's mind in the final lines with the effect of rendering what has come before hypothetical, fragile, or uncertain. In "Mont Blanc," for example, as the reader follows the mind's meditations upon the spectacle of Mont Blanc, he is offered a series of intuitions about the nature of things. Yet the poem ends with the question:

> And what were thou, and earth, and stars, and sea,
> If to the human mind's imaginings
> Silence and solitude were vacancy?
>
> (ll. 142–44)

9 · René Descartes, Meditation I of the *Meditations on First Philosophy*, in *Descartes' Philosophical Writings*, selected and translated by Norman Kemp Smith (London, 1952), 199.

Confronting us with this "If," the poem forces us to ponder the contingency of the empirical evidence on which we base our sublime flights of metaphysical assertion.

Wordsworth's "Lines Written in Early Spring" employs a similar "infernal method." The poem contains several propositions that might be mistaken for assertions of Wordsworthian (or even Romantic) ideology: the human heart grieves for "what man has made of man"; flowers, unlike corrupt men, enjoy the air they breathe; even the mere motion of birds, to a mind in tune with nature, contains "a thrill of pleasure." But the poem's concluding stanza brings such ideological cataloging up short, when it submits subtly to question the basic assumption behind the line of thought that generates such ideologies.

> If this belief from heaven be sent,
> If such be Nature's holy plan,
> Have I not reason to lament
> What man has made of man?
>
> (ll. 21–24)

The poem is suddenly revealed to be something closer to a dramatic monologue than to the mere calm, objective poem of meditation it had previously seemed to be. We are listening to a speaker trying to prove an argument, someone who anxiously wants to believe confidently in the doctrines he has been advancing. What we are maneuvered into thinking about, therefore, as in Shelley's poem, is the Romantic "If." What would one have to know, or at least simply choose to take on blind faith, in order to believe these doctrines about the gaiety of nonhuman nature and the inhumanity of man to man that the poem's earlier stanzas had so blithely articulated? The 1798 version of the concluding stanza of "Lines Written in Early Spring" accentuates the importance of this "If" factor.

> If I these thoughts may not prevent,
> If such be of my creed the plan,

> Have I not reason to lament
> What man has made of man?
>
> (ll. 21–24)

Emphasis falls more obviously here on thought process—if we cannot help thinking something, must it not be so?—than on the ideological product.

Often in Romantic poetry the corrosive technique operates in a less obvious fashion. Rather than posing the question directly, the Romantic poem will execute maneuvers that provoke the thoughtful reader to pose questions for himself. Wordsworth's "Anecdote for Fathers" exhibits a variation of this technique. The poem plays upon the reader's expectation that poetry is or should be somehow significant, grappling with important problems and arriving at important conclusions. By making the "anecdote" of his poem flirt with the inane, or what appears to be the inane, Wordsworth teases the reader into a state of half-irritated suspense. What is the point of all this muddling conversation between father and child? The poem simply ends abruptly, providing only the assertion that some kind of "lore" has been gained by the speaker.

> O dearest, dearest boy! my heart
> For better lore would seldom yearn,
> Could I but teach the hundredth part
> Of what from thee I learn.
>
> (ll. 57–60)

What precisely is this lore? Since we are not told, we are teased back into the anecdote again with a questioning mind, looking for hints. Small details of the poem become problematic, much in the way one of Blake's lyrics will begin to expand and shift shapes as one concentrates attention upon it. Perhaps the anecdote offers simply a lesson in lying; but Wordsworth has introduced some delicate touches that look symbolic (the "dry" walk, suggesting spiritual desiccation; the "gilded" weather vane, suggesting disguise), and thus make one uneasy about this easy reading, as they begin to suggest the possibility of an intuition of truth in the child's seemingly odd assertions. In the following chapter I will try to follow in more detail where such Wordsworthian maneuverings take us. Here I simply want to suggest broadly how Wordsworth's poem works upon our minds—how it exhibits a strategy designed to provoke corrosion of easy answers and comfortably held conclusions. By teasing the mind toward questions, the poem melts apparent surfaces away.

The most subtle of such corrosive techniques is that by which a Romantic poem sometimes seems to fulfill expectation, providing what at first glance appears to be a conclusion at the poem's climax—but which, upon examination, loses its conclusive force and so provokes renewed inquiry. A relatively stark example is provided by the question-answer structure of Keats's "La Belle Dame sans Merci." The poem begins with a question: "O what can ail thee, knight at arms, / Alone and palely loitering?" And then in the final stanza the question appears to be answered: "And this is why I sojourn here, / Alone and palely loitering" (ll. 45–46). But when we think about this conclusion, we find that *this* has no clear reference. Perhaps it refers to the effect of the knight's dream: having been warned in his dream, the knight has awakened from—escaped from—the spell that La Belle Dame sought to cast upon him. Or, considering the knight's sad present condition, perhaps the reason he still loiters is that he continues to be under the spell. Or maybe a spell has not been cast at all. The knight was warned against La Belle Dame in a dream. Perhaps the warning, then, was simply some fear or hesitation arising from within himself that caused him to lose his chance with one of the finer tones of life. The apparent answer with which Keats's poem concludes, in other words, dissolves into a multitude of questions. "La Belle Dame sans Merci," like Keats's famous image of the "large Mansion of Many Apartments," turns into a labyrinth of many open but dark doorways that teases the mind toward experiencing alternative possibilities of thought.[10]

---

10 · Keats to John Hamilton Reynolds, May 3, 1818, in *Letters of John Keats*, I, 280. Coleridge's "Rime of the Ancient Mariner" employs a similar technique of directing its reader toward an "answer" (the Mariner's "He prayeth well") that actually functions to provoke questions rather than resolve the poem's issues. See Gayle S. Smith, "A Reappraisal of the Moral Stanzas of *The Rime of the Ancient Mariner*," *SIR*, III (1963), 42–52. See also Richard

Our problem as careful readers of Romantic poetry is to recognize the factors in Romantic poems that, in the imagery of Keats's letter, open the dark doorways. Sometimes these are even less apparent than the ones discussed above. Near the conclusion of Wordsworth's "Michael," for example, we find the following passage:

> 'Tis not forgotten yet
> The pity which was then in every heart
> For the old Man—and 'tis believed by all
> That many and many a day he thither went,
> And never lifted up a single stone.
>
> (ll. 462–66)

Of this passage one might remark that "Wordsworth's Michael, after the unnatural city had captured his son Luke, 'never lifted up a single stone.'"[11] But this would not be quite accurate. It neglects the curious qualifying clause that Wordsworth employs in the passage: "And 'tis believed by all." If we focus our attention upon that clause, we will be drawn into the realm of questions. What is employed at this crucial point in Wordsworth's poem is a strategy designed to mark the distance that separates us, and even the poet narrator himself, from the actual truths of Michael's life. The poem is relating, not truths about Michael, but rather what other people (including the poet narrator) take to be truths about Michael, notions about Michael that are "believed by all." That phrase at the poem's conclusion functions to remind us of what we may have forgotten, or even neglected to note, in the poem's commencement. "Michael" is explicitly presented near the outset as a tale: "And hence this Tale" (l. 27). The poem, then, is a mirror held up, not to nature, but to ourselves. It positions us in a distanced space of conjecture, and if it tells us truths at all, those truths pertain to the tales we tell ourselves.

Haven, *Patterns of Consciousness: An Essay on Coleridge* (Amherst, Mass., 1969), which argues that Coleridge's Mariner "knows what happened to him, but he does not understand what happened" (21).

11 · Carl Woodring, "Nature and Art in the Nineteenth Century," *PMLA*, XCII (1977), 198.

Wordsworth's "'tis believed by all" is an instance of a recurring Romantic pattern. Here are a few further examples: "For all averred, I had killed the bird / That made the breeze to blow" (Coleridge, "The Rime of the Ancient Mariner," ll. 93–94); "Some say that gleams of a remoter world / Visit the soul in sleep" (Shelley, "Mont Blanc," ll. 49–50); "Some said / 'It is Urizen', But unknown, abstracted / Brooding secret, the dark power hid" (Blake, *The [First] Book of Urizen*, Plate 3). In their individual contexts these passages nudge the reader's thought in a number of different directions. But they unite in underscoring a common characteristic of Romantic literary art that has great significance: the tendency of that art is to present propositions, not as truths necessarily, but as things said, thought, or believed by some particular individual or party.[12]

When the Neoclassical poet Pope writes, "And spite of Pride, in erring Reason's spite, / One truth is clear, 'Whatever *Is*, is *Right*,'" he does not invite us to think about who says this, what individual or party is voicing this proposition ("An Essay on Man," I, ll. 293–94). Rather, the proposition simply seems to exist in its own right, independent of particular speakers or even believers. That is precisely the aura with which Pope seeks to surround his one clear truth—he would not wish us to think of it as his (or as anybody's in particular), because then contingencies would begin to arise. Had Pope written, for example, "The White Rabbit said, as he hopped into sight, / 'One truth is clear, Whatever *Is*, is *Right*,'" his famous proposition would have been transformed into an issue that raises questions. Attention shifts to dramatic context, and this shift demands inquiry into what we may suppose or what the literary work lets us know or suspect about the White Rabbit—his intentions, his quality of mind, and his relationship with hu-

---

12 · In a richly implicative essay, "The Mythographers and the Romantic Revival of Greek Myth," *PMLA*, LXXIX (1964), 447–56, Alex Zwerdling points out that, whereas seventeenth-century and early-eighteenth-century books on Greek myth commonly argued for one way of interpreting a given myth, such later-eighteenth-century works as *Bell's New Pantheon*, published in 1790, tended to be more like an encyclopedia. The late-eighteenth-century text offers multiple readings of a myth; and "the introductory phrases, 'according to some mythologists,' 'it is said,' and 'others affirm that,' create a more or less sceptical awareness of the nature of most mythological 'interpretations,' and focus attention on the story itself" (453).

man problems and concerns. Had Pope written, alternately, "I cannot but believe, while I gaze at the light, / That one truth is clear, Whatever *Is*, is *Right*," the transformation of doctrine into a question-raising issue would be more subtle, but it would still occur. One would be forced to think about the "I" believing, his state of mind and circumstances, and what the "I" might find himself believing if he had been gazing, instead, at the night. When propositions become explicitly associated with proposers and with propositional conditions in a literary text, doctrinal assertion tends to metamorphose into an issue that elicits inquiry from us.

This obvious point is easily forgotten if one comes to Romantic poems with dogmatic expectations. One can isolate, for example, propositions in Romantic poems like Keats's "O fret not after knowledge," or Shelley's

> Gentleness, Virtue, Wisdom, and Endurance,—
> These are the seals of that most firm assurance
> Which bars the pit over Destruction's strength.
> (*Prometheus Unbound*, IV, ll. 562–64)

One may forget, as it were, the White Rabbit—the fact that the propounders of these doctrines are a thrush and Demogorgon, not Keats and Shelley, and that in their poetic contexts these passages function dramatically to raise questions concerning a number of issues, as, for example, the relationship between human and nonhuman value systems. Much Romantic poetry makes use of the White Rabbit, through which maneuver the Romantic poet develops a poetic experience of propositional inquiry and exploration rather than dogmatic assertion.

In a letter written in 1817, Keats himself proposes a beauty-truth equation to his friend Benjamin Bailey.[13] But when that beauty-truth equation appears in a Keats poem eighteen months later, its proposer is no longer Keats but rather a Grecian urn. It may be (and has been) debated whether this indicates a shift in Keats's thinking about truth and beauty. What it does indicate, in any case, is that Keats's concern in his poem is to create a

---

13 · Keats to Benjamin Bailey, November 22, 1817, in *Letters of John Keats*, I, 184.

problematic experience for the mind that involves transforming an answer into a question-provoking issue. The proposition that "beauty is truth, truth beauty" is transferred from the mind to an object of the mind's contemplation. It is removed to a distance, and one is led thereby to ponder whether its emanation from a "friend to man" renders it applicable, finally, to the conditions of human life. Keats's Grecian urn, like Coleridge's Mariner or Byron's Witch of the Alps, is one of those many distanced voices the mind is made to encounter in Romantic poetry that *seem* to offer a haven for our sighs: "It may be / That I can aid thee" (*Manfred*, II, ii, ll. 150–51). The qualifying "may be" is crucially important.

In much Romantic poetry, such outer voices appear to be internalized: the propositions that appear in the poem are voiced by the poem's "I" rather than by some being or quantity encountered beyond the self. In such cases, the reader with dogmatic propensities may be still more readily tempted to forget dramatic contexts and assume that these propositions offer access to the doctrines and beliefs of the poet writing the poem. Some poems that seem to be of this type actually resolve themselves into the type discussed above. For example, when Blake writes in *The Marriage of Heaven and Hell* that "the tygers of wrath are wiser than the horses of instruction," it is important to remember that he is writing as a voice of the devil's party, that this doctrine is one of the "Proverbs of Hell," and that it helps constitute only one pole of that creative tension between heaven and hell that the poem is designed to generate (Plate 9). A more complex case in point is Byron's *Childe Harold's Pilgrimage*, wherein it is tempting to hear Byron himself in such effusions as "I live not in myself, but I become / Portion of that around me," until one remembers that he is professedly shifting back and forth between voices in his poem, projecting that indeterminate being positioned on the Bridge of Sighs into the role of "Self-exiled Harold," who "wanders forth again" to explore possibilities of the mind's creation (III, lxxii, xvi).

The most difficult cases in Romantic poetry are those in which the "I" of the poem—instead of resolving itself into some projected being like a devil or Childe Harold—gathers contingency factors to itself only through its association with mundane details of time, space, and dramatic circumstance.

Among Romantic poems, probably these are most likely to be distorted through the influence of preconceptions about Romanticism and order. In "Tintern Abbey," for example, when Wordsworth writes, "Knowing that Nature never did betray / The heart that loved her" (ll. 122–23), readers of a traditional inclination may suppose those lines convey what Wordsworth himself believes to be true. Alternately, some readers, especially those of the post–Geoffrey Hartman critical persuasion, may suppose those lines reveal what Wordsworth doubts but desperately wants to be true. That supposition leads toward various speculations about the anxieties of Wordsworth's personal and creative life. What both groups of readers tend to miss, however, is the fact that "Tintern Abbey," like the later monologues of Browning, is a self-consciously dramatic poem. "Tintern Abbey" emphasizes contingency factors in the same manner as my "while I gaze at the light" variation of Pope's couplet mentioned earlier. Wordsworth alerts us to the dramatic nature of his poem in its title: "Lines written a few miles above Tintern Abbey, on revisiting the banks of the Wye during a tour, July 13, 1798."[14] This insistently matter-of-fact title is not simply a Wordsworthian eccentricity: it functions significantly to inform us that what we are about to read (or, respecting the dramatic illusion, overhear) is a particular mind's activity in particular temporal and spatial circumstances. The poem does not convey, as one might be tempted, incautiously, to remark, "what Wordsworth thinks." Instead, the poem dramatizes a particular experience of thinking at a particular place and moment. Presumably, one might choose to consider this a representation of Wordsworth's actual experience at that given moment. But it should probably be thought of, cautiously, as the experience Wordsworth chooses to represent his "I" as having at that moment.

Wordsworth proceeds to develop in "Tintern Abbey," not only the title's highly particularized spatial and temporal circumstances, but also the particu-

---

14 · The word *written* in the 1798 title conveys more forcefully than *composed*, the formal term of Wordsworth's later, revised title, a sense that the poem we are reading is a document rather than a construction, a record of immediate experience more than an artistic reflection upon experience. Such an attempt to signal dramatization of the moment-by-moment experience of the mind thinking looks back to such eighteenth-century poems as Thomas Gray's "Elegy Written in a Country Churchyard."

lar mental bias of the "I" speaking: "For such loss, *I would believe,* / Abundant recompense" (ll. 87–88, italics mine). By the time we arrive, therefore, at the proposition "Knowing that Nature never did betray," we have long since been prepared to entertain it, not as a Wordsworthian truth, but rather as a piece of data in a Wordsworthian exploration of the mind's activity. It is a representation, in the familiar phrasing of the 1800 Preface, of how we associate ideas in a state of excitement. Wordsworth is inviting us to ponder questions, not conclusions, about the human mind's relationship with nature, by dramatizing something that the mind would have be true about nature in the context of a range of contingent factors designed to suggest that one might think, perhaps more reasonably though less agreeably, quite differently about the actual truth of nature.

"Tintern Abbey" offers a particularly complex illustration of the tendency of Romantic poetry, not to propound doctrine, but to employ it in a dramatic context designed to make the reader think skeptically, turning his attention toward factors involved in the activity of doctrine making.[15] Not all the poetry written by the Romantics works in this manner. The Romantics had moments of ideological infatuation, and they also had, more significantly, a strong bias in favor of defending traditional human values that they perceived to be endangered by fashions in contemporary thought. Shelley, for example, does not want us to question the value of mourning for Adonais, nor of condemning the "herded wolves, bold only to pursue; / The obscene ravens, clamorous o'er the dead," that he would have us believe hounded Keats ("Adonais," ll. 244–45). The Romantics were united in principle in their opposition to tyranny, though they disagreed in particular cases about what constituted tyranny. And they were united in defense of such fundamental human values as honesty, innocence, and love— though here again we need to be careful, recalling Blake's "The Human Abstract" in *Songs of Experience.*

> Pity would be no more,
> If we did not make somebody Poor:

---

15 · In a 1965 essay, "Romanticism: The Present State of the Theory," collected in *Triumph of Romanticism,* Peckham proposes that the concern of the Romantics was not simply to pur-

> And mercy no more could be,
> If all were as happy as we.
>
> (ll. 1–4)

Perhaps it is best to say that while the Romantics were cautiously supportive of many of our most traditional, fundamental human values, and while they were inclined to grant or at least explore sympathetically various clusters of provisional truths, nevertheless their minds generally continued to harbor an element of nagging uneasiness or suspicion. As in the case of Blake writing about pity and mercy, they were inclined—so long as they remained significantly under the influence of the Romantic situation—to keep probing for the prisons that might lie, hitherto unapprehended, behind palace walls.

THE Romantics recall Descartes in their impulse to move "downward" beneath surfaces that appear substantial but that melt when submitted to the corrosive question. Descartes, pursuing his downward course, thought he had reached a solid ground finally when he came upon his famous "Cogito, ergo sum." Having sought certain knowledge and having (as he supposed) discovered it in this *Cogito*, Descartes then proceeded to reconstruct the edifice of human knowledge. But important differences emerge between Descartes and the Romantics. For the Romantics, as for Descartes, the downward movement tends to lead toward the encounter of the "I" with itself. But whereas Descartes believed he saw a way to work back up from this encounter toward the surface, like a mathematician building up a series of theorems that follows necessarily from an axiomatic base, the Romantics tend to arrive at an "I" from which nothing further seems to follow of necessity. The Romantic *Cogito* involves itself alone.

The most stark example of this Romantic pattern, perhaps, is the late sonnet by John Clare that begins, "I feel I am, I only know I am," and ends abruptly with, "But now I only know I am—that's all."[16] A more famil-

---

sue metaphysics but rather to come to an analytic understanding of "metaphysical behavior," a project that involves meditation upon the fact that "one of the things human beings do is to construct . . . systems" (72).

16 · John Clare, "I Am," in Eric Robinson and Geoffrey Summerfield (eds.), *Clare: Selected Poems and Prose* (London, 1966), 222.

iar case would be that of Coleridge's Mariner, when he drops "Below . . .
below . . . Below," finally to discover himself "Alone, alone, all, all alone, /
Alone on a wide wide sea!" (ll. 232–33). Coleridge's lines suggest a complex pun that Ralph Waldo Emerson would later develop: to go down is to
lose all ground, to be "all at sea," and to become in the end only an I/eye
that is seaing/seeing. One thinks, further, of Shelley's sonnet "Lift Not the
Painted Veil"; behind that veil there is only fear and hope, "twin Destinies,
who ever weave / Their shadows o'er the chasm, sightless and drear"
(ll. 4–6). The seeing eye encounters its own antithetical inclinations of fear
and hope—a version of the recurrent Romantic contrariety—behind the
veil; but beyond this it finds only a chasm wherein nothing can be seen.
Melting apparent surfaces away, as Blake would say, or lifting the painted
veil, in Shelley's imagery, reveals, not a solid Something that has been hidden, but only a chasm.

It is easy to misapprehend the implications of this discovery. Is encounter
with the chasm cause for grief? Some Romantic poetry seems to suggest so.
In Shelley's rough draft of "Lift Not the Painted Veil," for example, the
sonnet's final two lines read: "I should be happier had I ne'er known / This
mornful man—he was himself alone." [17] However, if the Romantics did not
really want to find the chasm, it seems odd that they so frequently go out of
their way to provoke the encounter. Coleridge, for example, observes of his
hermit in "The Rime of the Ancient Mariner":

> He kneels at morn, and noon, and eve—
> He hath a cushion plump:
> It is the moss that wholly hides
> The rotted old oak-stump.
>
> (ll. 519–22)

The passage seems self-consciously designed to provoke suspicion that behind or beneath apparently substantial surfaces is not a solid core or firm
foundation but rather something rotten and insubstantial, a version of what
Shelley's sonnet images as a "chasm" and other Romantic works sometimes

17 · Shelley, "Lift Not the Painted Veil," in *Shelley's Poetry and Prose*, 312n7.

term an "abyss." Mary Shelley shows Elizabeth this abyss in *Frankenstein:* "Alas! Victor, when falsehood can look so like the truth, who can assure themselves of certain happiness? I feel as if I were walking on the edge of a precipice, towards which thousands are crowding, and endeavouring to plunge me into the abyss" (p. 93). The Romantics are almost inordinately fond of positioning their characters on the edge of the precipice. It seems naïve, therefore, to suppose that the Romantics themselves were not attracted to the discoveries they so frequently dramatize in their writings.

To assume that the Romantics would have avoided the abyss, were it possible, is to confuse the mental state of the writer with the mental states he is representing dramatically in his art. The Romantics were preoccupied with analysis of encounters with the abyss, probing the experience of such innocents as Mary Shelley's Elizabeth or Coleridge's Mariner as they find the bottom dropping out of the world of common experience that they had assumed to be stable and predictable. But the precipice from which the dramatic character shrinks, struggling in his innocence to preserve his notion that surfaces are not false appearances and that things hold together in a secure web of necessary relations, is the precipice that is attracting the author and toward which the author is maneuvering the reader. Coleridge's Mariner, for example, is

> Like one, that on a lonesome road
> Doth walk in fear and dread,
> And having once turned round walks on,
> And turns no more his head;
> Because he knows, a frightful fiend
> Doth close behind him tread.
>
> (ll. 446–51)

But Coleridge himself, in thus presenting his Mariner's experience, is teasing the reader's curiosity, and provoking him to look for what the Mariner refuses to see. The Romantic poet presses toward the precipice; and the abyss that is encountered is not an emblem of the poet's failure to find but, instead, the very thing the poet seeks. This is made most obvious in Blake's

Marriage of Heaven and Hell, when the downward journey of angel and speaker leads them "into the deep," where "by degrees we beheld the infinite Abyss." The angel plays the part of Romantic innocent, who, supposing his vision of the deep is true and substantial, learns that the abyss has no solidity of its own, and only lends itself to whatever "phantasy" that a dominant consciousness would "impose" upon it (Plates 18–20). The abyss is where consciousness realizes that its manacles are "mind-forg'd," and where visions of necessity are discovered to be mental creations of infinitely varying possibility.[18]

This is what Blake is aiming at in the passage from *The Marriage of Heaven and Hell* about corrosives that I quoted earlier. When Blake employs his infernal method to melt apparent surfaces away, he is pursuing, as he goes on to write, not some solid Cartesian ground that refuses to melt, but rather "the infinite which was hid" (Plate 14). The assertion calls to mind, among other passages in Romantic poetry, the one describing "flashes that have shewn to us / The invisible world," of which Wordsworth writes in the 1805 *Prelude* (Book VI, ll. 535–36). As in Blake, this hidden or invisible world of Wordsworth's is associated, not with some fixed essence that will serve as the stable foundation for a particular system of necessary truths, but rather with "infinitude": "Our destiny, our nature, and our home / Is with infinitude—and only there" (1805 *Prelude*, VI, ll. 538–39). It is this drive toward infinitude, or toward the abyss of infinitely varied possibility, that underlies the Romantic poets' preoccupation with generating particular orientations of thought that contain elements potentially destructive of those very orientations. Even as the mind is imposing some given fantasy upon the abyss, a competing fantasy offers itself as an equally viable candidate for imposition.

18 · Early Romantic scholarship tended to view the abyss as something the Romantics yearned to avoid, but recent scholarship has tended to conceive of the abyss more positively. Simpson, in *Irony and Authority*, for example, discusses the Romantic propensity to pursue "the deconstruction of habitual consciousness; a clearing of ground, a creation of empty space which might potentially be filled with something of greater integrity than what is displaced" (24). Weiskel, in *Romantic Sublime*, associates the Romantic conception of sublimity with the breaking down of "conventional systems, reading of landscape or text," and argues that "in that very collapse" it sought the "foundation for another order of meaning" (22).

It is also this drive toward infinitude that underlies many dramatizations of quest "failure" in Romantic poetry. When the Romantic "I" fails to find some object it seeks, or, finding it, fails to secure from that object the satisfaction it had anticipated, this hints at inadequacy, not of the questing "I," but of the object. If "our home / Is with infinitude, and only there," then our home is not with nightingales. The "I" tolled back from the nightingale to its "sole self" is being rescued from finite constructions and preserved for experience of the soul's destiny. This is why Romantic representations of the "I" that has been rendered solitary, all apparent surfaces melted away, the infinite abyss confronted, tend to be colored by spiritual associations. So, for example, the mournful man who was "himself alone" in the rough draft of Shelley's "Lift Not the Painted Veil" became an emphatically spiritualized being in the published version of the sonnet. This version develops the hint of "morning" light that underlies the dominant meaning "mournful" in the phrase "mornful man," and gives us a curiously heroic vision of the solitary being.

> Through the unheeding many he did move,
> A splendour among shadows—a bright blot
> Upon this gloomy scene—a Spirit that strove
> For truth, and like the Preacher, found it not.
>
> (ll. 11–14)

"Bright blot / Upon this gloomy scene" conveys intimations, if not quite of immortality, then at least of the spiritual light shining in darkness.

Wordsworth's version of this splendor among shadows is, most conspicuously, the child, father of the man. It is especially the "Child among his new-born blisses" in "Intimations of Immortality."

> See, where 'mid work of his own hand he lies
> . . . .
> See, at his feet, some little plan or chart,
> Some fragment from his dream of human life,
> Shaped by himself with newly-learned art.
>
> (ll. 88–93)

Here again the Romantic "I" is himself alone. In this case, however, the isolation unambiguously carries associations of spirituality and celebration. This child is not seeking some "truth," some solid ground beyond himself on which to find support. To the contrary, he is creating his own ground: "See, at his feet, some little plan or chart . . . Shaped by himself." He is absorbed in building his "dream of human life," what Blake would call the "phantasy," out of the space around him. The implication is that the abyss would be abysmal only to a being who has lost confidence in, or awareness of, his own power to cast light in the darkness.[19] For the creative soul— one may recall Blake's "Tyger! Tyger! burning bright" and Coleridge's "O Lady! we receive but what we give" in "Dejection: An Ode"—the abyss is an open space of creative opportunity wherein the soul, free from surrounding encumbrances, can exercise its ability to fill space with its own work. An interesting image in Shelley's "Hymn to Intellectual Beauty" plays upon a variation of this concept: "Thou—that to human thought art nourishment, / Like darkness to a dying flame" (ll. 44–45). If there is darkness without, the light within can manifest itself. The abyss permits the dream to appear as what it is: self-generated. Obstinate questionings of sense and outward things let spirit and inward things emerge.

This is why posing corrosive questions, melting away apparent surfaces in order to reach down to the abyss, is so important to the Romantics. It is only by touching the abyss that the soul comes to recognize its power, and, further, to see that those surfaces that the innocent takes to be true, necessary functions of an objective, real nature of things *seem* to be in fact mere products of the mind's own creativity. The systems of belief and value, then, that the naïve mind takes to be true are apparently systems that the mind has merely chosen to make true. Thus Byron's Manfred:

> The mind which is immortal makes itself
> Requital for its good or evil thoughts,—
> Is its own origin of ill and end
> And its own place and time.
>   (*Manfred*, III, iv, ll. 129–32)

19 · Concerning the creative, light-giving strain in Romantic thinking, see M. H. Abrams'

The fundamental Romantic irony is the mind's tendency to trap itself in the web of its own creations. Our being loses its clouds of glory, the bright fires die down to embers, as we begin to suppose that a particular system the mind has created has some sort of objective, independent existence to which the creating mind is subject. We forget to question, and lose the awareness that what our godlike power has brought into being, a dream of human life, can be altered or dissolved by that same godlike power. So Blake states in *The Marriage of Heaven and Hell:* "Thus men forgot that All deities reside in the human breast" (Plate 11). The child of Wordsworth's "Intimations of Immortality," on the other hand, still enjoys the bright fires, and for him it is still the activity rather than the product that is significant. Thus, importantly, he is busily shaping a "fragment." Before that fragment has developed into a system of such complexity and illusory force that it inhibits the shaping of alternative dreams of human life (one may recall Blake's myth of Albion falling into a dream of such weight that it has become a sleep of death), the Wordsworthian child is again at work, dreaming some other fragment:

> But it will not be long
> Ere this be thrown aside,
> And with new joy and pride
> The little Actor cons another part.
> (ll. 100–103)

Eventually, however, the Actor will lose himself in a given part: "And custom lie upon thee with a weight, / Heavy as frost, and deep almost as life!" (ll. 129–30). What remains is the embers, which, if properly nourished, can begin to burn away the frost and reach deep down toward what life remains within.

---

classic study *The Mirror and the Lamp: Romantic Theory and the Critical Tradition* (New York, 1953).

· *Three* ·

Wordsworth's Silent Thought

The History of an Encounter with

Romantic Questioning

IN the "Prospectus" to *The Recluse*, published with *The Excursion* in 1814 but probably composed between 1800 and 1802, Wordsworth lays claim to the human mind as the principle subject of his poetic concern.[1]

> Not Chaos, not
> The darkest pit of lowest Erebus,
> Nor aught of blinder vacancy, scooped out
> By help of dreams—can breed such fear and awe
> As fall upon us often when we look

1 · Beth Darlington offers a reasonable discussion of issues involved in dating the "Prospectus" in her edition for the Cornell Wordsworth series of *"Home at Grasmere": Part First, Book First, of "The Recluse" by William Wordsworth* (Ithaca, 1977), 19–22.

Into our Minds, into the Mind of Man—
My haunt, and the main region of my song.

(ll. 35–41)

The pairing of *fear* and *awe* here, echoing the eighteenth century's preoccupation with the sublime, is interesting. The way Wordsworth employs
John Milton in his high argument suggests that he was aiming at something
more important than a mere contest over poetic sublimity with his famous
precursor. When Wordsworth links the activity of probing into the mind
with Miltonic imagery of "Chaos" and the "darkest pit," he seems to imply
that mental inquiry may yield an experience like that of the rebellious angels when they found themselves deprived of a firm ground of heavenly
certitudes, and dropped into a realm of disorientation and confusion. Fear
and awe "fall" upon us, taking us by surprise and suggesting encounter
with something quite different from what was anticipated. Like Milton's
fallen angels, whose attempt to grasp foundations of power ended in loss of
all foundation, we may encounter within the mind only a sort of abyss instead of the substantial essence we had expected to discover. This experience, Wordsworth asserts, ultimately breeds awe, but it is apparently significant that the first term in the pairing is *fear*. The passage is designed to
convey the fear of emptiness, loss of substance or solid ground. We "look"
into our minds, but cannot see *things* there. The mind's depths are like a
"darkest" pit, or like aught of "blinder vacancy."

   This disturbing association between mental inquiry and dark or vacant
depths recalls the period of Wordsworth's mental crisis during the mid-
1790s. We do not really know much about that crisis. Evidences concerning
the precise effects of the Annette Vallon liaison upon Wordsworth's mind,
the exact history and intensity of Wordsworth's commitment to the French
Revolution, the extent of his infatuation and subsequent disillusionment
with Godwinism, and even the probable impact of personal monetary and
familial anxieties upon Wordsworth's mental stability all leave considerable
room for speculation; and they remain subjects open to critical debate.[2]

2 · The most balanced summary view of Wordsworth's early development appears in the first
volume of Mary Moorman, *William Wordsworth: A Biography* (2 vols.; Oxford, U.K.,
1957–65). The most significant critical analysis of Wordsworth's early career is Paul D.

But whatever may have been its causal background, the crisis produced in Wordsworth a period of doubt concerning the mind's powers that he chose to represent in *The Prelude* as related to his struggle to understand the failure of the Revolution in France. In Book X of the 1805 *Prelude,* Wordsworth looks back upon the hopes and fears he had felt for the Revolution, and re-creates the attempt he made to understand how the wondrous social and political dreams of the period turned to nightmare. What had gone wrong, and why? Wordsworth looked to the depths of his own mind for justification of the mind's ambitious claims.

> Dragging all passions, notions, shapes of faith,
> Like culprits to the bar, suspiciously
> Calling the mind to establish in plain day
> Her title and her honours, now believing,
> Now disbelieving, endlessly perplexed
> With impulse, motive, right and wrong, the ground
> Of moral obligation—what the rule,
> And what the sanction—till, demanding proof,
> And seeking it in every thing, I lost
> All feeling of conviction, and, in fine,
> Sick, wearied out with contrarieties,
> Yielded up moral questions in despair.
>
> (ll. 889–900)

Sheats, *The Making of Wordsworth's Poetry, 1785–1798* (Cambridge, Mass., 1973). On Wordsworth's relationship with Annette Vallon, see G. M. Harper, *Wordsworth's French Daughter* (Princeton, N.J., 1921); Emile Legouis, *William Wordsworth and Annette Vallon* (London, 1922); Herbert Read, *Wordsworth* (London, 1930); and H. I'A. Fausset, *The Lost Leader* (London, 1933). On Wordsworth's early educational environment, see Z. S. Fink, *The Early Wordsworthian Milieu* (Oxford, U.K., 1958), and Ben Ross Schneider, Jr., *Wordsworth's Cambridge Education* (Cambridge, U.K., 1957). In *Dissenting Republican: Wordsworth's Early Life and Thought in Their Political Context* (The Hague, 1972), Leslie F. Chard, III, explores how "the dissenting tradition" influenced Wordsworth in the early 1790s. On religious influences, see Richard E. Brantley, *Wordsworth's "Natural Methodism"* (New Haven, 1975), and *Locke, Wesley, and the Method of English Romanticism.* On political influences, see F. M. Todd, *Politics and the Poet: A Study of Wordsworth* (London, 1957), and Chap. 4 of Carl Woodring, *Politics in English Romantic Poetry* (Cambridge, Mass., 1970), 85–147.

The imagery of mental inquiry in this passage recalls the like imagery of the "Prospectus" passage. Wordsworth represents himself as looking within his mind for a "ground" that might be clearly seen, established "in plain day." He had sought mental substance, a secure foundation akin to the proverbial rock beneath the Church. In logical terminology, as his reference to "demanding proof" suggests, he had sought something like the traditional Cartesian *Cogito*. When the mind inquires suspiciously within itself, it should be able ultimately to hit rock bottom, as it were, finding a solid thing that cannot be questioned and upon which, therefore, a new edifice of stable, certain knowledge can be erected. However, Wordsworth encountered something unexpected—no solid ground at all, but only "contrarieties" and his own confusion and perplexity. Producing a result that recalls the fear of the "Prospectus," mental inquiry leads the questioning angel toward the margins of despair—toward chaos and the darkest pit.

In the mid-1790s, then, Wordsworth had looked "into our Minds, into the Mind of Man"; but at that time he had not encountered what he wished to find. Accordingly, he turned away from blind vacancy, yielding up moral questions in despair. This experience seems to mark Wordsworth's effective introduction to the problematic Romantic situation.

WORDSWORTH'S crisis cannot be dated with certainty, but it is likely that the culmination of the crisis period described in *The Prelude* occurred in late 1795 and/or early 1796.[3] Reverberations of the crisis appear in the imagery of depths, vacancy, and mental confusion that recurs in Wordsworth's poetry of the mid-1790s. One thinks, for example, of the following passage in "Salisbury Plain":

> The distant spire
> That fixed at every turn his backward eye
> Was lost, tho' still he turned, in the blank sky.

---

3 · Todd, in *Politics and the Poet*, suggests the crisis may belong to the Windy Brow period of 1794 (80 ff.), but see Moorman, *William Wordsworth*, I, 285–87, and Mark L. Reed, *Wordsworth: The Chronology of the Early Years, 1770–1799* (Cambridge, Mass., 1967), 174.

In the same poem are the lines "And vacant the huge plain around him spread," and "The woman told him that through a hollow deep / As on she journeyed, far from spring or bower."[4] This imagery suggestive of roaming through a hellish abyss is heightened in *The Borderers*, written in 1796 and 1797, particularly in Wordsworth's description of how an innocent mind falls into frightening depths of thought.

> Is not the depth
> Of this Man's crimes beyond the reach of thought?
> And yet, in plumbing the abyss for judgment,
> Something I strike upon which turns my thoughts
> Back on myself, I think, again—my breast
> Concentres all the terrors of the Universe:
> I look at him and tremble like a child.
>
> (ll. 780–86)[5]

It is tempting to think we hear Wordsworth himself behind these lines—a young, perplexed idealist fearfully plumbing the abyss in search of what he cannot find. Clearly we need to be cautious about this, however. It has been proposed, for example, that Wordsworth's own crisis must have been less intense than his poetry suggests, or at least that Wordsworth refused to yield to confusion and despair for very long, because the poetry he wrote in the years immediately following his presumed crisis hardly seems to exhibit a retreat from moral issues or a yielding to despair.[6] But what this actually implies is simply that Wordsworth's crisis was somewhat more complex, and its ultimate effects upon his poetry more subtle, than one might at first assume.

---

4 · Quoted from the Reading Text of "Salisbury Plain" in the Cornell Wordsworth edition of Stephen Gill (ed.), *The Salisbury Plain Poems of William Wordsworth* (Ithaca, 1975), ll. 39–41, 62, 163–64. A number of the recurring imagery patterns of the mid-1790s poetry have been examined by Enid Welsford, in *Salisbury Plain: A Study in the Development of Wordsworth's Mind and Art* (Oxford, U.K., 1966).

5 · For lines 783–84 I follow the reading in MS B; see Wordsworth, *The Borderers*, in *Poetical Works*, I, 159. On dating *The Borderers*, see Reed, *Chronology of the Early Years*, Appendix X.

6 · Sheats remarks upon this point in *Making of Wordsworth's Poetry*, 107.

We can begin to approach this complexity by noting the significant difference between Wordsworth's account of his crisis in the 1805 *Prelude* and his revised account of it in the 1850 version. In the latter version, the line "Yielded up moral questions in despair" stands as the climactic phrase of the verse paragraph that describes Wordsworth's mental quest, and *despair*, therefore, carries great and at least momentarily conclusive force. However, in the 1805 version the emphasis is different because the verse paragraph does not stop with the word *despair*.

> Yielded up moral questions in despair,
> And for my future studies, as the sole
> Employment of the inquiring faculty,
> Turned towards mathematics, and their clear
> And solid evidence.
>
> (ll. 900–904)

This earlier recollection of the crisis suggests a considerably different and more complex experience. Wordsworth may have yielded up *moral questions* in despair, but that is as far as the despair went. He appears to have determined only that moral questions are not subjects that can be profitably submitted to rigorous questioning. The "inquiring faculty" is better suited for pursuing problems in mathematics, where the evidence is "clear" and "solid." The 1805 *Prelude*, then, does not suggest that Wordsworth's crisis drove him into a state of utter despair concerning issues of morality. Nor does it even tell us he gave up moral convictions. All Wordsworth yielded up was the notion that the validity of moral convictions can be successfully submitted to close scrutiny.

This helps to explain why moral issues neither disappear nor become hedged round with despair in Wordsworth's poetry that follows close upon the crisis. Wordsworth's crisis was real and intense, apparently, but its effects found poetic expression in subtle ways. Wordsworth's entry into the problematic territory of Romantic questioning did not lead him toward nihilism. Instead, it aroused in him an initially disturbing but ultimately fruitful sense of the mystery of mental activity. How are we to understand the workings of the human mind? Surely we know things, including fundamental differences between good and evil, right and wrong, proper thinking and mental perversity—or, at the least, we can hardly help believing and acting as if we have such knowledge. And yet where actually is our foundation? The inquiring faculty of the mind seems to destroy rather than support, endangering what we suppose is our knowledge by revealing an underlying abyss instead of clear, solid ground. This unsettling perception exerts a powerful influence on the course of Wordsworth's subsequent poetic development. Basic shifts in the poet-reader relationship in Wordsworth's poetry during the 1790s suggest that this influence expresses itself in two relatively distinct phases, the first reflecting more the fear and the second more the awe that Wordsworth associates with mental inquiry in the "Prospectus."

Wordsworth's initial reaction to his crisis seems to have involved, not a retreat from the dogmatic inclinations of his early verse, but rather an anxious intensification of those tendencies. Behind this first poetic development would appear to be the idea that if the inquiring faculty presents a danger to our structures of knowledge, then it must be the poet's business to place careful limits upon the freedom of the mind's activity. Shades of the Augustan "Know thy own point" arise: if the mind is given free space, it may fall into some line of questioning that leads to the abyss. Earlier, Wordsworth had been relatively unworried about that problem. He had sought to please and instruct, in accordance with poetic tradition, and his inclination had been to instruct pleasingly. For example, in *An Evening Walk* (first published in 1793, but probably composed largely in the late 1780s), we encounter an early version of the recompense-in-loss theme that is so important to the poetry of Wordsworth's maturity. But the poetic stance in *An Evening Walk* is very different from that of the later verse. Later poems like "Tintern Abbey" build upon anxiety and poetic strain, underscored in such dramatic clauses as "If this / Be but a vain belief, yet, oh!" (ll. 50–51). In *An Evening Walk*, however, the poetic voice is primarily a companionable presence that, already in firm possession of saving truths at the poem's outset, is solicitously concerned to nudge the reader's mind toward clear-cut instructive goals.

> But why, ungrateful, dwell on idle pain?
> To shew her yet some joys to me remain,
> Say, will my friend, with soft affection's ear,
> The history of a poet's ev'ning hear?
>
> (ll. 49–52; 1793 quarto version)

As the poet here is guiding teacher, so the reader is presumed to be a willing, attentive student to whom truths can be presented without struggle or extensive argument: "Thus Hope, first pouring from her blessed horn / Her dawn far lovelier than the Moon's own morn" (ll. 407–408). The narrative details of an evening walk and instructive commentary about human life blend gracefully together because no contrary argument is exerting pressure upon the margins of thought, raising specters of "vain belief," as in "Tintern Abbey," that the mind must struggle to overcome. In *An Evening Walk* the poet can gently lead and expect his reader to gently follow.

This companionable instructive atmosphere begins to change, however, when the revolutionary world of doctrine and counterdoctrine starts to make its presence felt in Wordsworth's poetry. In "Salisbury Plain" (text of 1793–1794), for example, contrarieties are becoming a significant factor in the instructive situation.

> Nor only is the walk of private life
> Unblessed by Justice and the kindly train
> Of Peace and Truth.
>
> (ll. 442–44)

The poet is no longer simply inviting his reader to think with him along some particular line; he is also seeking to prevent the reader from thinking along alternative lines. On the far side of the negative constructions "Nor only is" and "Unblessed" lie dangerous antithetical dogmas and erroneous thought. Now the poet's duty is not merely to instruct but also to guard against false instruction. Accordingly, he is developing boundaries of negation that prevent the reader's mind from wandering into dangerous ideological territory.

This protective impulse seems to have gained added force from Wordsworth's own crisis of thought. Wordsworth's personal crisis did not make him retreat from moral issues. To the contrary, he became more fervently moralistic. The reader is instructed in "The Convict," perhaps written in 1796, and first published in the *Morning Post* in December, 1797, to think of the condemned man not as a villain but as a "Poor Victim!"[7] In "Adventures on Salisbury Plain," written from 1795 to *ca.* 1799, Wordsworth's weary sailor bears a large burden of moral imperatives.

> 'Tis a bad world, and hard is the world's law;
> Each prowls to strip his brother of his fleece;
> Much need have ye that time more closely draw
> The bond of nature.[8]

Underlying these imperatives is concern about contrary dogmas—that convicts are indeed enemies of society and that the good of society is best secured by encouraging each individual to pursue what appears to him his private advantage. The poet is now warring against dangerous inclinations of thought to which he believes his reader is susceptible.

> O, be wiser thou!
> Instructed that true knowledge leads to love,
> True dignity abides with him alone
> Who . . .
>> ("Lines Left Upon a Seat in a Yew-tree,"
>> ll. 55–58)

7 · Line 45 in the version of "The Convict" published in *Lyrical Ballads* (1798). Unless noted otherwise, in this chapter I will be quoting from the 1798 and 1800 versions of the poems that first appeared in *Lyrical Ballads.* My text is R. L. Brett and A. R. Jones (eds.), *Lyrical Ballads,* (New York, 1963; rev. ed. 1965), supplemented by the notes in De Selincourt and Darbishire (eds.), *Poetical Works.*

8 · Wordsworth, the Reading Text of "Adventures on Salisbury Plain" in *Salisbury Plain Poems,* ll. 658–61.

A similarly anxious lecture in proper thinking emerges from "The Old Cumberland Beggar":

> But deem not this man useless.—Statesmen! ye
> Who are so restless in your wisdom . . .
>
> ·
>   'Tis Nature's law
> That none . . .⁹

The poet, determined to hold thought rigorously in check, conceives of his reader as akin to an intellectually untrustworthy child, restless in presumption of wisdom. Behind this anxiety we can glimpse Wordsworth's uneasiness about the abyss. A restless mind risks falling victim to temptingly untraditional ideologies—from which follows, first, conflict between the new and the old, and second, the problem of resolving the conflict by calling on the mind to discover proofs. But as Wordsworth himself had found, the quest for proof can entangle the mind in a confusion that deprives it of "all feeling of conviction." The poet, therefore, must ward off that danger by firmly shepherding the restless reader back toward secure and proper thinking. The earlier poetry's gentle invitation ("Say, will my friend, with soft affection's ear") hardens into stern control. There are clear bounds beyond which thought must not be permitted to stray. Outside those bounds lies confusion.

This hardening of gentle guidance into stern control carries over into the *Lyrical Ballads* of 1798 and 1800 through poems that had been mainly composed prior to 1798—"The Convict," "Lines Left Upon a Seat in a Yew-Tree," and "The Old Cumberland Beggar." But in respect to their anxiety to impose definite limitations upon the range of the reader's thought, those poems are quite uncharacteristic of most of the poetry in the *Lyrical Ballads*. They represent, instead, vestiges of a poetic stance that Wordsworth seems to have put behind him rather abruptly between late 1797 and 1798.

---

9 · Ll. 67–74. "Lines Left upon a Seat in a Yew-Tree" was probably composed early in 1797. For composition date of "The Old Cumberland Beggar," see Reed, *Chronology of the Early Years*, Appendix XV.

In the poetry of the *Lyrical Ballads* that Wordsworth began writing in early 1798, he moved into a second, radically different stage of response to his earlier crisis of doubt. This response is much more fundamental and problematic, involving an about-face in how the poet treats mental activity. In most of the *Lyrical Ballads* poems, the poet is no longer the stern or even the gentle guide for the reader's thought, but rather a curiously provoking presence that refrains from providing the instruction that the earlier Wordsworthian voice had been so anxious to offer. Instead of guarding the reader's mind against the dangers of restless activity, the poet now seems determined to leave the reader groping with questions.

Most basically, the function played by doctrinal elements in the poetry changes. Doctrine ceases to stand out from the narrative content of the poem, serving for the reader as instructive commentary ("O, be wiser thou! / Instructed that"). Instead, doctrine dissolves into the narrative itself, as the authoritative voice of the earlier poetry becomes a dramatic voice that is caught up in qualifying conditions of particular times, places, and circumstances.[10] In "Expostulation and Reply," for example, we encounter an assertion about feeding the mind in a wise passiveness. But instead of addressing this assertion to the reader directly, Wordsworth has embedded it within a dramatic debate between two minds that think differently from each other; and the reader is positioned at a distance, as the reflective observer of the debate. In "Tintern Abbey" the reader is again the distanced observer: he is made to overhear the voice of the poem musing to itself, and

10 · Studies of Wordsworthian "philosophy" are almost as numerous as that poet's host of golden daffodils. The classic studies are Arthur Beatty, *William Wordsworth: His Doctrine and Art in Their Historical Relations* (Madison, Wis., 1922; rev. ed. 1927), and M. M. Rader, *Presiding Ideas in Wordsworth's Poetry* (Seattle, 1931). Recent contributions include Alan Grob, *The Philosophic Mind: A Study of Wordsworth's Poetry and Thought, 1797–1805* (Columbus, Ohio, 1973), and John A. Hodgson, *Wordsworth's Philosophical Poetry, 1797– 1814* (Lincoln, Nebr., 1980). Good corrective approaches, emphasizing the dramatic and manipulative nature of Wordsworth's art, include Stephen Maxfield Parrish, *The Art of the "Lyrical Ballads"* (Cambridge, Mass., 1973); James H. Averill, *Wordsworth and the Poetry of Human Suffering* (Ithaca, 1980); Jeffrey Baker, *Time and Mind in Wordsworth's Poetry* (Detroit, 1980); Jonathan Arac, "Romanticism, the Self, and the City: *The Secret Agent* in Literary History," *Boundary 2*, IX (1980), 75–90; and Charles Altieri, "Wordsworth's 'Preface' as Literary Theory," *Criticism*, XVIII (1976), 122–46.

seeking to persuade itself ("I would believe") that a doctrine of "abundant recompense" for sustained loss can deliver the mind from "somewhat of a sad perplexity" (ll. 89, 88, 61).

In "Lines Written in Early Spring," it is not quite certain whether the voice of the poem is arguing with itself or appealing to the reader, but in either case what is important is the factor of dramatic tension Wordsworth introduces into the poem. The poem contains and employs (quite different matters from inculcating) familiar contemporary doctrines about flowers enjoying the air they breathe and about man's inhumanity to man—that "man becomes the destroyer of man" had been William Godwin's more passionate version of the latter basic dogma in the 1794 preface to *Caleb Williams*. But these doctrines are being submitted to question by means of the poem's concluding stanza.

> If I these thoughts may not prevent,
> If such be of my creed the plan,
> Have I not reason to lament
> What man has made of man?
> (ll. 21–24; 1798 version)

This confronts the reader, not with an assertion that demands assent, but rather with a problem. What conditions, one is led to reflect, might actually constitute sufficient reason for believing that the thoughts that enter the mind are to be trusted?[11]

As doctrines become problematic data in these poems, the reader begins to find himself, like Wordsworth's image of Isaac Newton in Book III of the 1850 *Prelude*, "voyaging through strange seas of Thought, alone" (l. 63).

11 · H. W. Piper, *The Active Universe: Pantheism and the Concept of the Imagination in the English Romantic Poets* (London, 1962), examines the context of contemporary scientific thought in which Wordsworth would have encountered notions about the life principle in nature that he emplys in "Lines Written in Early Spring." On the "One Life" doctrine in particular, see Jonathan Wordsworth, *The Music of Humanity: A Critical Study of Wordsworth's Ruined Cottage* (London, 1969), 184–216; and Mary Jacobus, *Tradition and Experiment in Wordsworth's "Lyrical Ballads," 1798* (Oxford, U.K., 1976), 60–68. Both studies assume Wordsworth's subscription to the "One Life" doctrine, but I think the poetry shows that Wordsworth's interest was rather in thinking about what it means for a mind to believe such a doctrine.

The anxious guide of the earlier poetry seems to have disappeared, and the reader is confronted with questions of how to think about these dramatic representations of mental activity. Difficulties are still more conspicuous in the *Lyrical Ballads* poems that offer some stark "anecdote" or "incident" or "tale." In these poems the poetic voice generally intimates that something of considerable significance is being conveyed, but just what that significance may be is not revealed. In Chapter 2, I noted how elements in the anecdote of "Anecdote for Fathers," for example, hint at meanings that seem to overflow the simple assertion of the poem's original subtitle, "shewing how the art of lying may be taught." But the conclusion to this poem, instead of carefully instructing the reader in the manner of earlier Wordsworth poems, merely functions to underscore this sense of unexpressed significances.

> Oh dearest, dearest boy! my heart
> For better lore would seldom yearn,
> Could I but teach the hundredth part
> Of what from thee I learn.
> (ll. 57–60)

The authoritative voice of the early poetry has metamorphosed into a very different poetic voice. This poem's speaker learns many things from his boy, but the emphasis falls on his inability to "teach the hundredth part" of what he knows. The reader, accordingly, finds himself facing a challenge of expanding but indefinite thought. There is much to learn here. But the poet has lapsed into silence, and the reader no longer has a guide to direct his thinking.

In "Michael" the reader again confronts prospects of unexpressed significance.

> And hence this Tale, while I was yet a boy
> Careless of books, yet having felt the power
> Of Nature, by the gentle agency
> Of natural objects led me on to feel
> For passions that were not my own, and think

> At random and imperfectly indeed
> On man; the heart of man and human life.
>
> (ll. 27–33)

The tale the reader is about to be told has made the poet think of significant things. But just what were those thoughts, random and imperfect as they might have been, that Michael's story called forth from the young poet? And, still more important, what less random and imperfect thoughts should this story call forth from the mature mind of the reflective adult? The poet falls silent. While this introduction to the poem, then, stirs the mind to expectation, the substance of the poem concentrates upon the matter of the tale itself, concluding not with a reflective meditation but only with the poet pointing to the pile of rocks, the tree, and the brook of Green-head Gill. The reader is left to ponder as best he can or will the significance of these mute objects.

Wordsworth leaves the reader even more provokingly on his own in other poems, such as "The Last of the Flock" and "The Two April Mornings." Herein the poet is curiously silent concerning, not only the precise significance, but whether there is *any* significance in the incidents he relates. The very fact that the incidents are being related works to create some expectation—what is caught up in a narrative, and especially a poetic, frame must be important, must "mean something." But if this significance is not itself conventional and therefore obvious, one commonly expects the artist to provide help, indicating the direction that thought should take. So in "The Two April Mornings," for example, one looks for meaning in what appears to be the crucial moment in the poem, when Matthew, confronted with the "blooming Girl," exclaims, "I look'd at her and look'd again; / — And did not wish her mine" (ll. 43, 55–56). Yet the poet refrains from breaking in upon the narrative to direct the reader's thought. Instead, the poem merely concludes with a further narrative remark.

> Matthew is in his grave, yet now
> Methinks I see him stand,
> As at that moment, with his bough
> Of wilding in his hand.
>
> (ll. 57–60)

This conclusion stirs many readers to all sorts of interpretive flights. While literally the "bough / Of wilding" seems to be only the fishing pole that Matthew is carrying ("With rod and line my silent sport / I plied by Derwent's wave,") a reader is tempted to suppose it must mean something (ll. 29–30). So he begins constructing a reading upon it. Perhaps he aims at the notion that Matthew is untamed or "wild," and heroic: he is so devoted to his Emma's memory that he refuses to accept the merely natural resurrections that earth offers in its yearly blooming cycles. Or, contrarily, perhaps he aims at the notion that Matthew is a weak, pathetic figure, a branch broken from the tree of natural, ever-renewing life, who has gone "wild" with private suffering and is unable to recommit himself to the life process. One can arrive, in other words, at several, and contrary, readings. The poem thus works upon the reader in a manner strikingly different from that of Wordsworth's earlier poetry of strict reader control. Instead of being directed, one is being unsettled by absence of authoritative direction. The reader's expectations confront a poetry in which the poet has withdrawn into silences.[12]

Is the reader to assume that whatever notions of significance he may happen to conjure up in himself in response to the narrative content of the poem will be satisfactory? If so, that seems to encourage the very chaos of contrarieties among different readers (and perhaps even within the same reader at different moments) that the earlier Wordsworth had sought to avoid. Prior to 1798, Wordsworth's mental energies had been directed toward insuring that the mind would not go roaming restlessly into strange seas of thought. The concern had been to inculcate concepts of true knowledge that protect the mind from falling into an abyss. The poetic situation has now altered radically. Where does this leave, or, perhaps better, place the reader of the Wordsworth poem?

THE problem of how the reader is to understand and respond to the silences in Wordsworth's poetry was a disturbing issue in Wordsworth's own time, and what I take to be confusions of critical thought about that issue

12 · Such poetic designs call to mind some familiar strategies of radical twentieth-century art; see Brian Wilkie, "Wordsworth and the Tradition of the Avant-Garde," *JEGP*, LXXII (1973), 194–222.

today can be traced back to an approach to the issue that developed among Wordsworth's early readers. Wordsworth's silences placed many of his contemporaries in a state of perplexity or outright irritation. Reviews of the 1798 *Lyrical Ballads* frequently note that the volume showed signs of poetic genius, but they also register hints of uneasiness about the poetry. For example, one reviewer remarked of "Anecdote for Fathers" that "the dialogue is ingenious and natural; but the object of the child's choice, and the inference, are not quite obvious." Another went further: "Among his irregular verses, we are often surprised with beautiful expression, and sometimes displeased with a turgid obscurity." Robert Southey suggested the problem may have been simply that the poetic materials were inherently insignificant—the poet had tried to work his poetic experiments upon "uninteresting subjects."[13]

Gradually reviewers began to suspect, however, that their uneasiness had something to do, not so much with the poet's inadvertent errors in choice of subject matter or in his manner of developing it, but rather with his self-conscious, deliberate poetic designs. One reviewer of the 1800 *Lyrical Ballads* glimpsed this, for example, when observing that "there is a studied abruptness in the commencement and termination of several pieces, which makes them assume an appearance of mere fragments."[14] This suggestion that there seems to be "studied abruptness" in the poetry, the poet deliberately cutting elements from his poems and thereby creating odd structures that look like "mere fragments," anticipates what the influential critic Francis Jeffrey would later find so repellent about Wordsworth's poetic practice: "Love, and the fantasies of lovers, have afforded an ample theme to poets of all ages. Mr. Wordsworth, however, has thought fit to compose a piece, illustrating this copious subject, by one single thought. A lover trots away to see his mistress one fine evening, staring all the way at the moon:

13 · Dr. Charles Burney, *Monthly Review*, 2nd Ser., XXIX (June, 1799), 207; *New London Review*, I (January, 1799), 34; Robert Southey, *Critical Review*, 2nd Ser., XXIV (October, 1798), 204. These reviews, as well as those cited in footnotes 14, 17, and 19, can also be found in Donald H. Reiman (ed.), *The Romantics Reviewed: Contemporary Reviews of British Romantic Writers* (2 vols.; New York, 1972).
14 · *Monthly Mirror*, XI (June 1801), 389.

when he comes to her door, 'O mercy! to myself I cried, / If Lucy should be dead.' And there the poem ends!"[15]

Whatever may be thought of Jeffrey's criticism of "Strange Fits of Passion" as a whole, it is worth noting that he focuses attention upon a key factor: "And there the poem ends!" Jeffrey saw that Wordsworth was not just failing to write in a manner that fulfilled conventional expectation. Rather, he was writing as he did by deliberate design—he "thought fit" to avoid developing the "ample theme" as one would expect him to do, and he accentuated his refusal to develop his "copious subject" by cutting his poem off short, leaving his reader dangling, as it were, upon a statement the implications of which are by no means clear. It is interesting to note that a letter version of "Strange Fits of Passion" adds a final stanza to the poem that relieves much of the tension Jeffrey sensed in the abbreviated *Lyrical Ballads* version.

> I told her this; her laughter light
> Is ringing in my ears;
> And when I think upon that night
> My eyes are dim with tears.[16]

Jeffrey found the artistic maneuvering Wordsworth introduced into the *Lyrical Ballads* version unpalatable. He desired a poet to convey what he had to say clearly, or at least to develop a conventional theme along predictable lines if he had nothing significant to say on his own. And he was disturbed to find Wordsworth toying, as he saw it, with the poet's obligation to his reader.

Jeffrey saw that the reader's frustration was the product of some odd or perverse strategy that was apparently intentional. Many of Wordsworth's later reviewers, however, followed only Jeffrey's antagonism to what Wordsworth was doing, while developing a premise to account for it that

---

15 · Francis Jeffrey, review of *"Poems. By the Reverend George Crabbe,"* in *Edinburgh Review*, XII (April, 1808), 136.
16 · William and Dorothy Wordsworth to Coleridge, December, 1798, to January, 1799, in *Letters: The Early Years*, 238.

lost sight of Jeffrey's perception that Wordsworth's design was deliberate. It soon became commonplace to observe that Wordsworth's poetry did not communicate with its reader in ways that seemed satisfactory to conventional expectation, and the issue of what a poet owes his reader thus became a popular subject for discussion in Wordsworth's reviews. Ironically, reviewers gave Wordsworth lectures on how he should remember that he is a man speaking to men: "Surely Mr. Wordsworth cannot but perceive, that if a poet, in order to excite rational sympathy, must *express* himself as other men express themselves; by a still stronger reason it would seem to follow that *he must descend from his supposed height,* and *feel* as other men feel." They sought to remind him that other men might not be like himself: "Because he has discovered and maintained successfully, that good poetry may be written on a celandine or a daisy, he seems to have acted as if better poetry could be written on them than on subjects of a higher degree; he has neglected to take into the account that poetry is a communicative art, that the state of the recipient is to be considered, as well as that of the communicant."[17]

The important critical premise that begins to emerge from these reviews is that the communicative gap between poet and reader in a Wordsworth poem may be due, not so much to a manipulation, the poet's attempt to execute premeditated designs upon his reader, but rather to a Wordsworthian tendency to ignore or forget about his reader altogether. Jeffrey's recognition that, like it or not, Wordsworth was writing as he did by design gives way to the idea that the poet has become so enthralled by his own thought processes that he has lost track of the needs, desires, and expectations of our common humanity. Wordsworth becomes something like the poet of Gray's "Elegy Written in a Country Churchyard": "Mutt'ring his wayward fancies he would rove" (l. 106). Later-eighteenth-century myths of poetic sensibility—which will evolve into the more modern notion of the Wordsworthian "egotistical sublime"—enter Wordsworth criticism as a convenient means of accounting for Wordsworth's silences.[18]

17 · William Rowe Lyall, review of *Poems* (the first collected edition of 1815) and "The White Doe of Rylstone," in *Quarterly Review*, XIV (October, 1815), 208; review of "Peter Bell," in *British Critic*, 2nd Ser., XI (June, 1819), 588.
18 · For influence of later-eighteenth-century ideas about poetic sensibility upon the earlier Romantics, see Dekker, *Coleridge and the Literature of Sensibility*.

The unsympathetic critic, of course, would object to what seemed to him Wordsworth's presumption: *"he must descend from his supposed height, and feel as other men feel."* But other, more sympathetic minds readily embraced an appeal to poetic genius in defending the perplexing character of Wordsworth's poetic practice: "But, if we are not able to follow all the wanderings of his fancy, if he draws honey from flowers in which we can perceive, with our duller sense, neither fragrance nor flavour . . . so far we are losers, and so far Nature has endowed him with superior means of enjoyment and happiness."[19] This manner of thinking about Wordsworth carries powerful implications. The poem comes to be seen as the product of a superior sensibility or mentality—from which notion follows readily the proposition that it contains truths, profundities, visionary insights that are not to be perceived by readers with "duller sense." The ground is thus prepared for development of the idea of Wordsworth as mystic, philosopher, true believer, whose insights are conveyed within a poetry that only an elevated mind can successfully read. Thus if the reader finds himself perplexed, the onus falls on him rather than on the poet. Wordsworth was pursuing his own high experiences of thought and feeling in his poetry. Reading Wordsworth is transformed into a test of whether one is endowed, as is the poet, with "superior means of enjoyment and happiness." The key factor in the test is whether the reader is able to follow. To be unable to follow, or, like Francis Jeffrey, to resist following ("And there the poem ends!"), is to reveal one's failings—to show that one's own endowments are not of a sufficiently superior kind.

Something close to this manner of thinking underlies much of modern Wordsworth criticism. When Geoffrey Hartman writes of the procedure he adopted in his highly influential study of Wordsworth, "In short, I followed Wordsworth's self-interpretations as closely as possible," he exhibits the common product of assumptions that are now widely shared.[20] The modern critic tends to view a Wordsworth poem as a mystery or puzzle, and the poet's problematic silences as challenges that test the critic's ability to "follow" the poet "as closely a possible." The silences are thought to be like

19 · Review of "The White Doe of Rylstone," in *British Lady's Magazine*, II (July, 1815), 34.
20 · Geoffrey Hartman, "Retrospect 1971," in *Wordsworth's Poetry, 1787–1814* (1964; rpr. New Haven, 1971), xii.

labyrinths or veils; and the modern critic, like Shelley's "Alastor" poet, is striving to pass through them in order to gaze "on the depth / Of thy deep mysteries" ("Alastor," ll. 22–23). The critic is on trial: is he good enough, sensitive enough, superior enough to follow the poet and reach the secrets that lie behind the silence? Whether it be the philosophical critic pursuing some conception of a Wordsworthian philosophic system or the psychological critic pursuing some notion about the hauntings of Wordsworth's consciousness, the common assumption tends to be that the poetry is somehow hiding Wordsworthian truths and that the critic's problem is to *follow* Wordsworth in order to discover the hidden treasure. Accordingly, the modern critic generally engages readily in acts of interpretation, proposing readings that aspire to reveal those truths that Wordsworth has secreted behind the poetic veil. It is interesting to note how frequently "A Reading of" appears in titles of modern Wordsworth studies.[21]

However, as readings of Wordsworth, with their many and varied revelations of Wordsworthian secrets, pile up about our critical heads, it becomes increasingly apparent that our basic assumptions about reading Wordsworth may require revision. When a text seems particularly amenable to multiple readings and particularly resistant to attempts to determine that one reading is clearly more valid than another, we must begin to consider whether the text is hiding some given pot of propositional gold or is playing a rather different game with us. There are signs of a shift in Wordsworth studies back toward the line of thought anticipated (if with negative appreciation) by Francis Jeffrey: perhaps we need to think more about the intentionality of Wordsworth's poetry, noting that Wordsworth may have been a more self-consciously artifactual poet than one might first suppose. One may posit that Wordsworth's poems are less the effusions of a Solitary, warbling his egotistical woodnotes wild, and more the products of a poetic maker, who is designing constructs that will have certain predetermined effects

---

21 · A few examples: W. G. Stobie, "A Reading of *The Prelude*, Book V," *MLQ*, XXIV (1963), 365–73; Anne Kostelanetz, "Wordsworth's 'Conversations' A Reading of 'The Two April Mornings' and 'The Fountain,'" *ELH*, XXXIII (1966), 43–52; Frank D. McConnell, *The Confessional Imagination: A Reading of Wordsworth's "Prelude"* (Baltimore, 1974); Timothy Bahti, "Figures of Interpretation, the Interpretation of Figures: A Reading of Wordsworth's 'Dream of the Arab,'" *SIR*, XVIII (1979), 601–27.

upon the reader.[22] Indicative of this redirection of thought about Wordsworth is the fact that "Simon Lee," once one of the more neglected among Wordsworth's poems, is beginning to receive serious, extended critical attention.[23]

"Simon Lee" looks like a touchstone for considering Wordsworth's artistic designs. Critics inclined to favor psychological readings of artistic behavior are commonly tempted to suppose that silences in Wordsworth indicate stress, repression of some hidden truth, mental turmoil beneath the poetic surface.[24] But in "Simon Lee," when Wordsworth steps out from behind his silences for a moment to address our perplexity, we learn that he employed silence consciously to achieve strategic ends.

> My gentle reader, I perceive
> How patiently you've waited,
> And I'm afraid that you expect
> Some tale will be related.
>
> (ll. 69–72)

22 · See Parrish, *Art of the "Lyrical Ballads,"* on how Wordsworth sought to shape his own feelings through "the control of Art" in such a way as to "evoke responsive feelings in the reader" (32). Sheats, *Making of Wordsworth's Poetry,* argues for viewing the *Lyrical Ballads* poetry as "presentations of pre-selected artistic forms" designed to produce in an audience "highly complex and premeditated effects" (280n9). See also my essay "Wordsworth's Contrarieties: A Prelude to Wordsworthian Complexity," *ELH,* XLIV (1977), 337–54.

23 · Compare, for example, the relative lack of interest in "Simon Lee" exhibited by Hartman in *Wordsworth's Poetry* (148–50) with the serious, probing treatment the poem receives in the more recent essay by Andrew L. Griffin, "Wordsworth and the Problem of Imaginative Story: The Case of 'Simon Lee,'" *PMLA,* XCII (1977), 392–409. See also Don H. Bialostosky, *Making Tales: The Poetics of Wordsworth's Narrative Experiments* (Chicago, 1984), for an extremely interesting inquiry into the laws or principles of Wordsworth's narrative experiments; "Simon Lee" plays an important part in Bialostosky's argument (74–81).

24 · The main line of psychological probings into Wordsworth's mind and art include F. W. Bateson, *Wordsworth: A Re-Interpretation* (London, 1954); Hartman, *Wordsworth's Poetry;* Wallace W. Douglas, *Wordsworth: The Construction of a Personality* (Kent, Ohio, 1968); Richard J. Onorato, *The Character of the Poet: Wordsworth in "The Prelude"* (Princeton, N.J., 1971); and Donald H. Reiman, "Poetry of Familiarity: Wordsworth, Dorothy, and Mary Hutchinson," in Reiman *et al.* (eds.), *The Evidence of the Imagination* (New York, 1978), 142–77.

Wordsworth knew that he was withholding things that his reader would conventionally look for in a poem. He knew that his "gentle reader" expected to be treated gently—to receive instruction and delight in a readily apprehensible form from a poet who aimed to please. The concept of deity so well portrayed by Blake in "The Lamb" comes to mind.

> Gave thee life & bid thee feed
> By the stream & o'er the mead;
> Gave thee clothing of delight.
> (ll. 3–5)

Something very like this poet-reader relationship had been characteristic of Wordsworth's poetry before 1798. But now Wordsworth is intent upon creating a different relationship.

> O reader! had you in your mind
> Such stores as silent thought can bring,
> O gentle reader! you would find
> A tale in every thing.
> What more I have to say is short,
> I hope you'll kindly take it;
> It is no tale; but should you think,
> Perhaps a tale you'll make it.
> ("Simon Lee," ll. 73–80)

Wordsworth is warning his reader that there actually is a design in this poetry that seems so frustrating. The poet is in control of the poem and knows what he is doing (or, more precisely, what he is refusing to do) to his reader. What the poet seeks is to make the "gentle reader" become less gentle—to turn him into something closer to Blake's Tyger. Instead of being merely the passive receiver of the poet's thought, the reader must become a thinker, engaging through the active power of his own mind the silences of the Wordsworth poem.[25]

25 · Stephen K. Land, "The Silent Poet: An Aspect of Wordsworth's Semantic Theory," *University of Toronto Quarterly*, XLII (1973), 157–69, sees the silence of the Wordsworthian

Wordsworth's silence, then, playing a complex variation upon the Keatsian Grecian urn, is designed to tease the mind into thought. By arousing and then not fulfilling expectation, the poet provokes the reader's mind into action, inciting it to thought within the open space that anticipation has created. Wordsworth's employment of this design casts light on the curious movements of a number of his poems. In "The Idiot Boy," for example, Wordsworth first makes it appear that he is laying groundwork for description of Johnny's strange adventures in the forests of the night—pursuing one of those "deluges of idle and extravagant stories in verse" that he mentions in the 1800 Preface.[26] But then at a crucial point in the poem he abruptly turns the poetic voice into a bumbling incompetent—instead of the conventional seven-year artistic apprenticeship, this would-be poet has been "bound" to his muses "these fourteen years, by strong indentures"—who struggles comically with his own silence, accusing his muses of preventing him from revealing the exciting tale of Johnny's adventures: "O gentle muses! let me tell / But half of what to him befel" (ll. 347–48, 349–50). This appeal to the "gentle muses" reverberates in interesting ways against the appeal to the "gentle reader" of "Simon Lee," conveying a hint of relationship. The reader and the muse come together; the musings of the reader bring voice to the silence.

That Wordsworth may have had such a conceit in mind is suggested by the concluding line of "A Night-Piece," in which the mind is "left to muse upon the solemn scene" (l. 26). Distance between poet and reader begins to diminish. As the poet is "a man speaking to men," so the man is a potential poet, though he may not be quite aware of his potential.[27] He needs to be stirred out of his passive gentility into active musing. The poet thus teases the reader into activity by suspending the poem, as it were, at crucial moments. In "There Was a Boy," for example, when the poet's description of the child's life closes with an image of the poet standing by the child's grave,

narrator as a function of Wordsworth's suspicious attitude toward language. Griffin, in "Wordsworth and the Problem of Imaginative Story," seems more on track, when he emphasizes how Wordsworth employs language to engage the reader's active participation in the poetic experience.

26 · Wordsworth, Preface to *Lyrical Ballads* (1800), in *Prose Works*, I, 128.
27 · *Ibid.*, I, 138.

the contemporary reader would have anticipated a conventional graveside meditation—something in a manner, perhaps, of the concluding "Epitaph" of Gray's "Elegy Written in a Country Churchyard." But Wordsworth simply stops short: "A full half-hour together I have stood, / Mute—for he died when he was ten years old" (ll. 31–32). At the crucial moment that seems to demand poetic reflection, the poet falls mute, forcing the reader to muse upon the Wordsworthian silence.

This strategy continues to be an important factor in later poems. It seems probable that the oddly "simple" or stark lyrics Wordsworth wrote in the spring of 1802 exhibit his continued concern to force his reader into thought by refusing to develop the contexts of significance that the poet conventionally builds into his poem.[28] It seems clear that Wordsworth still had the maneuverings of silent thought in mind in 1802 when he wrote "Resolution and Independence." That poem closes enigmatically with the line, "I'll think of the Leech-gatherer on the lonely moor!" The statement, especially with its provoking exclamation mark, which seems to imply that something startling has just been asserted, teases the mind: just what is it that this poet-speaker is going to think? The reader is tempted to begin to muse—to become the muse. This strategy of provocation is still more apparent in the climax of "Intimations of Immortality": "To me the meanest flower that blows can give / Thoughts that do often lie too deep for tears" (ll. 204–205). The poet is almost playing with the reader. He claims that he himself is capable of reaching depths of thought. But the reader is only being led to the brink of these depths. Left there, he is tempted to enter them. Now the ambience of the situation is clearly more that of the awe than of the fear that Wordsworth had proclaimed in his "Prospectus." The poet is pressing the reader to "look / Into our Minds, into the Mind of Man," and to look further down than tears and fear. Thereby encountering what?

BEFORE the *Lyrical Ballads* period, Wordsworth was predominantly a prescriptive poet, concerned to tell his reader how and what to think. But when

28 · Useful studies of the 1802 period include Jared R. Curtis, *Wordsworth's Experiments with Tradition: The Lyric Poems of 1802* (Ithaca, 1971), and William Heath, *Wordsworth and Coleridge: A Study of Their Literary Relations in 1801–1802* (Oxford, U.K., 1970).

Wordsworth states in the 1800 preface to *Lyrical Ballads* that he has sought to make his poetic incidents and situations "interesting by tracing in them, truly though not ostentatiously, the primary laws of our nature: chiefly as far as regards the manner in which we associate ideas in a state of excitement," he exhibits a fundamental shift of goals.[29] The prescriptive impulse, anxiety to direct a reader toward true principles and into proper paths of thought, has yielded to the inquiring impulse of a scientific investigator. It is illuminating that the poet should be particularly interested now in how we associate ideas "in a state of excitement." Such a state would seem most likely to induce what the earlier Wordsworth would have considered erroneous, erratic, perhaps dangerous associations of ideas. But now Wordsworth is concerned not with how we *should* but rather with how in fact we *do* think—and especially, as his emphasis on a state of excitement suggests, with how we think before we have a chance to reflect and render our thought compatible with ideas we may have assimilated about "proper" thinking. Wordsworth's desire is to catch the mind by surprise: he seeks the "primary" laws of our nature, those laws that operate prior to the modifications that education may impose upon the basic impulses of the mind.

This shift in poetic orientation continues to be evident in some of Wordsworth's later discussions of his poetic aims. In an 1807 letter to Lady Beaumont, for example, Wordsworth insists that "there is scarcely one of my Poems which does not aim to direct the attention to some moral sentiment, or to some general principle, or law of thought, or of our intellectual constitution."[30] Wordsworth seeks to "direct the attention" of his reader. The aim has little to do with inculcating the doctrines of this or that system of dogma. A "moral sentiment" is not what the poem attempts to teach but rather what it provokes one to think about—the reader's attention is directed toward it, as toward a phenomenon worthy of study and contemplation. Here again the concern is that of scientific inquiry: Wordsworth

29 · Wordsworth, Preface to *Lyrical Ballads*, (1800), in *Prose Works*, I, 122.

30 · Wordsworth to Lady Beaumont, May 21, 1807, in Ernest De Selincourt (ed.), *The Letters of William and Dorothy Wordsworth: The Middle Years* (2 vols.; Oxford, U.K., 1969), I, 148. Parrish, *Art of the "Lyrical Ballads,"* 30–32, led me to recognize the significance of this letter.

pursues the "general principle," the "law" of thought, the nature of our intellectual "constitution." Questions about systems of doctrine have been set aside in favor of more fundamental questions about mental activity. The poet's aim shifts from the attempt to influence thought toward the attempt to probe the principles of thinking.

Broadly speaking, one can think of Wordsworth as following the scientific path of Newton, but he is actually undertaking an inquiry that seems to claim priority over Newton's.[31] If Newton was a mind voyaging through strange seas of thought toward what seem the general principles and laws of nature, Wordsworth is a mind voyaging into the principles and laws of thought itself. This Wordsworthian journey is a characteristic product of the skeptical bias in Romanticism: before we build or admit allegiance to some given system, we must seek to look at what underlies that system, inquiring into its foundations. "How do you know," asks Blake in *The Marriage of Heaven and Hell*, "but ev'ry Bird that cuts the airy way, / Is an immense world of delight, clos'd by your senses five?" (Plate 7). It is thus in this relationship between Wordsworth and Newton: before we think much about nature with Newton, we had best think with Wordsworth about human thought.

In the letter to Lady Beaumont discussed above, Wordsworth goes on to indicate the mental phenomenon he wished to investigate in the sonnet "With Ships the Sea Was Sprinkled": "Who is there that has not felt that the mind can have no rest among a multitude of objects. . . ? After a certain time we must either select one image or object, which must put out of view the rest wholly, or must subordinate them to itself while it stands forth as a Head."[32] What interests Wordsworth is the factor of obligation: how the mind *must* select, *must* put out of view, *must* subordinate. He is pursuing one of the laws of thought. The mind cannot remain disinterested indefi-

---

31 · Recent studies that have helped wean criticism of the once common, erroneous notion that Wordsworth was antagonistic to science include: Geoffrey Durrant, *Wordsworth and the Great System* (Cambridge, U.K., 1970); Sheats, *Making of Wordsworth's Poetry*; and James H. Averill, "Wordsworth and 'Natural Science': The Poetry of 1798," *JEGP*, LXXVII (1978), 232–46.

32 · Wordsworth to Lady Beaumont, May 21, 1807, in *Letters: The Middle Years*, I, 148.

nitely in the presence of a number of objects; eventually it has to focus attention upon one of them, ignoring the rest or reducing them to secondary status. At first reading, this commentary, like many that Wordsworth offered on his poems, seems disappointingly prosaic, even uninteresting— one suspects it did not strike Lady Beaumont as particularly illuminating. It does not seem to be a very "poetic" insight; and it is no match for the frequently sublime meditations on nature, human life, and the deep truths of the imagination that Wordsworth's readers have commonly derived from his poems. All of this suggests that we tend to misapprehend the nature of Wordsworth's artistic concerns. For Wordsworth, while the poem itself may be "poetic," it is designed to produce contemplations that are clear, simple, and precise—like the findings of a scientific investigator. The sublimity of a law of thought lies in the contrast between its simplicity and its implications.

What are the implications of the law of thought that Wordsworth was seeking to illustrate in this sonnet? Wordsworth saw the law as a sort of model that helps to account for the phenomenon of human belief. Given an intellectual environment characterized by a multitude of competing doctrinal systems, how is it that the mind exhibits the ability to find answers to questions it asks? How does it manage to arrive at fixed beliefs to which it confidently clings in the face of a number of competing possibilities of thought? This issue is important in the *Lyrical Ballads.* Many of the poems in those volumes involve dramatization of the mind arriving at or stubbornly seeking to maintain some fixed belief ("Have I not reason to lament / What man has made of man?").[33] Wordsworth's observation in his letter to Lady Beaumont implies that such mental behavior is to be understood, not as the product of the mind's ability to discover truths about the world, but simply as the product of the laws of thought itself, illustrating the nature of our human intellectual constitution. The mind must choose one option for belief among a multitude of possibilities, and then either ig-

33 · Hartman, *Wordsworth's Poetry,* observes that many poems in *Lyrical Ballads* show "people cleaving to one thing or idea with a tenaciousness both pathetic and frightening" (143). I suspect that Wordsworth himself saw, and that he hoped his reader would see, such activity as profound and intriguing rather than pathetic or frightening.

nore the others or somehow reconcile them with the option chosen. Thus we believe certain things, not so much because the mind has discovered that they ought to be believed, but rather because the mind must believe something. We do not reason and then choose. We choose, and then we reason our way toward justification of the choice.

As Wordsworth hints in the important passage from "Simon Lee" discussed previously, we tell ourselves stories: "It is no tale; but should you think, / Perhaps a tale you'll make it" (ll. 79–80). On first encountering these lines, one is tempted to place particular emphasis on the word *tale* and, following that, to begin seeking some particular tale (some "point," concept, doctrine) that is presumably hidden behind the veil of Wordsworth's silence. But it is more likely that Wordsworth's aim was to place as much, or perhaps more, emphasis on the word *make*. The tale itself is of secondary importance. What is primary is the tale-making power or impulse that the mind possesses and that (so Wordsworth supposes) it may be teased into exhibiting by means of the poetic maneuvers it is being confronted with in Wordsworth's poems. If we give the mind an incident, for example, and offer hints of potential significance concerning it, but then cut the poem off short, leaving the mind excited but unsatisfied, confronting the incident in silence, how will the mind respond? Do we not discover in that silence how the mind begins exerting itself, casting about to "make something," as we say, of the incident that confronts it? Thus the key phrase in the 1800 Preface is "the manner in which we associate ideas in a state of excitement." Ideas do not have associations in themselves; we make the connections. In Wordsworth's statement to Lady Beaumont, the mind "can have no rest" among a multitude of objects—it has to make sense of its experience.

Wordsworth's ambition was to induce conscious awareness of this law of mental activity—to direct the attention toward how the mind forms tales of meaning and significance that one commonly believes are somehow inherent in the outer world of things-in-themselves. The tale we make in the process of reading the Wordsworth poem is like a laboratory experiment, reproducing in a context wherein it may be studied the tale-making process we unconsciously engage in as we lead our ordinary lives. In life, as in poems, we make readings.

Wordsworth's silences are related to his celebration in *The Prelude* of the "creative soul" (XI, l. 256; 1805 version). They are thus further related to the more general Romantic preoccupation with how the mind's impulses mold (perhaps fulfilling, perhaps idealizing, perhaps distorting?) its awareness of the world around it. One thinks, most obviously, of Coleridge's secondary imagination, dissolving, diffusing, dissipating, in order to recreate.[34] Presumably Wordsworth had no such rigorous Coleridgean category in mind. But he did intend to provoke his reader to encounter the making impulse of the mind, and to induce reflection upon the significance of this general principle or law of mental activity.

THE young Wordsworth had been in many respects a conventional late-eighteenth-century intellectual: a developer, or at least an active supporter, of systems of doctrine. He had supposed the mind capable of discovering true systems of knowledge and of developing proofs in support of those discoveries. Even after he yielded up his moral questions in despair, he continued to cling for a time to what he could of that manner of thinking. True knowledge must be possible, even if the proofs are somehow lacking: "O, be wiser thou! / Instructed that true knowledge" ("Lines Left upon a Seat in a Yew-Tree," ll. 55–56). Perhaps the important thing is not to question but simply to hold tight to what we know. Mental inquiry can be fearsome; it makes the grounds of knowledge seem to disappear.

By 1798, however, Wordsworth began turning toward the mind again, and he began directing his reader inward as well, by means of poetic strategies involving silent thought. Beyond fear lies awe. The shift in Wordsworth's orientation is marked by a suggestive parallel in passages considered above. In *The Prelude*, when Wordsworth recreates his period of crisis and despair, he speaks of himself as "demanding proof, / And seeking it in every thing" (ll. 896–97). But then in 1798, when he addresses his reader in "Simon Lee," he urges, "O gentle reader! you would find / A tale in every thing" (ll. 75–76). The mind may not be able to find proofs, but it can find tales. And in 1798, instead of looking like a hindrance to the quest for truth,

34 · Coleridge, *Biographia Literaria*, I, 202.

the tendency of the mind to make things up begins to look awesome to Wordsworth.[35]

In the "Christabel" notebook of 1798–1799, there is a fragment that suggests the direction of Wordsworth's thought:

> In many a walk
> At evening or by moonlight, or reclined
> At midday upon beds of forest moss,
> Have we to Nature and her impulses
> Of our whole being made free gift, and when
> Our trance had left us, oft have we, by aid
> Of the impressions which it left behind,
> Looked inward on ourselves, and learned, perhaps,
> Something of what we are.[36]

The ultimate goal of our journey into our own thought—emerging for the "we" of this fragment from mental interaction with natural phenomena, and emerging for Wordsworth's "gentle reader" from mental interaction with the incidents and anecdotes of the Wordsworth poem—is an act of looking "inward on ourselves" in order to learn "something of what we are." The objective validity of our thoughts is not a matter of concern. It may or may not be true, for example, that flowers enjoy the air they breathe. The mental artifact reveals something, not necessarily about the nature of things that it represents, but about the maker of the artifact. What we make of things—the tale the mind spins to itself in musing upon natural phenomena—helps to reveal our nature to ourselves.

This orientation of thought underlies the assertions of a number of Wordsworth's poems. For example, a famous stanza in "The Tables Turned" proposes that

35 · Was Coleridge a direct or indirect influence on Wordsworth here? Averill, "Wordsworth and 'Natural Science,'" argues that "in early 1798, particularly, Coleridge's interest in science and his experimental habits of mind influence his partner in the *Lyrical Ballads*. The year of almost daily contact in Somersetshire causes Wordsworth to become aware of contemporary scientific inquiry" (235). See also John Beer, *Wordsworth and the Human Heart* (New York, 1978), on Coleridge as a source of "certain esoteric ideas which fascinated Wordsworth" (47).
36 · Wordsworth, Fragment vi, ll. 8–16, in *Poetical Works*, V, 343–44.

> One impulse from a vernal wood
> May teach you more of man;
> Of moral evil and of good,
> Than all the sages can.
>
> (ll. 21–24)

The assertion of this stanza is sometimes misunderstood, both by those who love Wordsworth for his supposed "nature philosophy" and by those who loathe him for being mindless enough to hold such a philosophy. But Wordsworth does not claim that an impulse from a vernal wood tells us anything about the wood, or, as commonly supposed, about some presence of nature behind the wood. The impulse only tells us something about ourselves.

Wordsworth's argument, ironically, is congruent with the argument that skeptics are fond of raising against what they mistakenly believe to be Wordsworthian philosophy: that the impulses we experience during our encounters with nature are molded by our mental inclinations—they are the tales we tell ourselves, as Wordsworth would state it. Wordsworth recognizes this, and he celebrates our tale telling precisely because it holds a mirror, not up to nature, but up to ourselves. So, for example, the concluding assertion in "Nutting" is

> Then, dearest Maiden! move along these shades
> In gentleness of heart with gentle hand
> Touch,—for there is a Spirit in the woods.
>
> (ll. 53–55)

This spirit is *in* the woods, not *of* the woods. It is not a wood sprite or presence of nature.[37] Rather, it hints at the creative spirit of mental activity that the human presence introduces into the woods—thus the pun "these shades." Like the Holy Spirit, the human mind brings light to the natural darkness. Or, if one presses further, the human mind, like God, can bring

---

37 · Durrant, *Wordsworth and the Great System,* suggests that the spirit mentioned in the final lines of "Nutting" is "literally no more than a mental event" (117).

shades to life—it can, for example, see an act of violation in removing nuts from a grove of trees.

As the concluding lines of "Nutting" imply, Wordsworth's ambition is to link discovery of what we are to intimations of spirituality.[38] That we build up associations between things that, but for our own creative power, do not seem to belong to those things in themselves, suggests the existence of some godlike spark within the mind. Thus we arrive at the basis of the awe that lies beyond fear in the "Prospectus" passage. Wordsworth goes on in the "Prospectus" to assert that

> by words
> Which speak of nothing more than what we are,
> Would I arouse the sensual from their sleep
> Of Death, and win the vacant and the vain
> To noble raptures.
>
> (ll. 58–62)

These references to the sensual, and the vacant and the vain, like his reference to the sages in "The Tables Turned," remind us that Wordsworth was engaged in an adversary relationship, conducting warfare against opposing currents of contemporary thought that he conceived to be dangerous and, almost literally, deadly. His antagonists were those proponents (or victims, Wordsworth would probably have said) of systems of thought that insist upon viewing human beings merely as creatures of sense (hence "the sensual"), subject like other mechanisms to the mechanical laws of a mechanically conceived universe. Wordsworth's aim was to trace, both by the tale-making impulse he dramatizes within his poems and by the like impulse he seeks to provoke from his "gentle reader," how the human mind seems to

---

38 · John Jones, *The Egotistical Sublime* (London, 1954), among others, observes that it is an error to think of Wordsworth as turning toward spirit and transcendence only in later life, the time of his supposed decline (see esp. 124). M. H. Abrams, *Natural Supernaturalism*, argues that Romantic writers generally reformulated traditional materials, but that their overriding aim was to "save traditional concepts, schemes, and values which had been based on the relation of the Creator to his creature and creation" (13).

struggle to create its own laws, or at least to be responsive to laws different from those that govern the merely natural creation.

This is why Wordsworth exhibits such interest in tensions that exist between the tendencies of human thought and the contrary tendencies of natural process. That our human impulses seem to be out of tune with the natural world makes human life subject to suffering. However, as Wordsworth remarks in "Intimations of Immorality," "soothing thoughts" can "spring / Out of human suffering" (ll. 184–85). That we are out of tune may imply that we are not of this world. In "Michael," the birth of the child Luke, so the poet asserts, "more than all other gifts, / Brings hope with it, and forward-looking thoughts"; then he immediately adds, "And stirrings of inquietude, when they / By tendency of nature needs must fail" (ll. 154–55, 156–57). The poem plays upon this basic tension: on the one hand, Michael's "forward-looking thoughts"—which find expression in his determination to preserve control over the land ("It looks as if it never could endure / Another Master," he tells Luke [ll. 389–90]), his struggle to build up a protective sheepfold from a pile of rocks, his desire to establish a covenant; and on the other hand, the nature of worldly experience, wherein things "by tendency of nature needs must fail."[39] The thoughts man has are, one might say, un-natural; or, alternately, as the multiple layers of religious imagery in the poem suggest, man's thoughts are supranatural. They lead him to devote himself to dreams of elevation that are alien to the world in which he lives.

In "The Ruined Cottage," when Wordsworth invites us to contemplate the old pedlar Armytage seeking to comfort the grieving Margaret, he directs attention to how the pair constructs a mental fortress to ward off encroaching dissolutions:

> long had we not talked
> Ere *we built up a pile of better thoughts,*

39 · Whereas early-twentieth-century studies tended to stress union between man and nature in Wordsworth's poetry, recent studies tend to explore the complex interaction between inclination toward unity and inclination toward separation or isolation in the poetry. See especially Jones, *Egotistical Sublime*; C. C. Clarke, *Romantic Paradox* (London, 1962); Hartman,

> And with a brighter eye she looked around
> As if she had been shedding tears of joy.[40]

This pile of thoughts built up by the pair recalls the pile of ruins from which Armytage is building up the entire tale of Margaret's sufferings. And Armytage's tale itself incorporates the tension between this impulse to build things up and the contrary tendencies toward dissolution that rule the natural world outside the mind:

> and her few books,
> Which one upon another heretofore
> *Had been piled up* against the corner panes
> In seemly order, now with straggling leaves
> Lay scattered here and there, open, or shut,
> As they had chanced to fall.[41]

The books, the thoughts, the material constructs that the human mind builds up in accordance with its impulse toward elevation, perpetuation, "seemly order," all tend to drop; and what is left, as here the "straggling leaves," slowly becomes absorbed into nature, like leaves that fall from the trees. But the human struggle against this tendency of nature, and even the very ruins of that struggle—a "ruined cottage," a "straggling heap of unhewn stones," the tears of the shepherd in "The Last of the Flock"—testify to the presence of something in humanity that rises above nature, acknowledging other, higher laws than those of the material world ("Michael," l. 17). The creative impulse to make tales, and to build up piles of thoughts

---

Wordsworth's Poetry; and Frederick Garber, *Wordsworth and the Poetry of Encounter* (Urbana, 1971). Roger N. Murray, *Wordsworth's Style: Figures and Themes in the "Lyrical Ballads" of 1800* (Lincoln, Nebr., 1967), offers a perceptive analysis of how Wordsworth employs complex linguistic maneuvers to draw "the human realm and the realm of nature into closer proximity in our thinking" (139).

40 · Quoted from Dorothy Wordsworth to Mary Hutchinson, March 5, 1798, in *Letters: The Early Years,* 206, italics mine. Cf. *The Excursion,* I, 686–89.

41 · *Ibid.,* 208; italics mine. Cf. *The Excursion,* I, 824–29.

or piles of rocks, offers intimations of the spirit not to be explained by the materialist sages and the sensual in their sleep of death.

This brings us to the frontier of the relatively unexplored territory often referred to, with a sad shake of the head, as the "later Wordsworth," which some people believe they encounter as early as 1805 or so and others somewhat later, about 1812 to 1814, perhaps. It was once commonly supposed that the later Wordsworth offers us only a sad story of the loss of creative power and a lamentable about-face from liberal toward conservative and even reactionary political, social, and artistic values.[42] Numbers of recent critics have proposed, however, that the later Wordsworth's major artistic and intellectual preoccupations do not constitute an abandonment of his earlier concerns. To the contrary, they represent a development or evolution of those concerns. We can argue interminably about whether we like Wordsworth's later poetry and about whether it measures up to standards of "great art." But once we tire of or wean ourselves of such vaporous aesthetic arguments and come back to the realm of analytic inquiry, we should recognize that there are in fact clear lines of continuity between the earlier and the later Wordsworth that suggest that the poet continued to pursue the implications of his poetic inquiry beyond the limits of his so-called "great decade."

The later Wordsworth's preoccupation with emblems, like, for example,

---

42 · The classic modern arguments, following Harper and Legouis, developing the decline-and-fall view of the later Wordsworth are Herbert Read, *Wordsworth*, and H. I'A. Fausset, *The Lost Leader* (London, 1933). W. L. Sperry, *Wordsworth's Anti-Climax* (Cambridge, Mass., 1935), offers one of the less simplistic discussions of reasons for the supposed decline. Other critics question whether there really was a Wordsworthian decline. See, for example, Edith C. Batho, *The Later Wordsworth* (Cambridge, U.K., 1933); Bernard Groom, *The Unity of Wordsworth's Poetry* (London, 1966); and Gordon Kent Thomas, *Wordsworth's Dirge and Promise: Napoleon, Wellington, and the Convention of Cintra* (Lincoln, Nebr., 1971). For discussion of particular aspects of the later Wordsworth's artistic complexity, see John Jones's analysis of the "baptized Imagination" in Chap. 4 of *The Egotistical Sublime* and James A. W. Heffernan's discussion "The Making of Emblems," in Chap. 6 of *Wordsworth's Theory of Poetry: The Transforming Imagination* (Ithaca, 1969). Peter J. Manning, "Wordsworth at St. Bees: Scandals, Sisterhoods, and Wordsworth's Later Poetry," *ELH*, LII (1985), 33–58, argues that Wordsworth's supposed decline should be understood, rather, as part of a general cultural shift. Wordsworth was simply responding to the same pressures that strongly influenced the work of the early Victorians.

the mysterious doe of "The White Doe of Rylstone," obviously evolves from his earlier preoccupation with the phenomenon of tale making in *Lyrical Ballads*. One thinks of the clipping tree or the pile of rocks in "Michael." Wordsworth's later attraction toward epitaphs, memorials, old abbeys, King's College Chapel—ecclesiastical architecture in general—would appear to constitute a development in the interests of a mind that had been inquiring in the late 1790s into the human propensity to build things, like, for example, a sheepfold (and at the same time a covenant) from a pile of rocks. The sonnet "Inside of King's College Chapel Cambridge" (XLIII of the *Ecclesiastical Sonnets*) celebrates that chapel's architecture by discovering in it signs of the mind's unwillingness to accept mutability.

> These lofty pillars, spread that branching roof,
> Self-poised, and scooped into ten thousand cells,
> Where light and shade repose, where music dwells
> Lingering—and wandering on as loth to die;
> Like thoughts whose very sweetness yieldeth proof
> That they were born for immortality.
>
> (ll. 9–14)

In the background of this poem are the "intimations" of the Immortality Ode, celebrating the mind's unwillingness to let the fires of life die out: "O joy! that in our embers / Is something that doth live" (ll. 130–31). Behind this in turn lies the resurrecting impulse that plays through many of the *Lyrical Ballads* poems—as, for example, through "Nutting."

> It seems a day,
> (I speak of one from many singled out)
> One of those heavenly days which cannot die.
>
> (ll. 1–3)

The dominant principle of evolution in Wordsworth's thought involves the poet's gradually increasing fascination with public as well as private manifestations of supranatural behavior in human life, reflected mainly in the human impulse to build and preserve in the face of nonhuman nature's tendency toward dissolutions. In his earlier poetry Wordsworth had been primarily concerned with common, everyday manifestations of that impulse, evident in games children play (one may recall "Rural Architecture"), in the struggles of a housewife to maintain her cottage world, in moments of private communication.

> thy mind
> Shall be a mansion for all lovely forms,
> Thy memory be as a dwelling-place
> For all sweet sounds and harmonies.
> ("Tintern Abbey," ll. 140–43)

In later life Wordsworth came to see that such yearning after a "mansion for all lovely forms" can be discovered and celebrated in public as well as private life. It appears in the ceremonies of church and state, in law and custom—constructs that generations of human minds have built up and sought to preserve. Underlying Wordsworth's later conservatism, then, is not so much some failure of will or imaginative vision, nor even a radical shift in moral convictions, but rather an expanded realm of metaphysical investigation. Preservation of church and state is merely preservation of the tale of Michael writ large.[43]

The history of Wordsworth's encounter with Romantic questioning, therefore, suggests an important consideration. Romantic questioning need not lead, as one might naïvely suppose, in the direction of solipsism, nihilism, or despair. For Wordsworth, and among the Romantics generally, it often leads in quite the opposite direction. The Romantics sometimes flirt

---

43 · This defense of human constructs finds manifestation in Wordsworth's later poetry in the tendency of the poems to reflect positively even upon the eighteenth-century poetic tradition that the young Wordsworth had been inclined to scorn. See David McCracken, "Wordsworth on Human Wishes and Poetic Borrowing," *Modern Philology*, XIX (1982), 386–99, for a good discussion of how Wordsworth's late poem "The Wishing-Gate" (1828) contains "poetic techniques, allusions, lines, and phrases that . . . lead back to the eighteenth-century poets Pope, Gray, and Johnson" (386).

with the negating muse, and sometimes questioning threatens to overwhelm desire and life itself. But the Romantics usually end up the masters rather than the slaves or victims of questioning. Questioning finally becomes for them a tool, a means of securing desired ends. These ends, as the case history of Wordsworth suggests, tend to be traditional and conservative rather than new and radical. Once the mind has wielded questioning to set at a distance the clamor of contemporary ideologies, it can turn its attention back toward past grace, traditional ceremonies of innocence, reaffirmation of old structures of thought and value that the contemporary mind has lost, forgotten, or foolishly cast aside. So, for example, Romantic writing gives us such artistic maneuvers as Shelley's "Conclusion" to "The Sensitive Plant." Therein Shelley insists, first, upon his personal ignorance: "I cannot say" (l. 4); "I dare not guess" (l. 9). This prepares ground for him to posit human inability to understand life generally.

> in this life
> Of error, ignorance and strife—
> Where nothing is—but all things seem,
> And we the shadows of the dream.
> (ll. 9–12)

This is designed, not to leave us in a state of utter skepticism, but rather to render us receptive to a "modest creed" that delivers us from despair and returns us to an old, traditional world of thought for which death is the illusion—"death itself must be, / Like all the rest,—a mockery"—and things we value are immortal: "For love, and beauty, and delight / There is no death nor change" (ll. 15–16, 21–22). Shelley's point is that if in fact we do not know answers to the most fundamental metaphysical questions, then we also do not know that such answers as we yearn to give to those questions are false. In the absence of knowledge, we are free to believe and dream our desired "modest creed."

· *Four* ·

Romantic Questioning and the Novelists of the

Romantic Period

IT is sometimes supposed that Romanticism in English literature must refer mainly to the poets of the Romantic period. The novelists, it is thought, and particularly (or at least) the so-called major novelists, Sir Walter Scott and Jane Austen, actually are quite different from the period's poets in their intellectual orientations. The preoccupation with reason, "proper thinking," and decorum that we find in Scott and Austen, so a familiar argument goes, implies mentalities that are fundamentally Augustan rather than Romantic. Or, again, it is sometimes claimed that Scott and Austen mark the distance between novels and poems in the Romantic period by virtue of the fact that their novelistic art is aggressively "realistic" and concerned to dispel "romantic" dreams.[1]

---

1 · Georg Lukács, in *The Historical Novel*, trans. Hannah and Stanley Mitchell (London, 1962), sees in Scott "a renunciation of Romanticism . . . a higher development of the realist literary traditions of the Enlightenment in keeping with the new times" (33). *Cf.* Edgar Johnson, for whom the hero of *Waverley* is not "the romantic hero of a romantic novel" but

Arguments of this sort, however, are functions of the dubious attributive theorizing about Romanticism discussed in Chapter 1. When we pursue the notion that Romanticism can be understood as a series of attributes that is antithetical to a list of Augustan attributes, we almost inevitably are tempted to forget the complexities of the literary evidence. This leads to erroneous conceptions of the Romantic period, particularly to the assumption that the art of the period's poets is fundamentally different from that of its novelists.

Clearing the mind of such attributive assumptions as that Romantic writing must be characterized mainly by feeling because Augustan writing is characterized mainly by reasoning, and turning to actual Romantic evidences, one notices immediately that there has to be something wrong with the idea that Romantics combat Augustan "realism" by celebrating dreams. Calling to mind Coleridge's person on business from Porlock or Wordsworth's "fond illusion of my heart" in the "Elegiac Stanzas" helps one remember that the Romantics are by no means sanguine about either the substantiality or the trustworthiness of a dream (l. 29). Similarly, attending carefully to the language of Wordsworth's preface to Lyrical Ballads—which employs such phrasing as "one property of all good poetry, namely good sense," the "gratification of a rational mind," and "the intelligent Reader," and which discusses poetic passages that "with propriety abound with metaphors and figures"—helps one remember that the Romantics are not utterly addicted to combatting Augustan reason with emotional outpourings and the categorical suspension of common sense.[2]

One might also demonstrate, of course, that Augustan mentalities were not so utterly devoted to right reason and decorum as attributive theorizing

the "realistic protagonist of a realistic novel" (Sir Walter Scott: The Great Unknown [2 vols.; London, 1970], I, 524). That the Romantic and realist impulses are not antithetical, however, is argued by, among others, Ian Watt in The Rise of the Novel (Berkeley, 1957), and George Levine in The Realistic Imagination: English Fiction from Frankenstein to Lady Chatterley (Chicago, 1981).

2 · Wordsworth, Preface to Lyrical Ballads, in Prose Works, I, 133, 137. On the meaning of spontaneity in Wordsworth's preface, see Paul Magnuson, "Wordsworth and Spontaneity," in Donald H. Reiman et al. (eds.), The Evidence of the Imagination (New York, 1978), 99–118.

generally tempts one to suppose. It is the early eighteenth century that gives us Belinda, lamenting the rape of her lock and wishing her attacker had stolen "hairs less in sight, or any hairs but these!" ("Rape of the Lock," IV, l. 176). The Romantics more often create Lucy and Belle Dame figures, whom we are not encouraged to think of as hairy in that hidden manner. Which visions of female grace, one muses, seem to have greater affinity with the ladies who inhabit the fiction of Scott and Austen?

My point is not that the hidden-hair argument has any more validity than other versions of attributive arguing. I suspect, rather, that we mostly confuse or bemuse ourselves whenever we start trying to think seriously along attributive lines. What one needs to consider are more basic factors, patternings or formal structures of intellection. For example, were we thinking attributively and directing our inquiry toward checklists of shared or contrary statements of belief, perhaps no two figures of the Romantic period would seem more alien to each other than the poet Blake and the novelist Scott. In Blake's poem "My Pretty Rose Tree," from the *Songs of Experience*, the speaker is offered "such a flower as May never bore" (l. 2). But he rejects this offering because he already possesses a pretty rose tree, and he virtuously reaffirms his commitment to his rose by promising to "tend her by day and by night" (l. 6). However, his virtue is all in vain: the only reward his rose pays him for resisting flowery temptation is her thorny jealousy. This poem's thrust seems compatible with a proposition Blake expresses elsewhere: since those who observe the Golden Rule end up the Golden Fool, one might better choose to "sport with Fortune Merry Blithe & Gay / Like to the Lion Sporting with his Prey" ("To S——D: 'You All Your Youth . . . ,'" ll. 3–4).

Such thinking does not look much like that of Walter Scott. Scott, for example, sets up a contrariety in *Waverley* between the exotic Flora MacIvor and the domestic Rose Bradwardine; and he positions Waverley between the two. But then, in apparent direct contrast to Blake, he proceeds to show Waverley amply rewarded for ultimately turning away from Flora and tending to Rose. From this analytic perspective, it may be tempting to disassociate Blake and Scott: Blake (and, by extension, the Romantic poets generally?) leans toward the Romantic exotic; Scott (and, by extension, the novelists of the Romantic period generally?) leans back toward Augustan common sense.

But it is important to look beyond this surface level of options chosen, and to direct inquiry toward what these examples from Blake and Scott have in common—the orientation of mind that leads both the poet and the novelist to think in terms of choices between the flower and the rose tree. Both writers are exhibiting the inclination to think in terms of contrariety, which arises from the pressures of the Romantic intellectual situation. This affinity between Blake and Scott is part of a larger pattern of relationship. Such preoccupation with contrariety and the questions that arise from it is a basic, recurring factor, not only in Romantic poetry, but in the novelistic art of the Romantic period, and particularly in the work of the period's major novelists, Scott and Austen.[3]

THE Romantic poets frequently associate contrariety with some variation of the notion of "party." Thus Blake, weaving one of his intricate webs of contrary thinking in *The Marriage of Heaven and Hell,* invites us to think of Milton as a would-be angel who was really "of the Devils party without knowing it" (Plate 6). Blake's statement about Milton is interesting, not so much because Milton himself would have claimed to belong with the angels, but because Milton would have been disturbed by the manner of thought underlying Blake's language. Milton would have wished to understand distinctions between angels and devils in terms of a division between truth and falsity, essence and illusion, and so forth. He would not have been comfortable with the idea that the difference between an angel and a devil was simply a matter of opposed party allegiances, commitment to differing principles of definition concerning truth and falsity. When Milton invoked the heavenly muse at the commencement of *Paradise Lost,* he did not suppose that he was merely announcing his party allegiance, enrolling himself in support of one party's platform and rejecting a contrary party platform. But that is precisely what Blake wishes us to think about Milton's action.

3 · Most critics are willing to recognize some degree of affinity between familiar conceptions of the Romantic and the so-called "gothic" strain in novels of the Romantic period. See, for example, Robert Kiely, *The Romantic Novel in England* (Cambridge, Mass., 1972). Relations

Blake's turn upon Miltonic thinking calls to mind Edmund Burke's famous definition of *party* in "Thoughts on the Cause of the Present Discontents," published in 1770: "Party is a body of men united for promoting by their joint endeavours the national interest upon some particular principle in which they are all agreed."[4] The "national interest" suggests a common goal, but as the phrase "some particular principle" implies, the means of promoting (or perhaps even of defining) that goal is viewed as a function of an indefinite number of differing lines of thought, each the produce of "some" principle that will constitute the fond gathering point of a given party.

Every party has principles—the party of the devil as well as that of the angel—and every party is working to advance the "national interest." But the inclination of each party is to believe that its principles are the only true ones and that the contrary party must be, accordingly, either wholly lacking in principles, and hence corrupt, or else sadly lacking in the faculty of right reason (or right feeling, or right intuition) necessary to discriminate between real principles and false ones. Thus William Godwin, musing on the contrarieties of late-eighteenth-century political and religious life, states

> No sentiment therefore is more prevalent, than that which leads men to ascribe the variations of opinion which subsist in the world, to dishonesty and perverseness. It is thus that a Papist judges of a Protestant, and a Protestant of a Papist; such is the decision of the Hanoverian upon the Jacobite, and the Jacobite upon the Hanoverian; such is the notion formed by the friend of establishments concerning the republican, and by the republican concerning the friend of the establishments. The chain of evidence by which every one of these parties is determined, appears, to the adherent of that party, so clear and satisfactory, that he hesitates not to pronounce, that perverseness of will only could resist it.[5]

---

between Romanticism and the period's major novelists, Scott and Austen, however, are a matter of considerable disagreement.

4 · Burke, "Thoughts on the Cause of the Present Discontents," in *Works*, II, 82.

5 · Godwin, "Of Difference in Opinion," in *The Enquirer*, 300.

This concluding observation of Godwin's calls to mind the situation that Wordsworth is exploring in "We Are Seven." The speaker of Wordsworth's poem offers a little cottage girl a "chain of evidence," as Godwin calls it, that seems to him "so clear and satisfactory" that only that wee creature's "perverseness of will" could account for her refusal to be convinced by it. Or, as Wordsworth has his speaker remark:

> 'Twas throwing words away; for still
> The little Maid would have her will,
> And said, "Nay, we are seven!"
> (ll. 67–69)

Romantic poetry is full of such contrary parties, each pursuing its own principles of doing arithmetic, and each, accordingly, distrusting the other's ability to count correctly.

If there is any significant difference between the poetry and the novels of the Romantic period in their preoccupation with issues of contrariety, it may be that the novels tend to render more clear facets of those issues that the poetry only teases us through delicate or subtle suggestion to discern for ourselves. In *Caleb Williams*, for example, Godwin does not invite us to contemplate the struggle between Tyrell and Falkland as a simple contest between truth and falsity, heroism and villainy, but rather as the confrontation of two fundamentally opposed systems of principles that make each man largely incapable of understanding the other: "One man thinks one way," Tyrell mutters to Falkland in a rare flash of insight, "and another man thinks another" (p. 28). In *The Fortunes of Nigel* Scott gives a similar speech to Nigel: "Old men and young men, men of the sword and men of peaceful occupation, always have thought, always will think, differently" (Chap. 29). Admiral Croft verges on such a perception in Austen's *Persuasion*: "Ay, so it always is, I believe. One man's ways may be as good as another's, but we all like our own best" (p. 127). Austen's *Emma* crosses the border completely: "One half of the world cannot understand the pleasures of the other" (*Emma*, p. 81).

Such conflicts of understanding between characters in novels of the Romantic period frequently introduce directly issues of principle and of logical system building. In Scott's *Waverley*, for example, Major Melville conducts his examination of Waverley in the presence of the clergyman Mr. Morton, "both because he thought he might derive assistance from his practical good sense and approved loyalty, and also because it was agreeable to have a witness of unimpeached candour and veracity" (Chap. 32). Scott thereby establishes the point that neither of these examiners is either a knave or a fool. But he then goes on to show that disagreement, nonetheless, arises from the examination, and he is particularly concerned to direct attention toward the cause of this disagreement: "Each mused over the particulars of the examination, and each viewed it through the medium of his own feelings. Both were men of ready and acute talent, and both were *equally competent to combine various parts of evidence, and to deduce from them the necessary conclusions.* But the wide difference of their habits and education often occasioned a great *discrepancy in their respective deductions from admitted premises*" (Chap. 32, italics mine).

In this case differing deductions follow from the same premises. In Godwin's *Caleb Williams* the premises themselves differ. Laura Denison confronts Caleb with the principle that "true virtue shines by its own light, and needs no art to set it off" (p. 299). That Caleb should disagree with this she finds incomprehensible; and so she tells him, "You have the *first principles* of morality as yet to learn" (p. 299, italics mine). The irony is that Caleb had held the same "first principles" earlier in the novel; but he has now learned, so he believes, to hold true ones. "Madam, Madam!" he cries, "It would be impossible for you to hold this language, if you had not always lived in this obscure retreat, if you had ever been conversant with the passions and institutions of men" (p. 300). But Laura and Caleb, for all their asserting toward one another, cannot achieve communication. They "hold," as Caleb significantly states, fundamentally different principles.

Conflict over first principles in novels of the Romantic period frequently involves, as in the encounter between Laura and Caleb, an argument over the language one should hold. Choice of language tends to be a function of the principles one holds, as we have discussed previously in particular reference to significant factors in Romantic poetry. Holding different languages can become a manifestation of the differences of principle that divide parties. In Scott's *Heart of Midlothian*, Davie Deans tells Mr. Saddletree, "I ken ye are one of those that are wise after the manner of this world." But Mr. Saddletree cannot make sense of that, answering, "I canna understand this, neighbor." But then neither can Deans really make sense of Saddletree: "'I ken little o' the language of Antichrist,' said Deans; 'and I care less than little what carnal courts may call the speeches of honest men'" (Chap. 12). In Scott's *Old Mortality* Burley asks Henry Morton, "And can you doubt of our principles . . . since we have stated them to be the reformation both of Church and State, the rebuilding of the decayed sanctuary, the gathering of the dispersed saints, and the destruction of the man of sin?" Morton only responds, "I will own frankly, Mr. Balfour . . . much of this sort of language, which, I observe, is so powerful with others, is entirely lost on me. It is proper you should be aware of this before we commune further together" (Chap. 21). That a speaker's language can be "entirely lost" upon an auditor, because the speaker and the auditor do not share the same principles, is a recurring issue in Scott. When Claverhouse in *Old Mortality* hears pleas to spare Henry Morton, he is incredulous. The only response he can think to offer is that "this is stark madness. . . . I *must* do my duty to Church and State" (Chap. 13). One thinks of the way the poet Blake plays with perceptions of madness: "As I was walking among the fires of hell, delighted with the enjoyments of Genius; *which to Angels look like torment and insanity*" (*The Marriage of Heaven and Hell*, Plate 6, italics mine).

In Austen these tensions find more subtle expression, because they are not decked out in such colorful mythic and political-historical costume. In *Pride and Prejudice*, for example, Elizabeth's sister Jane defends Charlotte Lucas' decision to accept Mr. Collins as her husband. But Elizabeth protests against such defending of what, to her, seems indefensible: "You shall not, for the sake of one individual, change the meaning of principle and integrity, nor endeavor to persuade yourself or me, that selfishness is prudence, and insensibility of danger, security for happiness." Jane replies to Elizabeth, "I must think your language too strong" (pp. 135–36). Jane's interesting phrase "must think" reminds us that language is not simply the medium of message in Austen's novels. It is often also the problem. Meanings of terms that seem so clear and reasonable to one party in Austen may not be at all clear and reasonable to another party.[6] One party employs one language, but another party "must think" in a different language.

In accordance with this contrariety, Austen's novels echo the same patterns of divisionary thinking that characterize so much other writing in the Romantic period. In *Persuasion* Anne Elliot tells her sister, "There is hardly any personal defect . . . which an agreeable manner might not gradually reconcile one to." Her sister responds, "I think very differently" (p. 35). What is important herein is the precise phrasing Austen gives to her character's speech. Our attention is directed, not to the simple issue of whether Anne's proposition is correct or incorrect, but rather toward the issue of the manner of thinking in which propositions are entertained. One sister thinks, not more or less accurately than the other, but only "very differently." To this extent, at least, Austen's characters would be quite at home in the world of Scott's fiction. In *The Heart of Midlothian*, the Duke of Argyle finds Jeanie's plea for her sister's life reasonable, but he expresses doubt about whether the relevant authorities will be similarly moved. To this caution Jeanie responds, "O but, sir, what seems reasonable to your honour, will certainly be the same to them" (Chap. 35). The Duke answers Jeanie in a characteristically Romantic manner—and one that appears both in the novels and in the poetry of the Romantic period: "I do not know that . . . ilka man buckles his belt his ain gate—you know our old Scotch proverb?" (Chap. 35).

If "ilka man buckles his belt his ain gate," then basic questions arise that challenge the most fundamental propositions of conventional, or, as Blake would say, Innocent ideology. How are we to decide how a man *ought* to buckle his belt? Is there some realm of objective truth that transcends the contrarieties of party doctrine, or is the question resolvable, if at all, only by counting up opposing party strengths? If more people (or bigger people?) buckle their belts in a given way, then perhaps that way in effect becomes

6 · For a subtle discussion of Austen's interest in words, see Stuart M. Tave, *Some Words of Jane Austen* (Chicago, 1973).

the rule for belt buckling. This seems innocuous enough, possibly, until one shifts the question to such issues as whether one ought to play pushpin or read books.

The situation has potentially disturbing implications, starkly captured in the bleak humor of Coleridge's anecdote in Chapter 12 of *Biographia Literaria*: "'I asserted that the world was mad,' exclaimed poor Lee, 'and the world said, that I was mad, and confound them, they outvoted me.'"[7] A literary product of such uncomfortable musings is preoccupation with Solitaries, which characterizes both the poetry and the novels of the Romantic period. One thinks of figures like Byron's Manfred, Godwin's Caleb Williams, Wordsworth's Solitary, Scott's Black Dwarf, and Mary Shelley's Creature in *Frankenstein*. Through such figures the writer can explore situations in which the isolated individual reacts against a world that outvotes him, testing the power of the one mind to remain free and constitute, as it were, a party to itself alone.

A few works of the Romantic period toy optimistically with this possibility. Byron's *Manfred*, for example, seems to aspire to such a vision of autonomy in its final scene. But Coleridge's "Kubla Khan" is probably more characteristic of Romantic tendencies: the stunning spectacle of individual transcendence of the mob ("Weave a circle round him thrice") is presented as a fragmentary moment, tragicomically undercut by the mundane power of the person on business from Porlock. Most writings of the Romantic period seem similarly doubtful about the ability of the one mind to sustain itself alone. Emphasis tends to shift, accordingly, toward the one mind's search for a friend, and toward the possibility that the one mind might enclose itself in a circle of other, like minds—securing thereby a more potent party position. "Points have we all of us within our souls / Where all stand single," writes Wordsworth in the 1805 *Prelude*; "this I feel, and make / Breathings for incommunicable powers" (III, ll. 186–88). But Wordsworth addresses *The Prelude* to his "Friend" Coleridge, and the climax of that epic poem reveals the poet's yearning to move from "I" to "we," gathering together a party: "What we have loved, / Others will love; and we may teach

7 · Coleridge, *Biographia Literaria*, I, 179.

them how'' (XIII, ll. 444–45). In ''The Nightingale'' Coleridge reveals like ambitions to extend his party beyond himself alone: ''My Friend, and thou, our Sister! *we* have learnt / A different lore'' (ll. 40–41, italics mine).

Similar patterns appear in novels of the Romantic period. Scott's Black Dwarf, for example, ''comforted himself, that, at the expiry of his imprisonment, he could form with his wife and friend a society, encircled by which he might dispense with more extensive communication with the world'' (*The Black Dwarf*, Chap. 15). In Mary Shelley's *Frankenstein*, Walton seeks the support of a friend: ''I desire the company of a man who could sympathize with me; whose eyes would reply to mine. You may deem me romantic, my dear sister, but I bitterly feel the want of a friend'' (p. 19). Later in that same novel it is just such a friend that Frankenstein seeks in Walton. Frankenstein wants Walton's eyes to ''reply'' to his own: he tries to make Walton see as he himself sees, recognizing in the Creature, not a being to be pitied, but a monster that must be destroyed. The Creature, though, insists that it is not monstrous at all, and it dreams of enrolling members in an opposition party of its own to support its way of seeing: ''I resolved to return to the cottage, seek the old man, and by my representations win him to *my party*'' (p. 137, italics mine). Unfortunately, however, Frankenstein's Creature, like, Coleridge's ''poor Lee,'' is outvoted.

THE recurrence of contrarieties, patterns of party conflict, and pursuits of party enrollment in literature of the Romantic period calls to mind the familiar critical notion that Romanticism is characterized by a ''quest for union.'' This concept, like most ideas about English Romanticism, is usually applied particularly to the Romantic poems. But issues concerning union also appear repeatedly among the period's novels. Austen's *Emma*, for example, concludes with the phrase ''the perfect happiness of the union.'' Similarly, the main narrative action of Scott's *Old Mortality* concludes with union: ''Lord Evandale, taking their hands in his, pressed them both affectionately, united them together, raised his face, as if to pray for a blessing on them, and sunk back and expired in the next moment'' (Chap. 44). These focuses upon union are not to be explained as merely a function of the period's notions about how novels should conclude. Both Austen and Scott play variations on the theme of union throughout their respective novels. *Emma* opens with the theme, as Austen announces that her heroine "seemed to unite some of the best blessings of existence"—the key word *seemed* creating a tension that will be maintained through the course of the novel (p. 5). In Scott's *Old Mortality*, Henry Morton is set up at the novel's outset as a sort of Everyman character confronted with temptations to unite his fortunes with one or another of the novel's contrary parties. Midway into the novel, Morton, worn out with this strain of party conflicts, yearns for a "union of the good, wise, and moderate of all parties" (Chap. 25). Maria Edgeworth, in her first novel, *Castle Rackrent*, plays Ireland off against England as her version of the theme of contrariety, musing upon "a problem of difficult solution": "whether an Union will hasten or retard the amelioration of this country" (p. 182). Mary Shelley takes the issue of union of parties beyond the political arena into the realm of metaphysical explorations, as Frankenstein's Creature laments to his creator that "the human senses are insurmountable barriers to our union" (p. 145).

The theme of union in Romantic writing is more complex than it might at first appear. One reason union is interesting to the period's writers, the above-quoted passage from Edgeworth suggests, is that it can create "a problem of difficult solution." It is a mistake to suppose that writers of the Romantic period see union as a saving grace that will heal the wounds of contrariety and make all one, as some of the more peace-loving Romantic critics seem to believe. Those critics forget such evidences as Blake's quip that "Jesus Christ did not wish to unite but to seperate" (*The Marriage of Heaven and Hell*, Plate 17). Unions can be interesting because they create problems rather than heal them.

The dubious notion that Romantic writers were questing after a problem-solving union of contrarieties seems to be traceable partly to the critical error of identifying the thinking of the dramatic character in a literary work with the thinking of the author of the work. Mary Shelley creates Frankenstein's Creature, and that Creature quests after a union that will ease its painful isolation. But Mary Shelley herself is submitting that quest to scrutiny, exploring the issues and problems that the quest brings to light, inquiring into the nature of the "insurmountable barriers" that the quest reveals. Many of the poems and the novels of the Romantic period deal with the nature and persistence of such barriers. In the concluding sentence of *Frankenstein* the Creature is "borne away by the waves, and lost in darkness and distance." The final vision of that novel is one of distance rather than union. In Wordsworth's *Excursion*, similarly, the aptly named Solitary remains so at the poem's conclusion, taking "the slender path that leads / To the one cottage in the lonely dale" (IX, ll. 773–74). In Keats's "Ode to a Nightingale," the bird with which the poem's speaker would unite is lost in distance at the poem's conclusion, and the speaker is tolled back to his "sole self." Much Romantic literature leaves us to contemplate visions of separation. One could argue, I suppose, that this means the Romantics were simply failed questers after a soothing unity. But that would be a little like claiming that *The Taming of the Shrew* shows Shakespeare to have been a failed advocate of women's rights.

In writings of the Romantic period that do bring their contrarieties into union, it is important to take note of the dramatic context in which those unions appear. As distinct from the culminating union in such eighteenth-century works as Henry Fielding's *Tom Jones*, wherein "there is not a Neighbor, a Tenant, or a Servant who doth not most gratefully bless the day when Mr. *Jones* was married to his *Sophia*," the achievement of unions in the Romantic period frequently take place in contexts of division that reveal barriers (Bk. 18, Chap. 13). In the conclusion of *Emma* the heroine and Mr. Knightley find the perfect happiness of their union within the confines of a "small band of true friends" (p. 484). As the subtly combative overtones of the word *band* suggest, just outside their little circle of friends lies a besieging force represented in the person of Mrs. Elton, who sniffs disparagingly at the simplicity of their wedding.[8] In Austen's *Persuasion* Anne Elliot's union with Captain Wentworth is associated with an even smaller

8 · Alistair M. Duckworth, *The Improvement of the Estate* (Baltimore, 1971), argues that this conclusion in *Emma* shows a healing of social fragmentation and reconstitution of society "around the central union" (27); but Lloyd W. Brown is closer to the mark in "The Business of Marrying and Mothering," in Juliet McMaster (ed.), *Jane Austen's Achievement* (London, 1976), 27–43, when he emphasizes "the isolation which seems to mark the Austen heroine" (36).

circle: "Their marriage, instead of depriving her of one friend, secured her two" (p. 251). Scott's *Old Mortality* binds Henry Morton and Edith together, not within a celebrating union of all parties, as in *Tom Jones*, but rather within a context of the death of other parties. Burley is dead, and Lord Evandale is dying, even as he unites the hands of the pair. Scott employs the circle-of-friends motif to underscore a stark contrast. Henry and Edith are united in a circle of lamentation over separation: "He was soon surrounded by his lamenting friends" (Chap. 44).

This preoccupation with enclosing circles in literature of the Romantic period commonly involves, not merely bringing things together inside the circle, but also excluding things outside. In *The Heart of Midlothian*, "A prison is a world within itself, and has its own business, griefs, and joys, peculiar to its circle" (Chap. 1). Fergus Mac-Ivor in *Waverley* "was, indeed, within his little circle, as perfect a politician as Castruccio Castrucani himself" (Chap. 19). In *Frankenstein* Victor's father anticipates his son's marriage to Elizabeth: "Our circle will be small but bound close by the ties of affection and mutual misfortune" (p. 90). In Romantic poetry the most famous instance of the pattern is probably the "dome of pleasure" in Coleridge's "Kubla Khan," wherein could be heard "the mingled measure / From the fountain and the caves" (ll. 33−34). There, as in the vision of "perfect happiness" at the conclusion of Austen's *Emma*, the circle of pleasure is a small, enclosed space, in which the pleasure is offset (though also perhaps heightened?) by the fact that no such pleasure is being shared by anyone positioned outside that charmed enclosure.

As these evidences suggest, Romantic union tends to direct attention, not merely toward the union itself, but also toward the divisions that union produces. In the Romantic period party union generally is dramatized in such a way as to remind us that it involves separation from other parties. Small touches in a poem by Wordsworth and a novel by Austen illustrate this dramatically. In Wordsworth's *Excursion* the characters set forth upon a stage of their excursion.

> Forth we went,
> And down the vale along the streamlet's edge

> Pursued our way, *a broken company,*
> Mute or conversing, single or in pairs.
>
> (IX, ll. 433–36, italics mine)

It is not only isolation but also the formation of pairs that can produce "a broken company." Austen touches a like chord in the Box Hill episode of *Emma:* "They separated too much into parties. The Eltons walked together; Mr. Knightley took charge of Miss Bates and Jane; and Emma and Harriet belonged to Mr. Churchill. And Mr. Weston tried, in vain, to make them harmonize better" (p. 367). Austen is particularly fond of this pattern. She employs it again in *Persuasion:* "Everything now marked out Louisa for Captain Wentworth. . . . In a long strip of meadow-land, where there was ample space for all, they were thus divided—forming three distinct parties" (p. 90). These pairs are created by acts of union, but from another perspective, which receives emphasis, such acts of union create divisions.

What seems particularly to interest both poets and novelists of the Romantic period is the generation of shared divisionary experience—divisionary unions, one might say. Involved in this interest is the speculation that perhaps the union of as few as two individuals might be sufficient to constitute an independent, self-sustaining "kind" or "race" or "species." The union of a male and a female in particular holds obvious attractions. If Frankenstein's Creature could secure a mate, Prometheus an Asia, Los an Enitharmon—if Adam could find an Eve—then this union might constitute (or, if not that, at least eventually produce) a distinct species that could define and defend its own system of thought and value. At its radical extreme this line of speculation finds expression in the incest or near-incest themes that attract Romantic writers. Byron's Manfred dreams of Astarte.

> She was like me in lineaments—her eyes
> Her hair—her features—all, to the very tone
> Even her voice, they said were like to mine.
>
> (*Manfred,* II, ii, ll. 105–107)

Coleridge teases thought toward flickering recollections of an Edenic state in which to "see the *stranger's* face" was to greet a "sister more beloved, / My play-mate when we both were clothed alike!" ("Frost at Midnight," ll. 41–43). The quintessential Romantic party is this Edenic one: a frail, holy enclosure, separated from a fallen world of alien parties outside, shared for a brief moment by an Adam and Eve who are, as in Eden before the Fall, clothed alike in nakedness.

Wordsworth's "Tintern Abbey" offers clear insight into the issue at stake in this familiar Romantic movement toward an Edenic divisionary union. In that poem's climax the troubled "I" becomes "we," as the speaker gathers to himself his "dearest Friend," who happens to be his "dear, dear Sister!" This Edenic party of two gathers together to transform the solitary faith of the isolated "I" into the more substantial substance of a shared proposition: "*Our* cheerful faith, that all which *we* behold / Is full of blessings" (ll. 133–34, italics mine). But this turn from "I" to "we" in the poem functions, not to render this cheerful faith suggestive of a universally accepted proposition, as one might at first suppose, but rather to set up a highly charged dramatic tension. A "dearest Friend" reminds us that there are other people beyond the "we," not all of whom are equally friendly, or perhaps even friendly at all. Wordsworth underscores this implication by referring to "evil tongues, / Rash judgments" and "the sneers of selfish men," thereby setting up a contrariety between "our" faith and the orientation of thought of opposition parties (ll. 128–29). Wordsworth thus formulates a dramatic proposition: that in the poem's situation of questioning indeterminacy—accented by such touches of doubt as "If this / Be but a vain belief, yet, oh!"—this cheerful faith of ours can become and remain true at least for us, impervious to assault from sneering parties outside the edenic bounds of our small, holy circle (ll. 49–50).

Novels of the Romantic period introduce similar maneuvers in which unions within a context of contrarieties become associated with assertions of "truth for us." In *Frankenstein* Mary Shelley arranges the circumstances of William's death in such a way as to suggest that, for all people can actually know with certainty, Justine might have murdered the child. This sets the stage for her to show Elizabeth uniting with Frankenstein in a small circle of faith that proclaims Justine's innocence. "I know, I feel she was innocent," she cries out to Frankenstein; "you are of the same opinion, and that confirms me" (p. 93). Elizabeth's drift from "know" to "feel" to "opinion" marks the epistemological fragility of her claim. But, just as the speaker of Wordsworth's "Tintern Abbey" restores himself by building up a "cheerful faith" with his sister, so Elizabeth finds her ground of confidence in sharing her faith with another consciousness, thereby establishing a "truth for us." James Hogg's *Private Memoirs and Confessions of a Justified Sinner* exposes the epistemological skeleton of the pattern yet more clearly, when Mrs. Logan asserts to her companion that "if you and I believe that we see a person, why, we do see him. Whose word, or whose reasoning can convince us against our own senses?" (p. 78). The claim is not that seeing a person means that the person objectively exists. It is simply that he is there for *us*, and this "truth for us" cannot be shaken by any contrary word or process of reasoning produced by parties beyond our own. Our word becomes, as it were, The Word within our own shared circle. One thinks of Shelley writing to Maria Gisborne, "*Let us believe* in a kind of optimism in which we are our own gods."[9]

The fundamental issue with these patterns of Romantic contrariety, then, does not appear to be whether one can bring them all together into some sort of grand union of all parties; nor is it whether one might be able to discern from among the varying truths of contrary parties which truth is somehow "really" or "more fundmentally" true; nor, the last and most subtle resort, is it to determine which truth finally ought to be accorded superior status, whatever relative degree of reality it claims.[10] Writers of the Romantic period seem more interested in questions concerning the nature and behavior of different parties, as exhibited by the activity of forming, seeking to maintain, or choosing between divisionary systems of truth. Such activity can offer insight into the distinctive nature of a quantity. It can cast light on issues of identity.

9 · Shelley to Maria Gisborne, October 13 or 14, 1819, in *Letters of Percy Bysshe Shelley*, II, 125; italics mine.
10 · Romantic scholarship's devotion to trying to discover which truths are "more true" in Romantic dramatizations of contrariety finds a good emblem in the history of critical analysis

"One Law for the Lion & Ox is Oppression," writes Blake in *The Marriage of Heaven and Hell* (Plate 24). Differing categories of being recognize or respond to differing laws. Exiling in Italy, Byron decided that even those seemingly degenerate, lawless Italians had in fact their own system of law: "Their system has it's rules—and it's fitnesses—and decorums—so as to be reduced to a kind of discipline—or game at hearts." Thus Wordsworth in the preface to the 1800 *Lyrical Ballads*, proposing inquiry into "primary laws," has in mind not those of nature or of the nature of things generally but rather the primary laws "of our nature."[11] He is interested in what defines *us*—the distinctive nature of, as it were, our human party. Investigation of how our minds work, and especially how our minds make choices among contrarieties, formulating "truths for us," may reveal something, not necessarily about the truth of our truths, but rather about what we are. A like inquiry appears to be going on in Romantic thought generally, and indications of it recur in both the poetry and the novels of the period. The behavior of a given individual or a given party of individuals in the context of some situation of divisionary truth offers a means of investigating the distinctive nature, the identity, of that individual or party. Differences in inclination or choice—attraction toward one option of truth, rejection of (or inability even to see or comprehend) an alternative option of truth—may serve to establish distinctions between and to suggest the properties of different "kinds" or "species."

This direction of Romantic inquiry suggests the ventures of a scientific investigator. One is reminded of how frequently images of scientific investigation appear in writing of the Romantic period (contra critical commonplaces about Romantic antipathy to science). In a letter to Sarah Jeffrey, for example, Keats speculates that traveling aboard an Indiaman ("An Indiaman

---

of Keats's *Lamia*. Two of the more interesting recent attempts to negotiate that Keatsian labyrinth are Garrett Stewart, "*Lamia* and the Language of Metamorphosis," *SIR*, XV (1976), 3–41; and Gene M. Bernstein, "Keats's 'Lamia': The Sense of a Non-Ending," *Papers on Language and Literature*, XV (1979), 175–92. Stewart is less uneasy than Bernstein about the possibility of arriving at clear judgments about the poem's contrarieties; Bernstein believes that *Lamia* "defies any schematic, allegorical reading" (190).

11 · Byron to John Murray, February 21, 1820, in *Byron's Letters*, VII, 43; Wordsworth, Preface to the 1800 *Lyrical Ballads*, in *Prose Works*, I, 126.

is a little world," he says) would be the "finest thing in the world" to strengthen the "energies of Mind": "To be thrown among people who care not for you, with whom you have no sympathies forces the Mind upon its own resourses, and leaves it free to make its speculations of the differences of human character and to class them with the calmness of a Botanist."[12] Keats's offhand remark suggests, first, the typically Romantic pursuit of the mind's freedom ("leaves it free to make its speculations"). It suggests, second, that strengthening the mind's resources is not so exclusively a matter of pursuing synthesis, unity, and reconciliation of opposites as Romantic criticism sometimes proposes. The mind also strengthens itself through activities of comparative analysis, focusing upon differences and learning to class them like a botanist. Finally, Keats's appreciative reference to botanists indicates that it is a mistake to identify Romanticism with such ideological statements as "We murder to dissect," in Wordsworth's "Tables Turned" (l. 28). That line occurs in the context of a dramatic debate between two speakers, neither of whom is quite Wordsworth himself.

Keats musing about the pleasures of analyzing people aboard an Indiaman is akin to Scott telling Robert Southey what seems to him interesting in studying the history of colonies: "The extremes of civilized and savage life are suddenly and strongly brought into contact with each other and the results are as interesting to the moral observer as those which take place on the mixture of chemical substances are to the physical investigator."[13] Scott's investigator, one notes, is a moral "observer," not a moralizer or a metaphysical reconciler. He is interested in mixing substances—the contrarieties we have been discussing—not in order to produce a healing medicine, but rather in order to study with scientific care the properties of those substances revealed when they are brought together.

This Romantic interest in inquiring into the natures of different substances helps to explain why particular mental orientations and dramatizations of crucial turns of thought in literature of the period are frequently marked by some manner of "species" identification. Probably the most con-

12 · Keats to Sarah Jeffrey, June 9, 1819, in *Letters of John Keats*, II, 115.
13 · Scott to Robert Southey, March 23, 1818, in H. J. C. Grierson (ed.), *The Letters of Sir Walter Scott* (12 vols.; London, 1932–37), V, 115.

spicuous example occurs in *Frankenstein*, where the title-character—after wavering between opposed poles of thought in a way that recalls the similar, aptly named title-character in Walter Scott's *Waverley*—finally finds himself (literally) in identification with his own species. "My duties toward the beings of my own species," Frankenstein tells Walton, "had greater claims to my attention, because they included a greater proportion of happiness or misery" (p. 217). This resolution of contrarieties in a commitment to "beings of my own species" has been building up through the entire course of Mary Shelley's novel, anticipated, not merely in the Creature's previously quoted exclamation concerning the insurmountable barriers created by Frankenstein's "human senses," but also in a dense texture of allusions to "race," "species," and "the human" that run through the novel—like, for example, "and often did my *human nature* turn with loathing from my occupation" (p. 55, italics mine). The issue in *Frankenstein* is not one of discovering the truth (who is "right," the creator or the created?); nor is it one of pronouncing moral judgment (there is a popular misconception that Frankenstein should have "taken responsibility" for his creation).[14] Instead, Mary Shelley's novel is, first, a study of how discovering truth and pronouncing moral judgment become highly problematic when different species are at issue, and second, an investigation of the boundaries between what we are and what we are not, the limits of our human circle or species.

As my reference to *Waverley* suggests, Scott's novels exhibit a similar concern with differences between species. When Scott positions Henry Morton in the middle of contrariety between covenant and crown in *Old Mortality*, for example, he marks Morton as the representative of "natural humanity": "I own I should strongly doubt the origin of any inspiration which seemed to dictate a line of conduct contrary to the feelings of natural humanity, which Heaven has assigned to us as the general law of our conduct," Morton declares to Burley (Chap. 6). Scott then proceeds to investigate how this "law" of natural humanity defines Morton in relation to parties that believe heaven has assigned to men other, quite different laws. "Thou art yet," Burley says to Morton, "in the court of the Gentiles, and I

---

14 · I discuss problems in such popular readings of Mary Shelley's novel in "Frankenstein's Monster."

compassionate thy *human* blindness and frailty" (Chap. 17, italics mine). What Mary Shelley illuminates with differences between human and non-human species, Scott explores with different species of human possibility itself. He is concerned to plot the shape of those barriers that both separate and give definition to our human contrarieties.

In one further example from the novelistic art of the Romantic period, *Caleb Williams,* Godwin sets up a contrariety between Tyrell and Falkland, thereby introducing an analysis of the opposed structures of thought and value inclination represented by those two subspecies of human possibility. Tyrell, observing his influence over those around him waning in favor of his enemy Falkland, "figured himself as about to be deserted by every creature in human form, all men under the influence of a fatal enchantment, approving only what was sophisticated and artificial, and holding the rude and genuine offspring of nature in mortal antipathy" (p. 46). Part of Godwin's intention is to show that Tyrell is not simply wrong or villainous. He is, instead, a man who behaves quite understandably in accordance with a particular mode of thought that characterizes a given party of men. Godwin has established previously that "Mr. Tyrell might have passed for a true model of the English squire" (p. 16). What interests Godwin is investigation of the identifying properties of this subspecies, isolating, for example, the notions it holds about the "human" and "genuine nature." When Godwin observes in his late essay "Of Self-Love and Benevolence" that different men are wont to pursue radically different ends in their lives, and then asks himself why this is so, he decides that "each man has an individual internal structure, directing his partialities, one man to one thing, and another to another."[15] This line of thought takes the principle of division much further than the earlier Godwin of *Caleb Williams* and most of the Romantics were inclined to go. But Godwin's notion about an "internal structure" is useful. When Godwin, like other writers of the Romantic period, sets up situations of contrariety, he is aiming like a scientific investigator at discovery and analysis of different internal structures.

This analytic impulse also characterizes the poetry of the Romantic pe-

15 · Godwin, "Of Self-Love and Benevolence," in *Thoughts on Man,* 212–13.

riod. In "Mont Blanc," for example, Shelley posits at his poem's outset that "the everlasting universe of things / Flows through the mind" (ll. 1–2), and his concern is to mark the boundaries that separate this universe of things and the "Power" that lies behind it from

> my own *separate* fantasy,
> My own, my *human* mind, which passively
> Now renders and receives fast influencings
> (ll. 36–38, italics mine)

The ambition, reminiscent of Wordsworth, is to discover what we are by revealing the internal structure of human thought as it seeks to grasp in "some faint image" or to "interpret" the Power that eludes our human visions (l. 47). "Mont Blanc" is not, as is sometimes supposed, a prime example of Romantic struggle to heal the division between subject and object. Quite the contrary, it is a prime example of Romantic concern to define ourselves by studying how our human nature reacts in response to a nonhuman species of nature—a variation of the more general Romantic preoccupation with analyzing, like a chemist, the properties of different substances when they are brought together.

Two further examples from the poetry of the Romantic period come to mind. In the "Elegiac Stanzas" Wordsworth portrays his mind turning from his own imagined, idyllic picture of Peele Castle and expressing preference for George Beaumont's troubled painting of the castle besieged by storm. In so doing, Wordsworth marks the species identification that he would have us associate with this mental choice. In preferring Beaumont's picture, the mind exhibits the behavior of a "humanized" soul, one that is unable to live "at distance from the Kind" (ll. 36, 54). Wordsworth's idea is not that one should suppose Beaumont's picture to be objectively true to the nature of nature; nor is it that one should simply decide the poet has changed his mind about what nature is really like. The point is, rather, that Beaumont's is the more "human" picture of nature—whatever nature in fact may be really like. Beaumont's reading of nature accords best with our "Kind," and our attraction toward it helps to reveal our human internal structure.

My final case in point is Keats's "Ode on a Grecian Urn." Keats's urn states that "Beauty is truth, truth beauty." But this is neither Keats's doctrine nor Romantic doctrine generally. Rather, it is an utterance marked by Keats with a species identification designed to set it at a distance from our human selves. Before Keats allows us to hear what the urn has to say, he carefully marks it as only "a friend to man." (l. 48). Ultimately the urn is nonhuman. It speaks a nonhuman language (or rather, more precisely, it has a grammatical logic that is teasingly close to but finally foreign to the internal structure of human thought). This is why we argue with ourselves over precisely what it is that the urn is saying, or whether it is saying anything meaningful at all. What Keats has achieved in this poem is to put us dramatically into the position of his knight-at-arms in "La Belle Dame sans Merci," making us hear the utterance of an alien species that seems to be offering "in language strange" something we desire (l. 27). But, as with the interpreting knight of that poem, the meaning we find in Keats's urn, if indeed we find any, tells us only something about ourselves—about how or what we human beings think.

The circles the urn speaks in lie outside our human circle of woe and generation. But our reaction to those circles can help us define our own boundaries. At the point where the urn teases us "out of thought / As doth eternity," we meet our border territory and begin to experience ourselves in contrast to the nonhuman (ll. 44–45).

WHEN Blake's singer in "My Pretty Rose Tree" passes a sweet flower by and receives only his rose's thorny jealousy in return for that constancy, it is tempting to read therein a Blake dogma about the importance of embracing free love when one has the opportunity. When Scott's Waverley overcomes his infatuation with Flora Mac-Ivor and settles down happily to cultivate his estate with Rose Bradwardine, it is tempting to read in that event a Scott dogma about the need to be sensible and embrace the orderly comforts of modern civilization. Thinking along such ideological lines leads to positing dramatic contrasts between Blake and Scott. However, this ignores important factors that lead to recognition of affinities between the poet and the novelist.

In "My Pretty Rose Tree," as in other poems from the *Songs of Inno-*

cence and of Experience, Blake is not concerned with objective truths. His focus, rather, is upon opposed perceptions of truth, different structures of "truth for us" that generate contrary visions of things experienced by two different species of mental orientation, Innocence and Experience. The poems of Innocence and the poems of Experience play upon the same world of data. For both Innocence and Experience there is, on the one hand, an enclosed realm of familiar things, and on the other, another realm beyond the enclosure that is largely unexperienced and is perceived only by glimpses. Distinctions between Innocence and Experience concern how these two realms are envisioned by the mind and what choices the mind makes in accordance with its visions.

The Innocent, for example, renders its vision of these realms into certain patterns of truth for Innocence. Blake's Introduction to Songs of Innocence dramatizes, among other things, the disposition of Innocence to believe that the passing moment of personal inspiration should be preserved, written down "in a book that all may read" (l. 14). To accomplish this task, the Innocent busies himself to make a "rural pen" (l. 17). This activity of pen making introduces us to one of the prevailing patterns of Innocent thought. Underlying the meaning of pen as writing instrument here is pen as enclosure: just as one preserves the moment's song in a book, one encloses the lamb in a sheepfold. For Innocence this seems a good thing to do. The pen becomes the lamb's familiar and protecting realm, variously represented throughout the Songs of Innocence as a "nest" ("Night," ll. 3–4), an "Angel-guarded bed" ("A Dream," l. 2), and a "green" ("The Ecchoing Green," passim; "Nurse's Song," l. 1). It is comforting and secure, warding off powers of the outer, unfamiliar world. That outer world is envisioned as dangerous and painful, and variously associated with "wolves and tygers" ("Night," l. 25), a "lonely fen" ("The Little Boy Found," l. 1), and a "tangled" waste wherein one becomes lost ("A Dream," l. 7).

Experience, in contrast, marks the emergence—or the puzzled beginnings of the emergence—of antithetical patterns of "truth for us," wherein the familiar world of enclosure begins to look dangerous, diseased, or deceptive, and the unknown world outside begins to appear enticing and attractive. In "The Tyger," for example, if creatures from the forests of the night that lie outside the domestic realm of the sheepfold are "fearful," they are also beautiful, possessing "symmetry"; and if they are "burning," they are also "bright"—which brightness shining in the forests of night calls up tentative memories of the promise of divinity. In accordance with the mind's temptation to lean toward the wild outside, dissatisfaction arises over the cultivated inside. The enclosure is now a prison, a place of "mind-forg'd manacles" ("London," l. 8); the bed of roses looks "sick" ("The Sick Rose," l. 1).

"My Pretty Rose Tree" dramatizes one of the many variations of this Experienced manner of thinking. The familiar cultivated garden has begun to look a little less overwhelmingly attractive: it contains not a lovely but only a pretty rose tree. In conjunction with this subtle shift to faint praise, what lies outside the garden now looks less like a tangle or lonely fen and more like a flower that might offer inconceivable joys—"Such a flower a May never bore" (l. 2). It is important to recognize that this particular vision is no more "true" than the vision Innocence would have. Rather it emerges from what Godwin would term the "internal structure" of Experience. It helps to explain that curious species of spiritual condition, a condition of unease and complaint, that Blake has termed "Experience." Blake's concern is analytical. He is interested in what makes minds think differently about the same data. What makes one mind respond to some given phenomenon like a rose (which combines the contrary characteristics of both beautiful petals and forbidding thorns) as if it were exclusively a floral beauty? What makes another mind respond to the rose as if it were exclusively a thorny torment? Blake is not preaching dogma about how people should think. He is probing the internal structures that account for basic variation in mental behavior.

Scott's novels, like Blake's poems, are concerned with how mental behavior in the presence of contrary options marks variations of identity. A common mistake in reading Scott is to suppose that he is seeking through this preoccupation with contrarieties to tell the reader—or perhaps even to decide for himself—which pole of the contrariety is the desirable one. This mistake leads to observations about Scott's own "ambivalence," as it is sometimes expressed, toward variations of the Flora/Rose dichotomy. Does

Scott favor lowlands or highlands, the present or the past, the comforts of a refined, but perhaps rather dull, civilization or the energies of a heroic, though instable, age?[16] Scott himself is not concerned to make choices in (or through) his novels. He is concerned, instead, with analysis of his characters making choices. His focus is directed toward different structures of thought and toward the ways in which confrontation can reveal the basic properties of differing species of mental orientation. To this end, his function as narrative voice, when that voice is indeed Scott's (or at least close to Scott's) rather than that of merely another dramatic character, is to keep reminding us that there is a contrary view or way of thinking.[17]

In Blake, the possibility of contrariety is conveyed by the way the two volumes of songs play off against each other. In Scott, the narrative voice is what reminds us that there is, as it were, another song that might be sung. Thus Scott *seems* ambivalent, because his voice is always shifting between contrarieties, thereby showing that there is something to be said for both sides of an argument, direction of thought, or perception of value. Scott's aim is not to exhibit his characters choosing things that are objectively good or evil, or sensible or foolish. It is, rather, to exhibit them choosing things that appear good or sensible for them—and at the same time to make the reader understand that there could be other choices that would be good or sensible to a competing species of human possibility.[18]

When the dramatic action in a Scott novel is moving to the rhythms of some version of Experience, Scott's narrator is wont to sing in the reader's ear a tune of Innocence, and vice versa. For example, one of the key moments in *Waverley* occurs on the eve of battle between the English and the

16 · See, for example, George Levine, "Sir Walter Scott: The End of Romance," *WC*, X (1979), 147–60, esp. Levine's discussion of how Scott's art "invariably manages to have things both ways" (148).

17 · More work needs to be done on the variety and complexity of narrative voices in Scott's novels. Mary Cullinan points the way in "History and Language in Scott's *Redgauntlet*," *Studies in English Literature, 1500–1900*, XVIII (1978), 659–75.

18 · In *Romantic Narrative Art* (Madison, Wis., 1960), Karl Kroeber observes that Scott "was the first artist to conceive of history as the organic evolution of competing styles of life" (169). This seems to me exactly right. Reading Scott, we need to think less about evolution of one structure from a previous one and more about how competing structures evolve.

Highlanders, when Waverley experiences a sort of epiphany as he looks upon the English army: "It was at that instant that, looking around him, he saw the wild dress and appearance of his Highland associates, heard their whispers in an uncouth and unknown language, looked upon his own dress, so unlike that which he had worn from his infancy, and wished to awake from what seemed at the moment a dream, strange, horrible, and unnatural" (Chap. 46). The situation Scott dramatizes has affinities with the one Keats dramatizes in "La Belle Dame sans Merci," when a knight-at-arms leaves his courtly life to experience the joys of a faery's child, but then is startled by a "horrid warning" from the world of kings and princes he has left behind (l. 42). Both artists are playing with the issue of language. Keats's knight abandons his own linguistic company when he joins La Belle Dame with her "langauge strange" (l. 27). Waverley, similarly, unites himself with a people who speak what is for him an "uncouth and unknown language." Neither Keats's knight nor Waverley, this emphasis on strange or unknown language suggests, really knows what they have given themselves up to. But Scott, like Keats, is not trying to imply that the world of familiar language his characters have left behind is somehow objectively better than this world of strange language that they now inhabit. Keats has the horrid warning of kings and princes come to his knight in a dream, "the latest dream I ever dream'd" (l. 35). In *Waverley* it is Scott's narrative voice that observes of Waverley's suddenly reversed sense of situation that it "seemed at the moment a dream, strange, horrible, and unnatural." The function of *dream* in both cases is to emphasize that we are encountering apprehensions of truth rather than truth itself in these dramatic shifts of consciousness. What each character experiences is his own dream of truth.

In "A Refutation of Deism" Shelley gives Eusebes the argument that "order and disorder are expressions denoting our perceptions of what is injurious or beneficial to ourselves, or to the beings in whose welfare we are *compelled to sympathize by the similarity of their conformation to our own.*"[19] Scott would have the reader gain a similar understanding of

---

19 · Shelley, "A Refutation of Deism," in *Complete Works of Percy Bysshe Shelley*, VI, 52; italics mine.

Waverley's experience. What Waverley has discovered is not objective truth—nor one of Scott's personal beliefs—but rather something significant about himself. Waverley has defined his own nature's conception of what is orderly and natural.

Scott's narrative voice functions in the example above and in other key scenes of *Waverley* to maintain our awareness that Waverley's experience reveals truths only about Waverley himself. In earlier chapters of the novel the Highlanders have been associated with the fallen angels of *Paradise Lost*, as when Scott describes how the gathered Highland chiefs and their followers "amused themselves" in various ways; "'Others apart sat on a hill retired,'—probably as deeply engaged in the discussion of politics and news as Milton's spirits in metaphysical disquisition" (Chap. 24). Once having suggested this association between the Highlanders and Miltonic infernal powers, Scott's narrator begins manipulating our awareness of the Highlanders in a way that sounds like a marriage of Virgil and Blake: "The mountaineers rous[ed] themselves from their couch under the canopy of heaven, with the hum and bustle of a confused and irregular multitude, like bees alarmed and arming in their hives. . . . Their motions appeared spontaneous and confused, but the result was order and regularity" (Chap. 44). Heaven does not play order to hell's confusion. The party of the opposition has its own "order and regularity." In the paragraph from Chapter 46 that immediately precedes Waverley's horrified comparison of what he suddenly feels to be Highland wildness and English order, Scott's narrator again intrudes to suggest: "Here then was a military spectacle of no ordinary interest or usual occurrence. The two armies, so different in aspect and discipline, yet each admirably trained to its own peculiar mode of war." In Scott, as in so much other literature of the Romantic period, national and political contrarieties both have their self-consistent, workable systems.

In other Scott novels as well as *Waverley*, statements, thoughts, and actions of a given character reveal, not Scott's ideology, but rather the nature of that character. Near the conclusion of *Old Mortality* Henry Morton is examined by the king's council, and he responds to an offer of the king's mercy with the words, "I have no other choice, my lord" (Chap. 36). But Scott wants to make clear that other choices are in principle conceivable. The narrator, accordingly, ironically notes Morton's awareness, "that, in the circumstances of his case, it was impossible for him to have escaped more easily" (Chap. 36). He then describes both Macbrier's heroic refusal to seek mercy and Cuddie's "unscrupulous" acceptance of an offer of mercy—which acceptance casts an ironic light upon Morton's similar acceptance of mercy: "'Blithely, sir,' answered the unscrupulous Cuddie; 'and drink his health into the bargain, when the ale's gude'" (Chap. 36). Through artistic maneuvers of this sort Scott maintains reader awareness that while his characters, like those in Romantic literature generally, behave in ways they themselves may suppose right, worthy, or inevitable, other orientations of mind could reasonably think quite differently about that behavior. In *Waverley* the Baron of Bradwardine glimpses this, as he reflects upon the defeat of his cause by what he calls, significantly, the "prevailing party": "'I did what I thought my duty,' said the good old man, 'and questionless they are doing what they think theirs'" (Chap. 65).

Waverley's choice of Rose Bradwardine over Flora Mac-Ivor, then, tells us nothing about Scott's own value choices—and hence nothing about whether Scott's thinking is or is not akin to the Romanticism of the Romantic poets. Waverley has simply revealed his own nature to himself in his choice of Rose. Earlier, Flora predicted to Rose that "high and perilous enterprise is not Waverley's forte. . . . I will tell you where he will be at home, my dear, and in his place,—in *the quiet circle of domestic happiness*, lettered indolence, and elegant enjoyments of Waverley Honour. And he will refit the old library in the most exquisite Gothic taste" (Chap. 52, italics mine). The passage returns us to Romantic preoccupation with the circle. Waverley's circle will be one in which he has his Gothic domestic rather than in the rough—in his library with his books rather than in the flesh. Scott's design is to make us think about our own reader's circle.

What Flora predicts for Waverley is the fate that we have in reading and that Scott has in writing *Waverley*. As many critics have observed, we seem to find ourselves in Waverley's circle. However, if this be so, our discovery is essentially an analytic rather than a celebratory one. We learn from the novel something about what we are, which knowledge also involves something about what we are not and apparently cannot be. *Waverley* bequeaths to us the problem of working out a balance sheet of our apparent gains and losses.[20]

The Fergus Mac-Ivors have disappeared from modern readers' and writers' lives. They have been replaced by the guiding influence of the Colonel Talbots. Is this to our advantage? Avrom Fleishman observes that "it is Waverley's guidance by Colonel Talbot that becomes the means by which he sees his Jacobite folly and the prudence of setting his course within the Hanoverian world. Talbot provides not only political realism but moral toughness as well."[21] This guidance into the modern-inclining Hanoverian world is not without its dangers. As Scott's narrator carefully notes when Talbot is first introduced into the novel, "Colonel Talbot was in every point the English soldier . . . he was a man of extended knowledge and cultivated taste, *although* strongly tinged . . . with those prejudices which are *peculiarly English*" (Chap. 52, italics mine). Scott's *although* is our warning. Talbot's "peculiarly English" system of "prejudices" makes him as blind in his own way as Fergus is blind in a contrary way. When Waverley, for example, protests to Talbot that he is judging the Highlanders too harshly, Talbot responds abruptly: "Not a whit, not a whit; I *cannot* spare them a jot; I *cannot* bate them an ace. Let them stay in their own barren mountains, and puff and swell . . . what business have they to come where people wear breaches, and speak an intelligible language?—I mean *intelligible in comparison to their gibberish*; for even the Lowlanders talk a kind of English little better than the negroes in Jamaica" (Chap. 56, italics mine). Talbot's repeated *cannot* marks him as a man who, like Mac-Ivor, or perhaps even more than Mac-Ivor, has fanaticism within him. Once more, this anatomy of blind conviction is associated with the issue of strange and familiar language. Waverley himself marks this parallel between Talbot and Mac-Ivor: "You and Mac-Ivor have some points not much unlike, as far as national prejudice is concerned" (Chap. 56).

The modern world, Scott seems to be suggesting, is not so utterly unlike the violent world of the past as it may seem. The prevailing party of Talbots

---

20 · Avrom Fleishman, *The English Historical Novel: Walter Scott to Virginia Woolf* (Baltimore, 1971), associates Scott's interest in balancing the claims of past and present with a preoccupation of the age's speculative historians (see esp. 49).
21 · Fleishman, *English Historical Novel*, 72.

that assures the security of our "quiet circle of domestic happiness," persuading us that we should lay down our arms and indulge our wildness only in the bounds of our exquisite libraries, retains its own dangerous possibilities in the prejudices and blind fervor of its protecting guidance. While we sit reading *Waverley* or treasuring pictures on our walls that depict the forsworn energies of our past selves—"It was a large and spirited painting, representing Fergus Mac-Ivor and Waverley in their Highland dress, the scene a wild, rocky, and mountainous pass, down which the clan were descending in the background"—we are being invited by Scott to cultivate a healthy skepticism about the actual security of our position (Chap. 71).[22] If we have gained comfort, we have lost power; and the guardians of our sheepfold have Tygerish potential.

Scott's novels, like other Romantic literature, are preoccupied with analysis of identities—not the least of which is the reader's identity. For Scott, as for Wordsworth, the conventional phrase "the gentle Reader" is loaded with serious and ironic implications. A sense of the fragility of the modern, gentle reader's calm casts interesting, disturbing shadows over what seem the obligatory happy endings of Scott's novels. Much has been written about the oddity—some would say the artistic failure—of the conclusions of Scott's novels.[23] Those endings, however, seem to have been intended by Scott to unsettle our complacency by revealing to us disturbing aspects of ourselves and our modern situation.

In the "Conclusion" of *Old Mortality* we are suddenly and disconcertingly wrenched away from the poignant scene of Lord Evandale's death amid the union of Henry Morton and Edith, and transported by violent contrast into our present world of domestic comfort, where we find ourselves sitting down to drink tea with Miss Martha Buskbody. George Levine suggests that this odd development is "actually amusing," but at the same time "embarrassingly incongruous."[24] The maneuver, however, serves an important function for Scott, which, if we recognize it, exerts a powerful im-

---

22 · See P. D. Garside, "*Waverley*'s Pictures of the Past," *ELH*, XLIV (1977), 659–82.

23 · So, for example, in "Scott's Endings: The Fictions of Authority," *Nineteenth-Century Fiction*, XXXIII (1978), 48–68, Francis R. Hart suggests that "Scott's imaginative authority seemed often to stop with catastrophe and discontinuity" (58).

24 · Levine, "Sir Walter Scott: The End of Romance," 153.

pact that disturbs but is not at all incongruous. Earlier in *Old Mortality* Scott has invited us to observe what kind of people are going to be the survivors of the world of sound and fury that the novel depicts—those, that is, who will live on to be the founding fathers of the modern reader's world. There is Henry Morton, following a line of conduct and belief dictated by "the feelings of natural humanity"—who, able to convince himself that he has "no other choice, my lord," can escape the consequences of his commitment to the rebel cause "more easily" than a Macbrier who chooses differently and accepts torture.[25] And there are others who both survive and prosper, such as Jenny, knowing "it's maybe as weel to hae a friend on baith sides" and expertly guiding Cudie into the circle of domestic bliss: "'And amna I the best guide ye ever had in 'a your life?' said Jenny, as she closed the conversation by assuming her place beside her husband and extinguishing the candle" (Chap. 24, Chap. 38).

Most significantly, perhaps, there is Niel Blane, the "town-piper" and landlord, "indifferent alike to the disputes about Church and State, and only anxious to secure the good-will of customers of every description" (Chap. 4). Niel Blane pipes the tune the developing town will follow. Near the end of *Old Mortality*, the "person and demeanour of Niel Blane, more fat and less civil than of yore, intimated that he had increased as well in purse as in corpulence" (Chap. 41). We recall that it is the prosperous descendants of Niel Blane who will beguile us with "Tales of My Landlord" that we buy to absorb our modern attention.

When Scott, therefore, abruptly delivers us over to the tea-drinking attentions of Miss Martha Buskbody at the conclusion of *Old Mortality*, he is confronting us with the species of mind that has been produced by those surviving, prospering characters. Further, since Miss Martha Buskbody is depicted as an avid consumer of novels as well as of her tea, she looks suspiciously like a parodic mirror image of our novel-reading selves—a frail, querulous creature of advancing age, demanding of and yet dependent upon the prosperous landlord novelist (more fat and less civil than of yore?) for

---

25 · Many critics disagree and find Morton more unambiguously heroic. See, for example, Johnson, *Sir Walter Scott*, I, 598.

the maintenance of domestic bliss. The end of *Old Mortality* makes us think about ourselves, revealing to us something of what we are by showing us what we no longer possess.

The most interesting of these Scott endings that disturb the reader's mind may be the long final section of *The Heart of Midlothian*, wherein Jeanie Deans and her party are transported into the charmed circle of the Duke of Argyle's Roseneath. With the move to Roseneath, as with other movements toward closure in Scott, critics have been bothered by the way Scott's "realism," as they tend to call it, seems to dissolve into something that looks suspiciously like fantasy or pure whimsy.[26] But Scott clearly had an artistic design in mind when he shifted the direction of his novel toward a curious form of idyll that contrasts dramatically with the preceding three-fourths of the book. Thus, introducing Roseneath, Scott at once marks the turn: "In these isles the severe frost winds, which tyrannize over the vegetable creation during a Scottish spring, are comparatively little felt. . . . Accordingly, the weeping-willow, the weeping-birch, and other trees of early and pendulous shoots, flourish in these favoured recesses in a degree unknown in our eastern districts" (Chap. 42).

Scott's imagery, "the weeping-willow, the weeping-birch," conveys the first hints of the odd theme that is being woven into this idyllic melody. Scott seems deliberately to be conducting us into an alternative world, akin to those islands of the heart's desire that Shelley dreams of in a poem like "Lines Written Among the Euganean Hills."

> Many a green isle needs must be
> In the deep wide sea of Misery,
> Or the mariner, worn and wan,
> Never thus could voyage on—.
>
> (ll. 1–4)

Actually, Scott apparently had *The Tempest* in mind, since the Duke of Argyle seems designed to remind us of Prospero: "This second surprise had

---

26 · See, for example, Arnold Kettle, *An Introduction to the English Novel* (2 vols.; London, 1951; rpr. New York, 1960), I, 120. See also Johnson, *Sir Walter Scott*, I, 660.

been accomplished for Jeanie Deans by the rod of the same benevolent enchanter, whose power had transplanted her father from the Crags of St. Leonard's to the banks of the Gare-Loch" (Chap. 43). That the gathering up of Jeanie's party into this "Highland Arcadia" is indeed a sort of enchantment is repeatedly emphasized by Scott (Chap. 45). It is, to take a single case in point, made clear at the outset of the Roseneath section of the novel: "It was too wonderful to be believed—too much like a happy dream to have the stable feeling of reality" (Chap. 42).

Scott appears to be teasing the reader's mind with fulfillment of his novel's ironic title. Roseneath is indeed the "Heart" of Midlothian, a vision of lovely rewards for heroic effort that the heart cherishes, though in fact the heart dwells within the prison house of a natural world in which, we know, such rewards are not forthcoming. As is commonly the case in Scott's novels, this natural world that we know (as distinct from the world that the heart *would* know) is carefully documented in the authorial notes that accompany the novel. Thus Scott's Introduction and Postscript to *The Heart of Midlothian* tell us something of the real history of Helen Walker, "the prototype of the imaginary Jeanie Deans" (Postscript). Therein we learn, as our minds would have suspected, that Scott's heroine never in reality received the rewards that Scott in his novel imagines for her (and for us): "That a character so distinguished for her undaunted love of virtue, lived and died in poverty, if not want, serves only to show us how insignificant, in the sight of Heaven, are our principle objects of ambition upon earth" (Postscript). Roseneath, therefore, offers us a visionary experience, what we human beings would have be true, in the face of the actual laws of nature that imprison us, and perhaps even in the face of the actual laws of heaven.

Many signals in *The Heart of Midlothian* invite our recognition of this theme. We see, for example, Madge Wildfire in her "madness" understanding her relationship and journey with Jeanie, not simply as an earthly quest with circumscribed earthly possibilities at its end, but rather as a spiritual journey, modeled upon the human mind's dream of paradisiacal attainments in *Pilgrim's Progress*: "—But we'll knock at the gate, and then the keeper will admit Christiana, but Mercy will be left out—and then I'll stand at the door trembling and crying, and then Christiana—that's you, Jeanie—

will intercede for me; and then Mercy—that's me, ye ken—will faint; and then . . ." (Chap. 31). Later in the novel Scott furnishes a conversation between Reuben Butler and Sir George Staunton that marks the distance between such a human dream and the "laws of nature."

> "Alas!" replied Butler, "what are we, that the laws of nature should correspond in their march with our ephemeral deeds or sufferings? The clouds will burst when surcharged with the electric fluid, whether a goat is falling at that instant from the cliffs of Arran, or a hero expiring on the field of battle he has won."
>
> "*The mind delights to deem it otherwise,*" said Sir George Staunton; "and to dwell on the fate of humanity as on that which is the prime central movement of the mighty machine." (Chap. 51, italics mine)

In the Roseneath section of *The Heart of Midlothian* Scott portrays how "the mind delights to deem it"—to the extent that the mind can be beguiled and lulled away from cool analysis toward delightful dreams by the yearning heart. But Scott, like Romantic writers generally, also gives us significant hints of the contrary to this idyllic dream—thereby keeping us aware that our delight is nothing more than a fragile toy, an enchanter's dream. Thus, for example, there is that odd note of the "weeping" willows and birches that hovers on the edge of consciousness as we are introduced into paradise. There are, as several critics have observed, further hints of danger or potential distress running through the Roseneath section: the Highland raiders and smugglers, the Whistler, the petty tyranny of the Captain of Knockunder. These create an aura of impending destruction that shadows the enchanter's art.[27] Beyond such obvious devices, there are more subtle hints of danger—for example, a passage that, preceding our introduction to Roseneath, warns us that the beloved creations of imaginative desire are transitory: "A lover's hope resembles the bean in the nursery tale,—let it once take root, and it will grow so rapidly, that in the course of a few hours

27 · See Fleishman, *English Historical Novel*, 94–95.

the giant Imagination builds a castle on the top, and by and by comes Disappointment with the 'curtail axe,' and hews down both the plant and the superstructure" (Chap. 39). This passage looks like a foreshadowing device. It prepares us to see the Roseneath enchantment dissolve at any moment, even as we continue to find it, moment after moment, somehow sustaining itself.

Even in small, unexpected spaces of the Roseneath section of the novel, Scott's art is directed toward manipulating our human desires, playing upon our hopes and fears for the safety of the charmed circle: "Ere they were well embarked, and ready to depart, the pale moon was come over the hill, and *flinging a trembling reflection* on the broad and glittering waves. *But* so soft and pleasant was the night, that Butler, in bidding farewell to Jeanie, *had no apprehension for her safety*" (Chap. 46, italics mine). Small hints of violence—the verb *flinging* followed by *trembling*—are balanced against the hopeful "But so soft." The very fact that Butler has no apprehension for Jeanie's safety makes us wonder whether we are being prepared for that "Disappointment with the 'curtail axe'" that Scott had earlier impressed upon our consciousness. We know, in other words, that this giant imagination's castle of Roseneath has to fall, and we find ourselves anticipating, though wishing not to find, the signs of the coming dissolution. Perhaps Effie will be the destroyer in some way, or maybe it will be Sir George. Or perhaps the uneasy union between Butler and Davie Deans, whose differences of "principle" in religion "often threatened unpleasant weather between them," will erupt into a fragmenting division of the little circle (Chap. 47).

But these seeming foreshadowings of disaster are only an artistic feint on Scott's part. In defiance of the laws of nature, as the novel has implied we should understand them, the enchantment holds. We are given a sort of miracle. Within the charmed boundaries of Scott's novel, "the enchanted princess in the bairn's fairy tale," as Jeanie calls herself, remains securely perched in her castle high (Chap. 49). The problem, therefore, is to determine what Scott supposed he was accomplishing by thus playing upon our minds in the Roseneath section of *The Heart of Midlothian*. Avrom Fleishman has offered the hypothesis that Scott was presenting Roseneath as "a symbolic landscape of modern Scotland"—that he was seeking to portray through Roseneath "a new Scottish national community" in which from an "array of limited positions Scott projects a universal value, formed by the synthesis of the best in partial truths."[28] But this does not seem to accord readily with the strong fairy-tale element in the Roseneath section. If Roseneath is in some sense modern Scotland (or perhaps, by extension, the modern world), then it is so only as a visionary dream of what we would desire. The novel forcefully impresses upon our minds that Roseneath is not the world according to nature in which we human beings unfortunately have to live. This otherworldly factor in Roseneath is what so bothers critics who object to the departure from realism of the novel's conclusion.

I suspect that Scott was thinking of Roseneath as a serious, poignant parody of the modern world that his optimistic reader wishes to believe he lives in. The thrust of Scott's strategy is to disturb this optimism, provoking realization that this vision of the modern world, wherein a synthesis of the best of partial truths seems to have been securely gained, is only a fragile dream. We actually live in the world of Helen Walker, not that of the enchanted Jeanie Deans; and Helen Walker, although she walked like a hero, "lived and died in poverty, if not want."

In company with other writers of the Romantic period, Scott is investigating what we are. In this instance he is measuring the distance that separates our dreams from life as we actually live it. We beguile ourselves with such modern notions as progress and the March of Mind, and we tell ourselves tales in which virtue and heroic effort are not merely their own reward. They are also amply rewarded with a large share of the world's goods. We like to believe that we have achieved, or at least are on the verge of achieving, a synthesis of the best that the past has to offer; and we like to think we have built a warm modern circle from this best, leaving the worst far behind. But in Roseneath Scott holds a mirror up to this dream of modern bliss and makes us sense upon our pulses that it is in fact only a dream.

THE work of the second major novelist of the Romantic period, Jane Austen, exhibits similarly close affinities with other Romantic writing. As Susan Morgan argues persuasively, a key issue in Austen's fiction is percep-

28 · Fleishman, *English Historical Novel*, 93, 88.

tion.[29] Characters in Austen's novels do not perceive things in the same ways. A closely related fact is that her characters also "feel" differently, as Austen is wont to phrase it. However, they are not generally aware of this difference. In *Emma*, for example, Mr. Woodhouse is described as a man who is "never able to suppose that other people could feel differently from himself" (p. 8). This brings into sharp focus a fundamental tension from which Austen's art derives much of its power and intellectual substance.

On the one hand, Austen's characters occupy a world of human relationships in which people do indeed feel differently. Austen's novels impress upon us strongly the sense that our supposedly common human nature exhibits a propensity to breed uncommonly diverse natures and that our supposedly common sense fragments into a welter of varying notions about what actually constitutes sense. In such a world, as the famous opening chapter of *Pride and Prejudice* makes clear, "a truth universally acknowledged" hardly is stated before it is lost in a flurry of contrary directions of thought and feeling.[30] Thus a recurring pattern of conversation in Austen involves structures of opposition. Sometimes these are relatively muted, as that between Mrs. Bennet and Mr. Bingley, for example.

> "But every body is to judge for themselves, and the Lucases are very good sort of girls, I assure you. It is a pity they are not handsome! Not that *I* think Charlotte so *very* plain—but then she is our particular friend."
>
> "She seems a very pleasant young woman," said Bingley.

29 · Susan Morgan, *In the Meantime: Character and Perception in Jane Austen's Fiction* (Chicago, 1980). Morgan develops a strong case for the value of reading Austen "through a perspective suggested by romantic concerns" (9). Among other critics who have begun to explore connections between Austen and Romanticism, see esp.: Karl Kroeber, "Jane Austen, Romantic," *WC*, VII (1976), 291–96; Nina Auerbach, "Jane Austen and Romantic Imprisonment," in David Monaghan (ed.), *Jane Austen in a Social Context* (Totawa, N.J., 1981), 9–27; and Patricia Meyer Spacks, "Muted Discord: Generational Conflict in Jane Austen," in Monaghan (ed.), *Jane Austen in a Social Context*, 159–79, esp. 164.

30 · Julia Prewitt Brown, *Jane Austen's Novels: Social Change and Literary Form* (Cambridge, Mass., 1979), argues that Austen's apparent lack of concern with class struggle traces to her interest in exposing "the less obvious gulf" between members of the same class and even of the family unit (17).

Romantic Questioning and the Novelists · 155

"Oh! dear, yes;—but you must own she is very plain."

(*Pride and Prejudice*, p. 44)

At other times the opposition is stark and direct. Jane asks, for example, "Can there be any other opinion on the subject?" And Elizabeth responds, "Yes, there can; for mine is totally different.—Will you hear it?" (*Pride and Prejudice*, p. 118).

On the other hand, however, as suggested by Jane's supposition that there could not possibly be "any other opinion on the subject," Austen's world is also one in which the characters tend, sometimes despite themselves, to be unable to suppose that others could differ from them. So, in *Mansfield Park*, for example, Edmund speaks to Fanny about Mary Crawford's treatment of him: "I do not consider her as meaning to wound my feelings. The evil lies yet deeper; in her total ignorance, unsuspiciousness of there being such feelings, in a perversion of mind which made it natural to her to treat the subject as she did. She was speaking only, as she had been used to hear others speak, as she imagined every body else would speak" (p. 456). Emerging in this speech is the familiar Romantic issue concerning what is natural. One recalls Scott's Waverley, for example, appalled by his involvement with a Highland army that strikes him suddenly as "unnatural." In Austen, as in Scott and other Romantic writers, we encounter an authorial preoccupation with characters who suppose that all human beings participate in a common human nature, and who therefore suppose that their own particular feelings, values, and modes of thought must be both natural and universal. Encounter with different behavior, accordingly, prompts surprise and then an explanation that such different behavior must be unnatural.

Underlying this authorial preoccupation in Austen, as in other writers of the period, is exploration of the hypothesis that our human nature is not common but divisionary. Different behavior appears natural to different species—and in Austen's case to different species of human nature itself. Thus Mr. Knightley, who is only sometimes a trustworthy perceiver, remarks to Emma of Frank Churchill: "Natural enough!—his own mind full of intrigue, that he should suspect it in others" (*Emma*, p. 446).

It is tempting to suppose that a character like Mr. Knightley always reflects Austen's own perception and that inability to recognize differences in other people is characteristic only of the apparent fools and perverts in Austen's fiction. But one finds Mr. Knightley himself, "a sensible man," arguing with Emma in the following suspect matter about Frank Churchill's behavior: "Depend upon it, Emma *a sensible man* would find no difficulty in it. He would *feel* himself in the right. . . . Respect for right conduct *is felt by every body*. If he would act in this sort of manner, on principle, consistently, regularly, their little minds would bend to his" (pp. 9, 147, italics mine). Emma's beautifully moderate response, "I rather doubt that," invites us both to smile and to catch the serious point. The sensible Mr. Knightley cannot perceive that everybody might not feel sensibly, like himself.[31] So Mr. Woodhouse, "never able to suppose that other people could feel differently from himself," represents only the extreme manifestation of a normal human condition in Austen. He differs from other characters merely in the absolute impenetrability of his nature.

A primary preoccupation of Austen's is the dramatization of interplay among characters who feel differently, but who do not immediately (and sometimes never) recognize the divisionary nature of their situation. In *Pride and Prejudice* Elizabeth is suddenly confronted with the fact, incomprehensible to her, that Charlotte Lucas intends to marry Mr. Collins. "It is unaccountable! in every view it is unaccountable!" she insists (p. 135). Elizabeth's "in every view" is one of Austen's warning signals. We are to recall the human passion for truths universally acknowledged that the novel's opening pages have already shown to be inapplicable to actual human experience. In response to Elizabeth's outrage, Jane gently suggests, "You do not make allowance enough for difference of situation and temper" (p. 135). This sort of exchange is a recurring theme in Austen's novels. In *Emma*, while Mr. Knightley is building up his system of universals to con-

---

31 · Recent critics have begun to note that Mr. Knightley is not so totally knightlike as at first he may seem. For a tentative move toward this perception, see Charles A. Knight, "Irony and Mr. Knightley," *Studies in the Novel*, II (1970), 185–93. James Kissane takes a firmer hold on the issue in "Comparison's Blessed Felicity: Character Arrangement in *Emma*," *ibid.*, II (1970), 173–84. The most determined effort to unseat Mr. Knightley totally from his noble steed is Alison G. Sulloway's "Emma Woodhouse and *A Vindication of the Rights of Women*," *WC*, VII (1976), 320–32.

demn Frank Churchill's supposed iniquities, Emma responds to him, "But you have not an idea of what is requisite in situations directly opposite to your own" (p. 147).

In *Pride and Prejudice*, as in *Emma*, the universalist keeps arguing. Elizabeth responds to her sister's reminder about difference of situation and temper by rejecting it in favor of a claim to shared feeling. "You must feel, as well as I do," she insists, "that the woman who marries him [Mr. Collins], cannot have a proper way of thinking" (p. 135). It is interesting that Elizabeth reaches out not to "every body," as does Mr. Knightley in *Emma*, but only to Jane. Like Mary Shelley's Elizabeth in *Frankenstein*, who seeks shared opinion with Frankenstein in a passage discussed previously in this chapter, Elizabeth is taking a first step down the road toward those small circles wherein a "proper way of thinking" means a shared way of thinking and truth is the "truth for us" of a few sharing friends. One may recall the "small band of true friends" at the conclusion of *Emma*.[32]

The situation in Austen that produces this dramatic pattern is, as in the work of other writers of the Romantic period, a multiplication of viable systems. Charlotte Lucas simply does not share the basic principles or axioms upon which Elizabeth's proper way of thinking is grounded. With fine economy Austen shows Charlotte explaining (or at least trying to explain) this to Elizabeth: "I am not romantic you know. I never was" (p. 125). This "you know" is a splendid touch, because of course Elizabeth does not and never did know. Nor will Elizabeth ever quite manage to know. When she visits the married Charlotte, she keeps trying to read her hostess' behavior in ways that will vindicate her own principles of proper thinking: "Charlotte took her sister and friend over the house, extremely well pleased, *probably*, to have the opportunity of shewing it without her husband's help. . . . When Mr. Collins could be forgotten, there was really a great air of comfort throughout, and by Charlotte's *evident* enjoyment of it, *Elizabeth supposed*

---

32 · In "The Spaces of Privacy: Jane Austen," *Nineteenth-Century Fiction*, XXX (1975), 305–33, Francis R. Hart, developing the connection between Rousseau and Austen that Lionel Trilling had suggested in *Sincerity and Authenticity* (Cambridge, Mass., 1972), points out that both Rousseau and Austen "are of the Enlightenment in their affirmation of society as the ground and sphere of human fulfillment; yet both dream of a small true society of intimates where privacies may be shared" (309–10).

he must be often forgotten" (pp. 156–57, italics mine). The words I have italicized mark Elizabeth's inability to believe that Charlotte's system of thought and value could really work successfully for her. It must be impossible to actually feel and think in Charlotte's professed manner; or, doing so, it must be impossible to live successfully unless one simply managed to forget the nature of the situation.

But Elizabeth is wrong. One of the most interesting and critically significant propositions that finds dramatic form in Austen's novels is that what looks to an angel like a proverb of hell often seems to support, and even to serve well, the devil who holds it. Charlotte appears to make a success of her life—according to her own definition of success. So does Frank Churchill. So even does Mrs. Elton. Mrs. Elton may not share Mr. Knightley's principles—"The nature and the simplicity of gentlemen and ladies, with their servants and furniture," he rebukes her firmly at one point in *Emma*, "I think is best observed by meals within doors"—but critics sometimes forget that the unregenerate Mrs. Elton reaches the finish line of the novel, alongside Emma and Mr. Knightley, with her views as active as ever and her limbs intact (p. 355).

One final case in point: in *Pride and Prejudice* Elizabeth may feel deeply humiliated and disgraced by her sister Lydia's behavior with Wickham. But Lydia herself feels quite different. More important, Lydia remains utterly untouched by Elizabeth's outrage. "Are you not curious to hear how it was managed?" Lydia asks the morally indignant Elizabeth; and Elizabeth responds by firing off a Knightley-like salvo of proper thinking: "I think there cannot be too little said on the subject." Lydia only responds in turn: "La! You are so strange!" (p. 318). Each person thinks the other strange, though Elizabeth would probably employ the term *unnatural*. But both people remain intact and satisfied within their own little circles.

Austen and Keats employ the discovery of strangeness in similar ways. As Keats uses the mind's encounter with the strange syntax of a Grecian urn to illuminate the values of our distinctively human nature, so Austen uses the strangeness of one character to another in her novels to mark boundaries between parties or species of thought and value within humanity itself, revealing fundamental divisions in human nature. In *Emma*,

Harriet Smith looks to Emma like a person who is easily understood. But near the end of the novel, when Harriet begins to exhibit odd turns of behavior, Emma glimpses that there is something about Harriet that "must ever be unintelligible" to her (p. 481). In *Pride and Prejudice* Kitty and Lydia "could not comprehend" their elder sisters' reaction to the departure of the regiment (p. 229). In *Persuasion* Captain Wentworth cannot comprehend how Benwick can turn his attentions upon Louisa so quickly after Fanny Harville's death: "A man does not recover from such a devotion of the heart to such a woman!—He ought not—he does not" (p. 183). Mutual incomprehension or mutual agreement upon a given definition of species (a *man* does not recover) forms the basis for party attachments on either side of party divisions: Benwick and Louisa on one side; Captain Wentworth and Anne on the other.

In a previously noted passage from *Mansfield Park* Edmund traces Mary Crawford's behavior toward him to "perversion of mind"—Mary is, according to Edmund's view, not quite of the same species as himself, not quite human. Hence, as Edmund proceeds to describe to Fanny how he departed from Mary, Austen shows his language turning Mary into the Belle Dame of a temptation scene: "I had gone a few steps, Fanny, when I heard the door open behind me. . . . 'Mr. Bertram,' said she, with a smile . . . a saucy playful smile, *seeming to invite*, in order to subdue me; *at least, it appeared so to me.* I resisted. . . . I have since—sometimes—for a moment—regretted that I did not go back; but I know I was right" (p. 459, italics mine). The italicized phrases warn us that to a different species of consciousness the truth about Mary Crawford might not have looked quite the way it appeared to Edmund. And the hesitating rhythms of his speech ("I have since—sometimes—for a moment—regretted") accentuate that possibility, dramatizing Edmund wavering on the brink of reexamining his firm conviction.[33] But then Edmund's abrupt "I know" shows him retreat-

---

33 · Edmund's wavering in *Mansfield Park* parallels similar patterns in Scott's dramatization of Waverley and Mary Shelley's dramatization of Frankenstein. In *Nightmare Abbey* Thomas Love Peacock beautifully captures the comic possibilities of this theme of Romantic wavering in a climactic confrontation scene wherein Scythrop finds himself trapped between the two women who have attracted him: "Scythrop was equadistant from both of them, central and

ing firmly to his own particular nature, reasserting the existence of perversity in Mary Crawford and the reality of his own triumph over dangerous temptation—which view accords nicely with his basic clerical axioms. Significantly, this chapter of *Mansfield Park* closes with the observation that "Fanny's friendship was all that he had to cling to" (p. 460). As many critics have observed with varying degrees of distaste, Fanny too has clerical axioms. Edmund and Fanny are drawing together, a happy pair within their clerical circle, while many of us critical readers sit outside, sniffing like Mrs. Elton in accordance with our rather different system of thought and value.

Readers for whom Austen belongs essentially to an eighteenth-century moralistic tradition—who see her delightedly gathering her three or four families in a country village in order to pronounce proper thinking upon their assembled heads—are wont to assert that she champions some truths (presumably familiar eighteenth-century ones in particular) and that she is subjecting other candidates for truth to satiric torment. But this view involves a misapprehension of Austen's art. Different characters in Austen's novels are shown to be holding on firmly to quite different notions of truth, forming divisionary unions of "truth for us." It is no doubt the case that our reading of Austen's novels leaves us yearning to curl up comfortably within some of these circles rather than others. No one—or am I here falling prey to one of those dubious truths "universally acknowledged" that Austen warns us about?—wants to go off with Charlotte Lucas to live with Mr. Collins. We all want to be close friends with Elizabeth, exude elegant decorums, and live in the big house with tasteful gardens. But the literary context in which we are being induced to embrace such a choice of truths is crucial. In Austen, as in the work of other writers of the Romantic period, we are made acutely conscious that one can think and choose differently, operating viably within the boundaries of other party unions.

Further, we are made conscious that what inclines one in the direction of some particular party's truths is the peculiar constitution or structure of

---

motionless. . . . Scythrop knew not what to do. He could not attempt to conciliate the one without irreparably offending the other; and he was so fond of both, that the idea of depriving himself for ever of either was intolerable to him: he therefore retreated into his strong hold, mystery" (Chap. 13).

one's own nature. In *Persuasion* Anne asks Captain Harville, concerning the issue of male versus female constancy, "But how shall we prove any thing?" He answers that "we never shall. We never can expect to prove any thing upon such a point. . . . We each begin probably with a little bias towards our own sex, and upon that bias build every circumstance in favour of it which has occurred within our own circle" (p. 234). What we learn, finally, in Austen is that there are other circles, and that they simply are not ours. We learn, with Anne Elliot, "the art of knowing our own nothingness beyond our own circle" (*Persuasion*, p. 42). This knowledge teaches us our boundaries and the nature of our circle in relation to others.

In *Julian and Maddalo* Shelley's Julian dreams of being able to sit "in Maddalo's great palace," where Maddalo's wit "and subtle talk would cheer the winter night / And *make me know myself*" (ll. 559–61, italics mine). In Austen the aim of movement toward revelation is similar. It primarily concerns, not so-called objective truths about the outer nature of things, but rather subjective truths about the nature of one's self. Thus, at a crucial moment in *Pride and Prejudice* Elizabeth cries out, "Till this moment, I never knew myself" (p. 208). This applies equally to the reader of an Austen novel. When Austen persuades us through her art to yearn for Elizabeth's circle rather than for Charlotte Lucas', she is discovering a claim, not about the objective truth of things, but about our nature as readers. Charlotte Lucas is "not romantic you know." That, Austen slyly suggests, is why Elizabeth, who *is* romantic, can never quite put herself in Charlotte's circle. And we readers, who hold out our hands toward Elizabeth rather than toward Charlotte? Austen, a Romantic writer, is writing for a romantic reader.

· *Five* ·

From the Romantic Gleam to the Victorian Game

I F "Victorian" connotes mainly heavy-handed utilitarianism, earnest imitation of Mrs. Grundy, and a perhaps hypocritical fondness for solemn and interminable moralizing, then Victorianism would appear to be fundamentally opposed to Romanticism. Were one inclined, therefore, to seek out the later fortunes of Romanticism in the Victorian period, one would probably look, not among the eminent Victorians, but rather among those in the more exotic subcultures of the Victorian world: the Pre-Raphaelites, Walter Pater, Algernon Charles Swinburne, Oscar Wilde.[1] In recent decades, however, Victorian scholars

---

1 · The old idea that Romanticism was either dying or dead in the Victorian period is characteristically expressed in the title of John Heath-Stubbs's study *The Darkling Plain: A Study of the Later Fortunes of Romanticism in English Poetry from George Darley to W. B. Yeats* (London, 1950); the first chapter of this study is titled, significantly, "The Defeat of Romanticism." See also C. M. Bowra, in *The Romantic Imagination* (Cambridge, Mass., 1949), who argues that after the deaths of Keats and Shelley, poetry "contracted its ambitions and was content to combine mild instruction with grace and charm" (197). A less narrow view of the Romantic inheritance during the Victorian period informs Mario Praz, *The Romantic Agony* (1933; rpr. London, 1951). On the complex relationship between the later-nineteenth-century Aesthetic movement and the second-generation Romantics, see Louise Rosenblatt, *L'Idée de*

have succeeded in setting aside most of the cruder notions about Victorianism that were once popular; and some conceptions of a Romantic-Victorian antithesis, accordingly, have been rendered untenable. We now know that there is far greater diversity in Victorian literary thought than was once recognized, that most of the greater Victorian writers feel no more at ease with Mrs. Grundy than did the Romantics (Mrs. Grundy was in fact a creation of the Romantic period—she is mentioned in a play called *Speed the Plough* by Thomas Morton, published in 1798), and that the mainstream of Victorian literature exhibits patterns of thought and tendencies toward doubt and ambivalence that suggest the existence of close affinities between the Victorians and the Romantics.[2]

The main thrust of contemporary criticism is more toward merging the Victorians with the Romantics than toward separating them. Today, when

l'art pour l'art dans la littérature anglaise pendant la période Victorienne (Paris, 1931); and Jeffrey R. Prince, "The Iconic Poem and the Aesthetic Tradition," *ELH*, XLIII (1976), 567–83. For the influence of Keats in particular on the Victorians, see George H. Ford, *Keats and the Victorians* (New Haven, 1944).

2 · Classic studies that combat antique stereotypes of the Victorian period include Jerome Buckley, *The Victorian Temper: A Study in Literary Culture* (Cambridge, Mass., 1951); Walter E. Houghton, *The Victorian Frame of Mind* (New Haven, 1957); and E. D. H. Johnson, *The Alien Vision of Victorian Poetry* (Princeton, N.J., 1952). Much recent Victorian scholarship emphasizes conflicting psychic inclination among Victorian literary artists; see, for example, Charles Altieri, "Arnold and Tennyson: The Plight of Victorian Lyricism as Context of Modernism," *Criticism*, XX (1978), 281–306. That this Victorian psychic conflict has affinities with Romanticism is argued by Masao Miyoshi, *The Divided Self: A Perspective on the Literature of the Victorians* (New York, 1969). Other wide-ranging investigations of relationships between Romanticism and Victorianism include Langbaum, *Poetry of Experience*, and two studies by Morse Peckham, *Beyond the Tragic Vision: The Quest for Identity in the Nineteenth Century* (New York, 1962), and *The Triumph of Romanticism*. Studies investigating Romantic influence on the Victorian novel in particular include Jerome H. Buckley, *Season of Youth: The Bildungsroman from Dickens to Golding* (Cambridge, Mass., 1974); Walter L. Reed, *Meditations on the Hero: A Study of the Romantic Hero in Nineteenth-Century Fiction* (New Haven, 1974); and Levine, *Realistic Imagination*. Studies considering various aspects of Romantic influence on the Victorian poets and writers of nonfictional prose include Patricia M. Ball, *The Science of Aspects: The Changing Role of Fact in the Work of Coleridge, Ruskin and Hopkins* (London, 1971); U. C. Knoepflmacher, "Mutations of the Wordsworthian Child of Nature," in U. C. Knoepflmacher and G. B. Tennyson (eds.), *Nature and the Victorian Imagination* (Berkeley, 1977); and Woodring, "Nature and Art in the Nineteenth Century."

we think of Matthew Arnold, we look back to Wordsworth; when we think about Alfred, Lord Tennyson or Browning, we look back to Keats and Shelley. When Thomas Carlyle writes about custom in the "Natural Supernaturalism" chapter of *Sartor Resartus*—"'Custom,' continues the Professor, 'doth make dotards of us all. Consider well, thou wilt find that Custom is the greatest of Weavers; and weaves air-rainment for all the Spirits of the Universe'"—he recalls Wordsworth addressing the spiritual child of "Intimations of Immortality."

> Full soon thy Soul shall have her earthly freight,
> And custom lie upon thee with a weight,
> Heavy as frost, and deep almost as life!
>
> (ll. 127–29)[3]

John Ruskin delivers a cautionary address to his reader in *Proserpina:* "For, as my reader must already sufficiently perceive, this book is literally to be one of studies—not of statements. . . . I work down or up to my mark, and let the reader see process and progress, not caring to conceal them. But this book will be nothing but process. I don't mean to assert anything positively in it from the first page to the last. Whatever I say, is to be understood only as a conditional statement—liable to, and inviting, correction."[4] One is reminded of the frequently unsettling narrative strategies of Coleridge, of the movement from systematic toward conditional thinking in the later essays of William Godwin, and, in general, of the primacy of inquiry over dogmatic assertion in Romantic literary art.

3 · In "Toward a Theory of Romanticism," Peckham discusses Carlyle's *Sartor Resartus* as a work that, placed next to Wordsworth's *Prelude* and Coleridge's "Rime of the Ancient Mariner," illuminates basic patterns of Romantic thought. In *Natural Supernaturalism* Abrams employs *Sartor Resartus* as a key Romantic paradigm. See also Janice L. Haney, "'Shadow-Hunting': Romantic Irony, *Sartor Resartus*, and Victorian Romanticism," *SIR*, XVII (1978), 307–33.
4 · John Ruskin, *Proserpina*, in E. T. Cook and Alexander Wedderburn (eds.), *The Works of John Ruskin* (39 vols.; London, 1903–12), XXV, 216. A useful discussion of Ruskin's inclination toward discursive structure appears in Chap. 4 of Jay Fellows, *The Failing Distance: The Autobiographical Impulse in John Ruskin* (Baltimore, 1975).

Today the difficult task is not so much to discover continuities between the Romantics and Victorians as it is to rediscover significant grounds of distinction between them. Now that it has become popular to conceive of Romanticism as a vast tidal wave of thought and/or sensibility sweeping over everything between the French Revolution and the present moment, we confront the problem of regaining analytic balance. No doubt investigators used to go much too far in setting up their stark contrasts between the Romantics and Victorians, but today we need to guard against the overcompensating urge to lean too far in the opposite direction. Victorian scholars have been particularly sensitive to this problem. Sensing that their field of study faces the prospect of becoming merely a redundant or secondary phenomenon in the overriding "triumph" of Romanticism, they have begun exploring new definitions of the Victorian literary impulse in order to reaffirm basic contrasts between the Victorians and the Romantics.[5] This task is hard because the scholar is dealing with a process of gradual, relatively undramatic evolution. Nothing approaching the concentrated magnitude of a French Revolution occurs in the movement from the Romantic to the Victorian period. Gradual changes do not lend themselves to easy analysis. The best approach is to start with acknowledgment that there are obviously patterns of continuity between the Romantics and Victorians. But if these patterns are explored, they begin to reveal points at which divergence appears.

IN Victorian as in Romantic literature the strategies of questioning are frequently employed as a means of evasion. Much has been written about the

5 · The inclination of Romanticists either to appropriate or to ignore Victorianism is deplored by Park Honan in "On Robert Browning and Romanticism," in William S. Peterson (ed.), *Browning Institute Studies*, I (1973), 147–72, and by Jerome J. McGann in "Romanticism and the Embarrassments of Critical Tradition," *Modern Philology*, LXX (1973), 243–57. Significantly, the title of a recent collection of critical essays, (George Bornstein, ed.), *Romantic and Modern: Revaluations of Literary Tradition* (Pittsburgh, 1977), seems to imply that revaluation revalues the Victorian factor out of existence. Victorian scholarship's response to the encroachment of Romantic critics is registered by Michael Timko, "The Victorianism of Victorian Literature," *New Literary History*, VI (1975), 607–27, and by Gerald R. Bruns, "The Formal Nature of Victorian Thinking," *PMLA*, XC (1975), 904–18. For a reply to Bruns, see Charles W. Hagelman, Jr., "Victorian Thinking," *PMLA*, XCII (1977), 129–30.

anguish and doubt of Victorian writers. But, like the Romantics in their maneuvering, the Victorians tend to use apparent negatives to secure positive results. Anguish and doubt are turned into weapons that can oppose encroaching systems of dogma that are deemed oppressive. For example, Tennyson expresses doubt in *In Memoriam*.

> So runs my dream: but what am I?
> An infant crying in the night:
> An infant crying for the light:
> And with no language but a cry.
> (LIV, ll. 17–20)

But it is because of, not in spite of, this doubt that the poem arrives, finally, at an optimistic, even visionary, conclusion in which our thought is directed toward

> That God, which ever lives and loves,
> One God, one law, one element,
> And one far-off divine event,
> To which the whole creation moves.
> (Epilogue, ll. 141–44)

Tennyson's strategy in *In Memoriam* is gradually to build up an argument that we are all, so far as we can know, only infants crying in the night and that, if this is so, then no given cry would appear to be demonstrably more valid than another. The poem weaves repeated variations upon the theme that time looks like a "maniac scattering dust" (L, l. 6) and that nature seems to say, "A thousand types are gone: / I care for nothing, all shall go" (LVI, ll. 3–4). The years, the birthdays, the Christmas seasons, the visions on the lawn are forever passing away—as are all things: "The hills are shadows, and they flow / From form to form, and nothing stands" (CXXIII, ll. 5–6). This all-encompassing metamorphosis implies, further, that all our human ideologies are similarly unstable, and this is the crux of Tennyson's argument. He announces it in the Prologue: "Our little systems have their day; / They have their day and cease to be" (Prologue, ll. 17–18). The effect of this assertion, once it begins finding repeated support in the mutability theme of the poem, is to sever the mind's ideological chains. Tennyson's bewildered "I" (which becomes "us" in our reading of the poem) may be only an infant in his cry. But the "They" that seems to loom so large to an infant is also infantile—"little" systems have their day. Perhaps it is not necessary, then, to submit like a meek child to systems of seemingly authoritative scientific thought that give rise to such nightmares as the poet encounters in the poem.[6] Those nightmares that deny the humanistic beliefs we used to cherish pass away, as we do: they have no privileged ontological status. All human thought, then, begins to look like the dream of an infant in the night. And from this follows the proposition that one is free to choose the dream one wishes to hold.

> But in my spirit will I dwell,
> *And dream my dream, and hold it true;*
> For tho' my lips may breathe adieu,
> I cannot think the thing farewell.
> (CXXIII, ll. 9–12; italics mine)

The vision of "that God, which ever lives and loves" with which *In Memoriam* concludes represents an act of will by the dreamer. It is being presented, not as a truth in the ordinary sense, but rather as the product of the dreamer's desire. As in Romantic literature, this act of will is marked by a species indicator (as discussed in Chapter 4): "But *in my spirit* will I dwell."[7] To choose this dream is definitive of the poet's nature. The nature

6 · In theory, at least, Victorian science itself would have been no more sympathetic to authoritative systems of thought than was Tennyson. In an 1866 paper, "On the Advisableness of Improving Natural Knowledge," Thomas Huxley argues that the scientist "absolutely refuses to acknowledge authority, as such. For him, scepticism is the highest of duties" (*Methods and Results* [New York, 1898], 40).

7 · *Cf.* John Sterling, asserting in an 1842 essay, "Characteristics of German Genius," that "there is a godlike within us, that feels itself akin to the gods; and if we are told that both the godlike and the gods are dreams, we can but answer that so to dream is better than to wake and find ourselves nothing," in Julius Charles Hare (ed.), *Essays and Tales, by John Sterling* (2 vols.; London, 1848), I, 420.

in which the poet finds himself may "care for nothing, all shall go"; but the poet's nature is spiritual—and it obeys other laws.

A maneuver similar to that of *In Memoriam* lies behind Arnold's famous image in the "Stanzas from the Grande Chartreuse."

> Wandering between two worlds, one dead,
> The other powerless to be born,
> With nowhere yet to rest my head.
>
> (ll. 85–87)

The speaker's lonely condition seems lamentable, but actually Arnold is developing a powerful skeptical weapon. To be able to think of oneself as occupying the interstice between worlds allows the mind, as the Romantics knew, to put all worldly claims at a distance. Once we envision worlds being born and dying, we are able to give their claims the appearance of mere passing fashions (like styles of clothing, in Carlyle's terms, which custom makes popular only for a season). The effect—as in the case of Tennyson's "little" systems—is to diminish the authority of those claims. Arnold goes on to praise people who, unlike himself, will be able to participate enthusiastically in the new worlds that are to be born.

> We admire with awe
> The exulting thunder of your race;
> You give the universe your law,
> You triumph over time and space!
> Your pride of life, your tireless powers,
> We laud them, but they are not ours.
>
> (ll. 163–68)

But as "exulting thunder," "triumph," and "pride" suggest, this praise is hyperbolic and ironic. Positioning himself as a wanderer between worlds and drawing the reader into his perspective (the earlier "I" of the poem has expanded into "We" in the present passage), Arnold is maneuvering the reader's mind in the direction of acute skepticism toward nonwandering mentalities that blindly give themselves up to the prevailing dogmas of their passing age. Those system builders of the mutable moment, who give the universe their law, call to mind Shelley's Ozymandias. They "thunder" and command a dangerous power; but ultimately, like Shakespeare's sound and fury, they signify nothing.

Accordingly, "Stanzas from the Grande Chartreuse" closes with a scene of stirring noise and colorful activity that is momentarily appealing for its energy but disturbing for its uncertain direction. Armies and troops of hunters pass through a forest in different directions, armed with banners and bugles that entice the lonely mind: "Banner by turns and bugle woo: / *Ye shy recluses, follow too!*" (ll. 191–92). As the word *woo* implies, this is a seduction scene, an intriguing inversion of the traditional temptation motif in which the hero is invited to lay down his arms and linger in a Bower of Bliss. Now it is not the retreat but the quest that is perceived as dangerous. Strong knights with emblems on their shields who go pricking purposefully across the plain are subject to suspicion: "Pass, banners, pass, and bugles, cease; / And leave our desert to its peace!" (ll. 209–10).

In theory at least, it is not law giving or devotion to cause itself that is objectionable. Some sort of law would presumably be welcome—in one of the paradigmatic images of Victorian literature, the Arnoldean Scholar-Gipsy awaits a "spark from heaven" ("The Scholar-Gipsy," l. 171). But this yearning for a transcendent authority points toward the problem. Here on earth, our human lawmakers have lost our trust because they are fundamentally at odds with one another. The Victorians continue to struggle with a situation that troubled the earlier Romantics: our world seems to have too many answers in it. There are plenty of banners and bugles appealing for our allegiance, and behind their splendid show we can glimpse armies marching mindlessly to war against each other. One may recall "Dover Beach": this world that "seems / To lie before us like a land of dreams" is really only a "darkling plain" where "ignorant armies clash by night" (ll. 31, 35, 37). Literary preoccupation with this problem ranges in expression from the rather solemn dramatization of the mind wrestling with "the various modes of man's belief" in Browning's "Christmas Eve" (XX, l. 11) to such emblematic images as the boisterously comic response to *Hamlet* in

Dickens' *Great Expectations:* "Whenever that undecided Prince had to ask a question or state a doubt, the public helped him out with it. As for example; on the question whether 'twas nobler in the mind to suffer, some roared yes, and some no, and some inclining to both opinions said toss up for it; and quite a Debating Society arose" (Chap. 31).[8]

Underlying the Victorian Debating Society are epistemological issues that the Victorians share with the Romantics—issues that give rise to a number of similar literary patterns. In Mary Shelley's *Frankenstein,* Elizabeth appeals anxiously to Frankenstein to help form some solid foundation for her belief in Justine's innocence: "She was innocent. I know, I feel, she was innocent; you are of the same opinion, and that confirms me" (p. 93). But Mary Shelley's reader would remember Frankenstein's earlier moment of doubt, his thought that perhaps "nothing would or could ever be known"; and as events in fact develop, the innocent Justine is condemned at her trial (p. 41). The imagery of trials, law courts, and lawyers, and of securing shared opinion, building up cases on the one side of an issue or on the other, and making judgments from the presentations of evidence, all become important among the Romantic writers as vehicles for exploring conflicts between orientations of thought and issues of the mind's ability to arrive at resolutions. If Elizabeth's "I know" is gounded only on "I feel" and on an appeal to shared opinion, then Justine (and justice?) becomes fair game for the legal Debating Society. Echoes reverberate through Victorian literature. In *Our Mutual Friend,* for example, the part of Elizabeth is played by Lizzie Hexam and that of Justine by Lizzie's father: "Of her father's being groundlessly suspected, she felt sure. Sure. Sure. And yet, repeat the words inwardly as often as she would, the attempt to reason out and prove that she was sure, always came after it and failed," (Book 1, Chap. 6). In Browning's great trial poem *The Ring and the Book,* the corresponding roles are played by Pompilia and Caponsacchi. When Pompilia begins giving her evidence, she first aspires to prove Caponsacchi's innocence. But soon she realizes the dilemma.

---

8 · Unless indicated otherwise, references to Victorian novels that appear in the text in this chapter are to one-volume editions, listed in the bibliography, in which the chapters are numbered consecutively throughout the volume.

> Wherefore should I blame you much?
> So we are made, such difference in minds,
> Such difference too in eyes that see the minds!
> That man, you misinterpret and misprise—
> The glory of his nature, I had thought,
> Shot itself out in white light, blazed the truth
> Through every atom of his act with me:
> Yet where I point you, through the crystal shrine,
> Purity in quintessence, one dew-drop,
> You all descry a spider in the midst.
>
> ("Pompilia," ll. 911–20)

The reader of *The Ring and the Book* finds himself in the position of a judge listening to witnesses present their varying and contradictory testimonies in accordance with this "difference in minds" that Pompilia has seen. To be placed in the role of judge is to be rendered suspicious. The maneuver functions to alert us to the fact that what we are hearing from a witness of the moment is only one side of an argument, only one limited and perhaps biased perspective, and that the testimony of different witnesses might require us to think quite differently about the issue at hand. While this design upon the reader is probably most commonly associated with Browning, many other Victorian writers employ it as well. One thinks, for example, of how the Brontë sisters employ their dramatic narrators. In *Wuthering Heights*, Emily Brontë has Mrs. Deans "esteem" herself "a steady, reasonable kind of body," who insists that "I have undergone sharp discipline which has taught me wisdom" (Chap. 7). These protestations are designed to make the reader suspicious of the validity of Mrs. Deans's perspective. Later in the novel Emily Brontë reinforces this suspicion and extends it to Lockwood, when Mrs. Deans remarks to him, "But you'll not want to hear my moralizing, Mr. Lockwood; you'll judge as well as I can, all these things; at least, you'll think you will, and that's the same" (Chap. 17). The reader realizes that the judgments that are to be made on "all these things" he has been overhearing are by no means obvious—different minds would perhaps judge the events differently, and yet each would be as confident about its own wisdom as is Mrs. Deans. The problem of judging the judges in the novel is thus laid upon the reader—with the added weight that comes from his awareness that he too is probably subject to the weakness of believing too confidently, like Mrs. Deans, in his own wisdom.

Charlotte Brontë also likes to make her reader experience the Debating Society upon his pulses. In a crucial moment in *Jane Eyre*, for example, she makes her heroine appeal to the reader for judgment: " 'Show me, show me the path!' I entreated of Heaven. I was excited more than I had ever been; and whether what followed was the effect of excitement, *the reader shall judge*" (Chap. 35, italics mine). Here, as in many other passages in *Jane Eyre*, the reader confronts a witness who is by turns cajoling, coy, and indignant—and whose motives and degree of self-awareness and self-interest, accordingly, become difficult subjects for skeptical inquiry.[9]

Further, modern criticism is gradually establishing that the authorial voice in Victorian fiction is also employed frequently to serve a dramatic rather than authoritative function. In George Eliot's *Adam Bede*, this authorial voice straightforwardly presents herself as a witness who seeks "to give a faithful account of men and things as they have mirrored themselves in my mind. The mirror is doubtless defective; the outlines will sometimes be disturbed, the reflection faint or confused; but I feel as much bound to tell you as precisely as I can what that reflection is, as if I were in the witness-box narrating my experience on oath" (Chap. 17). The passage is ingenious, and it leads us for the moment to think simply that we are hearing in *Adam Bede* as close an approximation to the "real truth" as is humanly possible. But the concluding image of the witness-box and narration on oath alerts one to the fact that George Eliot is really raising the issue of perspectives and making one ponder how a different mind would reflect the men and things that the present trial witness is seeking to give her own faithful account of. George Eliot's authorial voice is not an intrusive, irritating quirk of the novelist's personality; it is designed to enrich our experience of the novel by maintaining our awareness that we are hearing one particular perspective and not The Perspective.

9 · An acute anaysis of Charlotte Brontë's use of her reader in *Jane Eyre* appears in Sylvere Monad, "Charlotte Brontë and the Thirty 'Readers' of *Jane Eyre*," in Richard J. Dunn (ed.), *Jane Eyre*, Norton Critical Edition (New York, 1971), 496–507.

Anthony Trollope also comes to mind. His authorial "intrusions," as readers who dislike the phenomena are fond of terming them, establish and maintain a distance between the events and characters of the Trollope novel and the judgmental experience.[10] Trollope often marks this distance merely with an "I think." The reader is thereby reminded that judgment upon a thing is not somehow inherent in the thing itself but, instead, requires the activity of a thinking "I." To say, for example, "This wine is bad" is quite different from saying, "This wine, I think, is bad." The former statement invites us to ignore or forget the problem of making judgments; it tends to lull the skeptical impulse into slumber. But the latter statement rouses the skeptical impulse from slumber and puts it to work. Trollope is interested in providing a lot of such work: "For myself, I think it as well that clergymen should not hunt; but had I been the parson of Clavering, I should, under the circumstances, have hunted double" (*The Claverings*, Chap. 2).

This "I think" and its variations are also employed by the characters in Trollope's novels. One of the main occupations of Trollope's characters is thinking differently from the way other characters think: " 'I think you are wrong,' said Stanbury" (*He Knew He Was Right*, Chap. 9); "When a man sees a thing clearly himself he cannot always realize that others do not see it also. I think I perceive . . ." (*John Caldigate*, Chap. 50); "Try to think of this thing rightly" (*Ayala's Angel*, Chap. 44). This creates situations in which the possible ways of thinking about a given issue become increasingly complex and confusing, and a mind called upon to take sides on the issue faces a hard problem: " 'Well! Mr. Grey, what do you think about it—eh? This was a comprehensive question, but Mr. Grey well understood its purport. What did he, Mr. Grey, think of the condition to which the affairs of Tretton had been brought" (*Mr. Scarborough's Family*, Chap. 19). So many witnesses in Trollope's novels offer so much contrary testimony that the reader is forced to wonder what clear truths, if any, are to be salvaged from the diversity of human experience.

Behind Victorian interest in this sort of problematic situation lies a similar Romantic interest. Scott, for example, observes of the Porteous trial

---

10 · See Kincaid, *Novels of Anthony Trollope*, 32–45; see also Peter K. Garrett, *The Victorian Multiplot Novel: Studies in Dialogical Form* (New Haven, 1980), 182–85.

in *The Heart of Midlothian* that "a great part of his [Porteous'] defence was . . . founded on the turbulence of the mob, which witnesses, according to their feelings, their predilections, and their opportunities of observation, represented differently" (Chap. 3). And underlying this Romantic preoccupation with different testimonies are such fundamental Romantic inquiries into the mind's operation as the "Memorable Fancy" in Blake's *Marriage of Heaven and Hell,* wherein a devilish narrator and an angel take turns imposing upon each other their differing "phantasies" of their eternal lots (Plates 17–20). One line of Victorian literature tends to accommodate such interest in the mind's creative propensities to traditional issues concerning appearance and reality. The *Bildungsroman* seems inclined to lean in this direction.[11] Pip's great expectations lead him to create a fantasy about Miss Havisham that is *only* an appearance, and in this case legal rhetoric plays a role in educating Pip.

> "And yet it looked so like it, sir," I pleaded with a downcast heart.
> "Not a particle of evidence, Pip," said Mr. Jaggers, shaking his head and gathering up his skirts. "Take nothing on its looks; take everything on evidence. There's no better rule." (Chap. 40)

But there is another, somewhat more interesting line that extends from the Romantics into Victorian literature. This line inclines more toward inquiry into how one appearance clashes with another appearance, and one testimony with another testimony, without leading to any resolution of debate. In Romantic literature, one thinks of stark anecdotal narratives like Wordsworth's "We Are Seven": "The little Maid would have her will, / And said, 'Nay, we are seven!'" (ll. 68–69). In Victorian literature, this simple conflict between individuals often expands into large familial or societal controversy in which the machinery of lawcourts and trials is brought into play. This machinery helps dramatize the hypothesis, not only that opposing arguments may be developed on any given issue, but also that the contrary "proofs" so readily built up by a prosecution and defense tend

11 · See, Buckley, *Season of Youth, passim.*

to balance each other out, thus failing to direct the judging mind to a verdict either of acquittal or of condemnation. In *Orley Farm*, one of Trollope's many novels that deal with a legal proceeding, Lady Mason is guilty of falsifying a will; but we observe the process of a trial that ends in pronouncing her not guilty. Trollope's interest is not so much in exposing the corruption or inadequacy of law and lawyers as in delving into fundamental questions of mental conviction. Thus he has one of his lawyers remark: "A man with what is called a logical turn of mind may prove anything or disprove anything; but he never convinces anybody. On any matter that is near to a man's heart, he is convinced by the tenour of his own thoughts as he goes on living, not by the arguments of a logician, or even by the eloquence of an orator" (Chap. 69).

What, though, if a man has no heart? The Romantics worried some about that question—Wordsworth, in his anxious anatomy of Oswald's sensibility in *The Borderers*, is a prime example. The Victorians, more completely caught up in the mind's dialogue with itself, worry about it more. Wordsworth's Oswald was subjected to a heart-wrenching torment, and his villainy reflects the heart's impulses, inasmuch as he is directing his energies against those impulses. But the Victorians begin flirting with a more truly motiveless and directionless malignancy. How will a man with Trollope's "logical turn of mind" who has little or no heart behave? In *Our Mutual Friend*, Mr. Boffin is introduced to Eugene Wrayburn, and seeking to make innocent, companionable conversation, he remarks that "there's nothing like work. Look at the bees." Eugene Wrayburn immediately pounces on the remark and objects to the analogy: "I object on principle, as a two-footed creature, to being constantly referred to insects and four-footed creatures" (Book 1, Chap. 8).

> "But I said, you know," urged Mr. Boffin, rather at a loss for an answer, "the bee."
> "Exactly. And may I represent to you that it is injudicious to say the bee? For the whole case is assumed. Conceding for a moment that there is any analogy between a bee and a man in a shirt and pantaloons (which I deny), and that it is settled that the man is to learn

from the bee (which I also deny), the question still remains, What is he to learn? To imitate? Or to avoid?" (Book 1, Chap. 8).

Eugene Wrayburn possesses one of those legalistic, logical minds that is able, as Trollope says, to "prove anything or disprove anything." He presses to a disturbing extreme the key question of the Romantics, "How do you know?"

Wrayburn hovers on the edge of alienation from human values in general, but he is pulled back into the human community by Lizzie Hexam, who succeeds in stirring his heart. Another character in Dickens, however, goes over the edge: Steerforth in *David Copperfield.* He, in a sense, occupies the free space that the Romantics had coveted, but in that free space as he experiences it, the constructive, humanistic impulse that Romantic questioning had sought to tap has been left behind. Steerforth remarks to the innocent David: "I have never learnt the art of binding myself to any of the wheels on which the Ixions of these days are turning round and round. I missed it somehow in a bad apprenticeship, and now don't care about it.— You know I have bought a boat down here?" (Vol. 1, Chap. 22). Steerforth sees all the ordinary pursuits of human life as torturous "wheels." He represents the dark possibility toward which Romantic humanistic skepticism can drift: perhaps the mind might so completely free itself from all mind-forged manacles that it finds itself left with no humanistic impulses upon which to build. Steerforth thus takes us a step beyond Arnold's Scholar-Gipsy, who at least had hope of a "spark from heaven."

In taking us this further step Steerforth brings into focus the problem in the Scholar-Gipsy himself. At first encounter, the Scholar-Gipsy seems a product of the familiar Romantic impulse to distance the mind from the oppressive contrarieties of human thought: "But fly our paths, our feverish contact fly! / For strong the infection of our mental strife" ("The Scholar-Gipsy," ll. 221–22). However, it is forebodingly significant that having removed himself from mental strife, the Scholar-Gipsy discovers no spark flaming up from within his being—instead, he must wait for one to drop from heaven. The Romantics had envisioned a quite different scene: if we could only evade the numbing frost of custom (or Urizen, or Jupiter), then our inner spark ought to reveal itself: "O joy! that in our embers / Is something that doth live." But Arnold's Scholar-Gipsy has no fires of his own. The spark has returned to heaven, and instead of rising up like a second Prometheus to pull it down again, the Scholar-Gipsy is only a patient supplicant. The next stage in this metamorphosis finds a representative in Dickens' Steerforth. He not only lacks a heavenly spark; he lacks desire for one.

Hints of Steerforth can be found in Romantic works. The most interesting of these appears in Byron's *Childe Harold's Pilgrimage.*

> And from the planks, far shatter'd o'er the rocks,
> Build me a little bark of hope, once more
> To battle with the ocean and the shocks
> Of the loud breakers, and the ceaseless roar
> Which rushes on the solitary shore
> Where all lies founder'd that was ever dear:
> But could I gather from the wave-worn store
> Enough for my rude boat, where should I steer?
>   (Canto IV, Stanza CV)

However, in Byron there are still faint traces of desire (" a little bark of hope") and of value commitment (things are remembered as "dear"). The plaintive question "where should I steer?" bespeaks a mentality that wishes to believe that some directions of travel must be preferable to others. But Dickens' Steerforth has transcended or lost this anxiety: he aims merely at steering forth, without worrying about direction. A mind that seems able to prove or to disprove anything, and that views commitment as the torment of Ixion turning round and round upon a wheel, must either lose itself in pure apathy and paralysis or, like Steerforth, simply move—without regard for issues of value and consequence.

I will venture a sweeping generalization: the Romantics tend to be haunted by madness; the Victorians by an alienation of mind that finds expression either in boredom and paralysis or in activity that in theory is amoral but that in practice tends to gravitate toward endangerment of traditional humane values. Romantic madness is characterized by obsessive clinging to things. The Romantics incline toward the hypothesis that once the mind is freed of (deprived of?) things, dogmas, and values that it covets, it will begin building up replacements. We are mythmakers, tale makers, builders of havens for human values, even despite ourselves. Danger lies not in the possibility that we may fail to exert the power of creation and so find ourselves left in vacancy but, instead, in the fact that we have a propensity to become blinded by or trapped within the structures we have created: "Thus men forgot that All deities reside in the human breast" (*The Marriage of Heaven and Hell*, Plate 11). We risk going mad pursuing the oppressive fantasies of our own creation—one thinks of the relationship between Frankenstein and his creature in Mary Shelley's novel. A different danger emerges among the Victorians. Steerforth's problem in Dickens' novel is that he has no tendencies toward such madness. Better the madness of Mr. Dick innocently flying his kites than Steerforth's clear-eyed sanity that everywhere perceives Ixions trapped in meaningless circles, "turning round and round."

Again, hints of such vision can be found among the earlier Romantics. Blake, for example, explores the nightmare of human torture within natural cycles in "The Mental Traveller." However, Blake also has confidence in the possibility of a quite different program of travel: rising out of nature's cycles into a Jerusalem of human creativity. In *Prometheus Unbound* Shelley's Demogorgon throws out hints of cosmic cycles when he replies cryptically to Asia:

> —If the Abysm
> Could vomit forth its secrets:—but a voice
> Is wanting, the deep truth is imageless;
> For what would it avail to bid thee gaze
> *On the revolving world?*
> (II, iv, ll. 114–18; italics mine)

It would avail nothing to bid Asia gaze on the revolving world because she would not really be able to see it. For Asia, the "deep truth is imageless." Like that of Prometheus, her sensibility is alive to

> lovely apparitions dim at first
> Then radiant—as the mind, arising bright
> From the embrace of beauty.
> (III, iii, ll. 49–51)

Such apparitions prevent and protect her from viewing dark vistas of endless revolutions, and thus immunized, she is able to cultivate the characteristic Romantic

> hope that can never die,
> Effort, and expectation, and desire,
> And something evermore about to be.
> (1805, *Prelude*, VI, ll. 540–42)

The Romantic writer who probably comes closest to the Victorian view is Keats, whose poetic career exhibits an ongoing—though perhaps, in the end, losing—struggle to keep the Romantic hope from dying. In his "Ode on Indolence," Keats seems to be verging on the perspective of Steerforth, as he represents love, ambition, and even his "demon Poesy" as ghostly temptresses who can no longer successfully tease his mind.

> So, ye three ghosts, adieu! Ye cannot raise
>   My head cool-bedded in the flowery grass;
> For I would not be dieted with praise,
>   A pet-lamb in a sentimental farce!
> (ll. 51–54)

Indolence becomes the last minimal refuge for the humane sensibility. Beyond it lies either suicide (slight hints of which arise in the image "head cool-bedded in the flowery grass") or bitter attack upon a world that appears to have proven itself false to the despairing mind ("pet-lamb in a sentimental farce" has a suggestion of anger in it—a hint of refusal to submit meekly to sacrifice—that threatens to disturb the state of indolence within which Keats is seeking to protect what little grace remains to him). However, even in this poem the final lines exhibit a pull against the tone of renunciation and suggest a faint rebirth of Romantic confidence in "something evermore about to be."

> Farewell! I yet have visions for the night,
> And for the day faint visions there is store;
> Vanish, ye phantoms, from my idle spright,
> Into the clouds, and never more return!
> (ll. 57–60)

Perhaps, even yet, there are distinctions to be maintained between phantoms and visions, and so to dismiss the phantoms from one's sight is not to cast away everything. Keats is not quite ready to see all acts of commitment as invitations to the torment of Ixion, turning round and round.

In the Victorian period, there are more optimistic ways of thinking about cyclic movement than the one Steerforth espouses. The hopeful strain in Victorian literary thought explores the possibility of dreaming of progress—holding it true that although we may appear to be moving only in circles and getting nowhere, actually our revolutions are propelling us in some desirable, evolutionary direction. In "Locksley Hall," Tennyson develops the drama of a mind attaching itself to this manner of thinking: "Forward, forward let us range, / Let the great world spin for ever down the ringing grooves of change" (ll. 181–82). Dickens reflects this sort of optimism when he revises the characteristic pattern of Romantic conclusions in the final paragraphs of *Little Dorrit*. The Romantics liked to envision the concluding unions between their heroes and heroines as occurring in the context of elevation from the stresses of the world; Prometheus and Asia retire to the environs of a cave in *Prometheus Unbound*; Jeanie Deans and Reuben Butler escape to the isle of Roseneath in *The Heart of Midlothian*; Emma and Mr. Knightley find their perfect happiness within their band of true friends, leaving the Mrs. Eltons of the world outside, in *Emma*. But Dickens insists upon returning his happy pair in *Little Dorrit* to the turmoils of the world, making them go "down" into a life that—with shades of Tennyson's "Forward, forward"—he presents as full, not simply of activity, but of accomplishment: "Little Dorrit and her husband walked out of the church alone. They paused for a moment on the steps of the portico, looking at the fresh perspective of the street in the autumn morning sun's bright rays, and then went down. Went down into a modest life of usefulness and happiness. Went down to give a mother's care" (Book 2, Chap. 34).[12] Other Victorian writers work variations upon this revision of Romantic transcendence. For example, instead of making the happy union occur at the conclusion of the literary work (as Austen does in *Emma*), Tennyson in *The Idylls of the King* places it at the outset, and then explores the accomplishments that the union generates. Emma and Mr. Knightley surrounded by their band of true friends become Guinevere and Arthur surrounded by their Round Table.[13]

But the brooding melancholy of *The Idylls of the King* suggests the frailty of this optimistic strain. *The Idylls of the King* actually brings us back to Steerforth's Ixions turning on their wheels. Tennyson's great poem traces a pattern of rise and fall through a series of narrative poems in which the recurring imagery of seasonal cycles implies that human endeavor, like natural growth, is bound to the revolution of the spheres.

> The sudden trumpet sounded as in a dream
> To ears but half-awaked, then one low roll
> Of Autumn thunder, and the jousts began;
> And ever the wind blew, and yellowing leaf,
> And gloom and gleam, and shower and shorn plume
> Went down it.
>
> ("The Last Tournament," ll. 151–56)

---

12 · On this pattern of downward movement in literature of the Victorian period, see George Levine, "High and Low: Ruskin and the Novelists," in U. C. Knoepflmacher and G. B. Tennyson (eds.), *Nature and the Victorian Imagination* (Berkeley, 1977), 137–52, wherein Levine argues that "much of the energy of Victorian fiction was consciously directed at endowing the lowlands with the feelings that so much of popular Romantic tradition had reserved for the heights" (142).

13 · See Patricia M. Ball, *The Heart's Events: The Victorian Poetry of Relationships* (London, 1976), in which Ball argues that a distinctively Victorian concern is the exploration of the psychological repercussions that follow from the joining of two lives.

The Idylls of the King is framed by the narratives "The Coming of Arthur" and "The Passing of Arthur." In the former, we find the young Arthur firmly announcing to "those great Lords from Rome, / The slowly-fading mistress of the world," that "the old order changeth, yielding place to new" (ll. 503–504, 508). In the latter, we are confronted with a less joyous echo.

> And slowly answer'd Arthur from the barge:
> "The old order changeth, yielding place to new,
> And God fulfills himself in many ways,
> Lest one good custom should corrupt the world.
> Comfort thyself; what comfort is in me?"
>
> (ll. 407–11)

This recalls Carlyle's clothes philosophy and, behind that, Wordsworth's warning about the numbing frost of custom; but Tennyson makes it difficult to find that argument consoling in this context. Set off against the burden of custom in Wordsworth is the prospect of the soul rediscovering its freedom, at least in thought, and in Carlyle the emphasis falls on the prospect of building something new from ruins. Tennyson, however, subtly directs thought away from such prospects. Having induced his reader to follow through the course of the idylls the process of a new order and a good custom becoming old and bad, Tennyson leaves the reader wondering whether change offers something desirable or only a nightmare prospect of repetition. When we hear the old king in "The Passing of Arthur" repeat his words, "The old order changeth, yielding place to new," we are brought back, as it were, to the beginning; and the poem offers no grounds for supposing that the new order on the horizon will offer anything other than a repetition of the poignant, painful moment of joyous power and the hour of sad decay that we have already experienced. Change in *The Idylls of the King* promises a new Ixion and a new wheel, but the old round.

There is an interesting passage in Ruskin's *Modern Painters* that concerns change. Alluding to Wordsworth's immortality ode, Ruskin argues that it is fruitless to hope that the pursuit of change might offer an escape from the heavy weight of custom: "If we grow inpatient under it [the weight of custom], and seek to recover the mental energy by more quickly repeated and brighter novelty, it is all over with our enjoyment . . . if we try to obtain perpetual change, change itself will become monotonous; and then we are reduced to that old despair, 'If water chokes, what will you drink after it?'"[14] Suspicion that change may lead not to something new and different but only a repetition of entrapment is one variation of a fundamental Victorian penchant for thinking that alternatives to negative conditions may simply lead back to negatives. When we try to go somewhere, perhaps we only move in circles. The mariners in Tennyson's "Voyage" sail round the world in pursuit of their vision.

> Again to colder climes we came,
>   For still we follow'd where she led:
> Now mate is blind and captain lame,
>   And half the crew are sick or dead,
> But, blind or lame or sick or sound,
>   We follow that which flies before:
> We know the merry world is round,
>   And we may sail for evermore.
>   (Stanza 12)

The poem recalls such examples of the Romantic quest motif as that in Shelley's "Alastor." But the basically linear movement in Shelley (from ocean through river, cavern, and stream to an elemental resting point) has been transformed into a frenzied circular movement that follows the "round" of the "merry world." There is a touch of stubborn heroism in the activity, perhaps, but the poem leaves its reader with a bleak parable suggesting that the expenditure of effort, expectation, and desire tends to collapse upon itself, as the pursuit of vision becomes the pursuit of pursuing.

Tennyson's most famous commentary on this theme is probably his ear-

---

14 · Ruskin, *Modern Painters*, III, Part 4, Chap. 17, Para. 23, in *Works of John Ruskin*, III, 370.

lier poem "Ulysses." Having returned from his epic adventures to Ithaca, Ulysses is bored and restless with "the sphere / Of common duties"; he is determined, therefore, to break away from tedium and set out questing again (ll. 39–40).

> Yet all experience is an arch wherethro'
> Gleams that untravell'd world, whose margin fades
> For ever and for ever when I move.
>
> (ll. 19–21)

While this rhetoric is stirring and attractive to politicians, it is designed to make one uneasy. The margin of Ulysses' untraveled world fades forever when he moves because—as the later, less subtle poem "The Voyage" states with a more bitter irony—Ulysses is going around in a circle. Ulysses exclaims, "How dull it is to pause, to make an end" (l. 22). The poem teases the mind with the disquieting idea that Ulysses' alternative to making an end promises, not an escape from a sphere, but merely entrapment within a larger sphere.

The Romantic mind, it has been argued, tended to reject the old dichotomy of either-or in favor of a manner of thinking characterized by both-and.[15] The Victorians seem fond of postulating a third pattern: neither-nor. Staying in one's proper sphere, as we say, is frequently associated with the entrapment of tedious repetition, as in Ulysses' vision of Ithaca in Tennyson's poem. Or, as a second example, there is Dickens' claustrophobic picture of Mrs. Flintwinch's situation in *Little Dorrit*: "The house in the city preserved its heavy dulness . . . and the invalid within it turned the same unvarying round of life. Morning, noon, and night, morning, noon, and night, each recurring with its accompanying monotony, always the same reluctant return of the same sequences of machinery, like a dragging piece of clockwork" (Book 1, Chap. 29). But escape from this "unvarying round" through energetic quest after some alternative object or value is also often associated with going in circles. In Browning's poem "Meeting at Night," night falls and a lover comes in from the sea to embrace his mistress on the shore; but

15 · See E. D. Hirsch's chapter "Both-And Logic in the Immortality Ode," in his *Wordsworth and Schelling: A Typological Study of Romanticism* (New Haven, 1960).

when the sun and the tide rise in the companion poem "Parting at Morning," the lover leaves for the sea again, feeling "the need of a world of men for me" (l. 4). The passions of Browning's persona seem equally bound to the unvarying round of day and night.

Many of the quests that appear in Victorian literature dramatize attempts to escape some version of an unvarying round, which end in efforts to escape the condition of escape. In *Middlemarch*, Dorothea Brooke escapes from the drudgery of ordinary life, throwing herself, like Saint Theresa, into what she supposes will be an epic life of sacrifice and dedication to a great cause; but Casaubon's "Key to All Mythologies" itself becomes a drudgery for her, and she escapes back into the world she had earlier forsworn. In a less solemn vein, Dickens' Mr. Wemmick constructs a fortress to escape into: "After I have crossed this bridge, I hoist it up—so—and cut off the communication" (*Great Expectations*, Chap. 25). But this fortress that shuts things out also begins to shut Mr. Wemmick in, and by the end of the novel he delivers himself, the Aged Parent, and his cherished privacy up to communication with the outer world in the considerable person of Miss Skiffins. In Tennyson's "Palace of Art," the soul leaves the world for a lordly pleasure-house, but finding that it loses its pleasure, she leaves it to return to the world. And yet—a nice final touch on Tennyson's part—she decides in the poem's last moment that perhaps she will return to the palace.

> Yet pull not down my palace towers, that are
> So lightly, beautifully built:
> Perchance I may return with others there
> When I have purged my guilt.
>
> (ll. 293–96)

This poem is frequently read as a lesson that Tennyson was trying to teach himself about the inability of the soul to live in splendid isolation within a world of art; but I suspect Tennyson was probing a more complex issue. Perhaps we cannot live in a palace of art, but it may also be true that we cannot live without that palace either.

A sort of emblem of the Victorian dilemma is John Harmon's attempt to make his way through Limehouse Hole in Dickens' *Our Mutual Friend*.

"Did we go by this alley? Or down that little lane?"

He tried both, but both confused him equally, and he came stray-
ing back to the same spot. . . .

He tried a new direction, but made nothing of it; walls, dark doorways, flights of stairs and rooms, were too abundant. And, like most
people so puzzled, he again and again described a circle, and found
himself at the point from which he had begun. "This is like what I
have read in narratives of escape from prison," said he, "where the
little track of the fugitives in the night always seems to take the shape
of the great round world, on which they wander; as if it were a secret
law." (Book 2, Chap. 30)

Unless he can somehow maintain a state of suspended supplication, the Victorian fugitive confronts a problem. To seek escape within a protective circle
such as the Romantics fondly envisioned is for the Victorians a dubious enterprise, because Romantic circles threaten to metamorphose into Victorian
traps. "The Palace of Art" revises "Kubla Khan" by offering the aspiring
soul, not just the momentary glimpse of a pleasure dome, but the actual
experience of living in one—only to show that the haven turns into a
stifling prison. However, to seek escape from prison can be equally frustrating. The Romantics liked to think that one might move in a relatively
straight line toward some goal, or at least that one might perhaps wander
freely—one recalls, for example, Coleridge: "But *thou*, my babe! shalt
wander like a breeze / By lakes and sandy shores" ("Frost at Midnight,"
ll. 54–55). But Victorian thought curves toward the dark possibility that
"the little track of fugitives in the night always seems to take the shape of
the great round world." Herein are shades of Steerforth's wheels and the
torture of turning round and round.

Alice asks the Cheshire cat, "Would you tell me, please, which way I
ought to go from here?"; and the cat answers, "That depends a good deal on
where you want to get to" (*Alice's Adventures in Wonderland*, Chap. 6).
Behind this exchange is the orientation of thought that was fostered by the
earlier Romantics. Under the pressure of skeptical inquiry, the question of
obligation dissolves into a question of choice: "ought" yields to "want."

Once the claims of dogmatic systems have been set at a distance, we will be free—so the Romantics were inclined to believe or hope—to choose our direction according to the deep impulse of our own human nature. But the Victorian Lewis Carroll is not so confident about this. Alice and the Cheshire cat continue their exchange: "'I don't much care where—' said Alice. 'Then it doesn't matter which way you go,' said the Cat.''

Alice has begun to exhibit the tug of the Victorian current that produces the indifference of Steerforth. Once the obligatory "ought" is set aside, perhaps it will develop that the mind will only discover that it does not much care about where to go, and from this proposition emerges the "it doesn't matter" of an alienated sensibility. Alice, however, continues to cling to the remnants of the old notion that some form of "ought" might be derived from gaining information and thus determining where to go according to distinctions between available options. So she asks the Cheshire cat, "What sort of people live about here?" And "in *that* direction," the Cat said, waving its right paw round, "lives a Hatter: and in *that* direction," waving the other paw, "lives a March Hare. Visit either you like: they're both mad." Alice is caught in the Victorian circle. In the end, it may not really matter whether one cares about which direction to take; alternative directions may lead to the same phenomenon.

In *David Copperfield*, Steerforth plays the Cheshire cat to David's Alice. David has been instructed by his Aunt Betsy Trotwood to "look about" and settle upon some profession to follow; but, he admits to Steerforth, he has been neglecting his charge. So Steerforth ironically recalls David to his duty: "'Well! look about you now, and make up for your negligence,' said Steerforth. 'Look to the right, and you'll see a flat country, with a good deal of marsh in it; look to the left, and you'll see the same. Look to the front, and you'll find no difference; look to the rear, and there it is still'" (Vol. I, Chap. 23). The innocent David responds with laughter at Steerforth's "balancing all callings and professions so equally," but there is really nothing funny about Steerforth. Steerforth has fallen (or, depending perhaps on one's metaphysics, risen) into a perspective from which energy and desire look more like the senseless attributes of the Lamb than the sublime properties of the Tyger. One might try leaps of faith—proposing that a man's reach should exceed his grasp or what's a heaven for—but it appears that, short of such leaps, the prospect in every direction looks equally flat and marshy. Only an unseeing Lamb, therefore, would be inclined to worry about where it ought to go, and would set out earnestly and energetically in pursuit of some particular profession. The Victorian Tyger exhibits a propensity toward boredom. In *Vanity Fair*, Lord Steyne tells Becky Sharpe that she is a "silly little fool" for wanting to get somewhere in society. "Everyone is striving for what is not worth the having!" he tells her. "It's not half so nice as here. You'll be bored there. I am" (Chap. 48).

ONE basic factor in the evolution of questioning between the Romantic and Victorian periods is emergence of the suspicion that escape from systems may not offer the promise of humanistic salvation. To reach a free space between the claims of competing ideologies is not to discover the creative power of our distinctively human nature; instead, it is to risk falling either into a state of almost metaphysical paralysis or into a state of perverse activity that seems antagonistic to humanistic impulses. When the individual steps outside systems, he does not find himself; instead, he is lost: "Amid the seeming confusion of our mysterious world, individuals are so nicely adjusted to a system, and systems to one another and to a whole, that, by stepping aside for a moment, a man exposes himself to a fearful risk of losing his place forever. Like Wakefield, he may become, as it were, the Outcast of the Universe." This passage is from the final paragraph of Nathaniel Hawthorne's tale "Wakefield," published in the *Twice-Told Tales* in 1837. It reminds us that developments in England were not an insular phenomenon. In England, the heroic journey in *Childe Harold's Pilgrimage* metamorphoses into Steerforth's journey toward ennui and depravity. In America, the metamorphosis produces such an outcase as Hawthorne's Wakefield or Herman Melville's Bartleby the Scrivener, in whom the factor of passivity is accentuated. In Russia, it produces more active outcasts such as Fëdor Dostoevski's Man Underground, devoted to cutting capers.

The metamorphosis gives rise to the fundamental Victorian dilemma of mutually unsatisfactory alternatives: on the one hand, that of committing the self to some given occupation, value system, or quest, and thereby becoming an Ixion, turning round and round in torturous circles; and on the other hand, that of rejecting all such commitments, and thereby risking the possibility of becoming Steerforth or one of his variations, lost to humanity and drifting toward paralysis or corruption. Among Victorian attempts either to deny the validity of this dilemma or to discover an evasion of it, the most interesting development involves experimenting with a basic shift in the way the mind thinks about experience. If people who give themselves up to the ordinary human commitments of life seem to be going in circles, it does not necessarily follow that we need to think of them as undergoing the torture of endlessly striving and yet endlessly going nowhere. We can transform our image of a circle into the image of a ring, and then think of the activities that take place in that ring as constituting in their circularity some kind of holistic achievement—an act of completion—as in, for example, a theatrical performance. Spinning round and round, therefore, is no longer a meaningless activity that leads nowhere. To the contrary, it is the miraculous showmanship of performers in the ring, whose mastery of the circle elevates our spirits and restores us to our humanity. Hence, for example, when we find ourselves becoming trapped within the utilitarian spin of Gradgrind's "circle of the sciences" in Dickens' *Hard Times*, we can close Gradgrind and open Sleary's circus: "Mr. Gradgrind sat down forlorn, on the Clown's performing chair in the middle of the ring" (Book 1, Chap. 3; Book 3, Chap. 7).

Dickens is especially attracted in his less somber moments toward such thinking. In *Great Expectations*, for example, we are confronted with the circular argumentation of Joe.

"Well," said Joe, passing the poker into his left hand, that he might feel his whisker; and I had no hope of him whenever he took to that placid occupation; "your sister's a master-mind. A master-mind."

"What's that?" I asked, in some hope of bringing him to a stand. But Joe was readier with his definition than I had expected, and completely stopped me by arguing circularly, and answering with a fixed look, "Her." (Chap. 7)

What might become torment is being transformed into humor here. In *Great Expectations*, Dickens invites us to conceive of people as players performing in comic games or pageants. Pip encounters a "pale young gentle-man" who insists for no apparent reason that Pip "come and fight": "'Laws of the game!' said he. Here, he skipped from his left leg on to his right. 'Regular rules!' Here, he skipped from his right leg on to his left. 'Come to the ground, and go through the preliminaries!' Here, he dodged backwards and forwards, and did all sorts of things while I looked helplessly at him" (Chap. 11).

It is not quite clear just what this game is, but apparently it has laws and "Regular rules." The threat of torment is deflected by the stirrings of curi-osity concerning the game that is being played and the odd performances of the players. Miss Havisham is unable to appreciate this. Lost in her torpor, she tells Pip, "I want diversion, and I have done with men and women. Play." Pip, however, is paralyzed: "I felt myself so unequal to the perfor-mance that I gave it up, and stood looking at Miss Havisham in what I sup-pose she took for a dogged manner" (Chap. 8). The interesting irony here is that the diversion Miss Havisham seeks would be readily available to her through encounter with the ordinary activities of the men and women she has decided to "have done with." The child Pip cannot be made to perform on demand, but the characters who populate the world of *Great Expecta-tions* perform without being asked.

> To my unutterable amazement, I now, for the first time, saw Mr. Pocket relieve his mind by going through a performance that struck me as very extraordinary, but which made no impression on anybody else, and with which I soon became as familiar as the rest. He laid down the carving-knife and fork . . . put his two hands into his dis-turbed hair, and appeared to make an extraordinary effort to lift him-self up by it. When he had done this, and had not lifted himself up at all, he quietly went on with what he was about. (Chap. 23)

There is an echo here of the Romantic notion, passed on to the Victorians by Carlyle, among others, that if we could manage to see things afresh, then the most common things around us would appear miraculous. Because he is observing Mr. Pocket's performance for the first time, Pip is astonished by it, but the others, familiar with Mr. Pocket's behavior, take no notice. That

is presumably the problem that confronts Miss Havisham: her past association with men and women prevents her from looking upon them with fresh
vision. Brooding upon the betrayal she has suffered, she clings to the past:
"Before she spoke again, she turned her eyes from me, and looked at the
dress she wore, and at the dressing-table, and finally at herself in the
looking-glass. 'So new to him,' she muttered, 'so old to me; so strange to
him, so familiar to me; so melancholy to both of us!'" (Chap. 8). But while
it is true that Pip finds Miss Havisham and her environment melancholy, he
also finds them awesome in their strangeness. Miss Havisham cannot see
the strangeness in things, and so instead of being diverted, she sinks further
and further into her torpor.

Poetry, Shelley claimed, "lifts the veil from the hidden beauty of the
world, and makes familiar objects be as if they were not familiar."[16] Continuing to test this possibility that the power of art might successfully
render the familiar unfamiliar—thereby warding off the Steerforthian tendency of thought to see only a flat country, with much marsh in it, extend-
ing in all directions—the Victorians grow fond of employing art to make us
think of life as an entertainment or show. Edward Fitzgerald's *Rubáiyát of
Omar Khayyám* holds up a mirror to the perplexity of the skeptical Victorian mind, and it aspires to transform the image of that perplexity into
something lovely, an exotic entertainment.

> We are no other than a moving row
> Of Magic Shadow-shapes that come and go
>   Round with the Sun-illumined Lantern held
> In Midnight by the Master of the Show.[17]

The image suggests that, although we "go / Round," we can think of ourselves as being magical shapes in a strange, exotic show. Or again, there is a
slightly different image.

---

16 · Shelley, *A Defense of Poetry*, in *Shelley's Poetry and Prose*, 487.
17 · Edward Fitzgerald, *The Rubáiyát of Omar Khayyám*, in *The Variorum and Definitive
Edition of the Poetical and Prose Writings of Edward Fitzgerald*, collected and arranged by
George Bentham (5th ed., 7 vols.; New York, 1902; rpr. 1967), III, 26, Stanza 68. The following extract is from Stanza 69.

> But helpless Pieces of the Game He plays
> Upon this Chequer-board of Nights and Days;
> Hither and thither moves, and checks, and slays,
> And one by one back in the Closet lays.

Both images are designed to make us see our human condition in an unfamiliar, intriguing light. One thinks for a moment of Shakespeare's *King Lear*, perhaps: "As flies to wanton boys, are we to the gods, / They kill us for their sport" (IV, i, 38–39). But Shakespeare and Fitzgerald are really moving in different directions. The stark assertion Shakespeare gives to Gloucester on the heath is designed to emphasize the helplessness of humanity (at least according to Gloucester's perception) and to deny the possibility of consolation. But Fitzgerald's lines, while they by no means ignore this helplessness, accentuate the imagery of the show and the game, and accordingly, they invite us to view this helplessness from the perspective of an audience. We become an entertainment to ourselves. The artist functions as magician, diverting attention from despair toward the imaginative satisfactions of contemplating the imagery of "Magic Shadow-shapes" and the "Chequer-board of Nights and Days."

Other Victorian writers execute similar maneuvers. For example, the bleak implications of William Makepeace Thackeray's *Vanity Fair* are both underscored and transformed in that novel's concluding paragraph: "Ah! *Vanitas Vanitatum!* which of us is happy in this world? Which of us has his desire? or, having it, is satisfied?—come, children, let us shut up the box and the puppets, for our play is played out." The initial thrust of the paragraph is to sum up the running theme of frustration in *Vanity Fair*. But then, picking up a thematic undercurrent of the novel, Thackeray concludes by inviting us to shift our way of thinking by seeing the events of "this world" (the ambiguous "this" blurs the border line between the world of the novel and the world we readers live in) as a theatrical performance—a modest, Sleary-circus version of Fitzgerald's magic lantern show in *The Rubáiyát of Omar Khayyám*.

During the course of the novel, Thackeray has been laying the ground for this shift in perspective: "If Rawdon Crawley had been then and there present, instead of being at the club nervously drinking claret, the pair might have gone down on their knees before the old spinster, avowed all, and been forgiven in a twinkling. But that good chance was denied to the young couple, doubtless in order that this story might be written, in which numbers of their wonderful adventures are narrated" (Chap. 16). Thackeray offers us, in his authorial voice, a P. T. Barnum variation of the master of the show, who functions to develop in his audience the ability to perceive the show as a show. The conclusion of *Vanity Fair* implies that this ability be exercised in reference to the world at large. *Vanity Fair* trains us to see that vanity *is* fair—entertaining, and capable of rousing us from torpor or disgust. The countryside is by no means equally flat and marshy in all directions. To the contrary, "There are scenes of all sorts; some dreadful combats, some grand and lofty horse-riding, some scenes of high life"—a wealth of diverting entertainment, so long as one learns to look at the performances ("Before the Curtain").

A somewhat subtler but not essentially dissimilar maneuver is being executed by Lewis Carroll in *Alice's Adventures in Wonderland*. The work suggests that when we grow up (as Alice does both mentally and physically in the concluding chapter), we might learn to see the tormenting trials of life in the way Alice finally sees the trial in which she has become entangled: "'Who cares for *you?*' said Alice (she had grown to her full size by this time). 'You're nothing but a pack of cards!'" (Chap. 12). We can learn to respond to life as if it were a game of cards. The wonder of *Alice's Adventures in Wonderland* lies in the way Carroll diverts our minds from the nightmarish aspects of the world by showing us possibilities of discerning elements of game in experience.[18]

Early in the twentieth century, when the children of the Victorians were busy burying their eminent Victorian fathers instead of praising them, it became popular to propose that the Victorians were hypocritical, insensitive, or dull-witted. Tennyson, for example, was proposed to have a magnificent ear for poetic effects but no mind. Dickens, it was discovered, drowns us in

---

18 · *Cf.* Kathleen Blake, *Play, Games, and Sport: The Literary Works of Lewis Carroll* (Ithaca, 1974), esp. 64–77 and her concluding chapter, "A Victorian Gospel of Amusement."

awkward sentiment. Browning insults the mind with stunningly naïve maxims. It is probably more true to say that the Victorians saw and thought a little too well. The Romantics wanted to believe that we have all one human heart and that if we could only lay bare the naked dignity of man, we might rediscover our humanistic bearings. In the service of this high argument, they produced a literature of inquiry that is highly complex, intellectually demanding, and designed to probe beneath the surfaces of ordinary structures of thought and value. Beneath those surfaces might lie an abyss, but from that abyss would rise a saving grace of some kind. Wordsworth calls it "Imagination" in *The Prelude*.

> Imagination—here the Power so called
> Through sad incompetence of human speech,
> That awful Power rose from the mind's abyss
> Like an unfathered vapour.
>   (1850 *Prelude*, VI, ll. 592–95)

This awful power becomes more vaporous during the course of the nineteenth century. For many of the Victorians, the abyss is a danger: it hides either nothingness or some version of Mr. Hyde. Once this notion of the abyss develops, the writer's duty toward the human community (such community as there is left) may begin to change. To inquire is to uncover a monster; to divert is to hold the monster in check. The beauty of a line from Tennyson is not mindless; it is rather, one might say, mind-transcending. It is the product of a writer who perceives the need to divert the mind with beauty.

In *Hard Times* (an unhappily appropriate title with which to conclude our own inquiry), Dickens relates a conversation between Sissy Jupe and Louisa Gradgrind that contains an important defense of a literature of diversion. Sissy has been telling Louisa that she used to read her father "wrong books"—books that Louisa's father would certainly detest but in which, Sissy insists, she didn't see any harm. Louisa responds by giving Sissy "a searching gaze" and asking whether Mr. Jupe had liked such wrong books. Sissy replies: "O very much! They kept him, many times, from what did him real harm. And often and often of a night, he used to forget all his troubles in wondering whether the Sultan would let the lady go on with the story, or would have her head cut off before it was finished" (Book I, Chap. 9). When humanity finds itself in a dangerous situation like that of *The Arabian Nights*—in which the choice is either to tell tales of wonder that divert the mind or else to yield the stage to beheadings—then it is a literature of diversion that may appear to claim first prize for the defense of humanism.

Selected Bibliography

Primary Materials, Editions Used in Citations

Arnold, Matthew. *The Poetical Works of Matthew Arnold.* Edited by C. B. Tinker and H. F. Lowry. London, 1950.

Austen, Jane. *The Novels of Jane Austen.* Edited by R. W. Chapman. 3rd ed. 5 vols. Oxford, U.K., 1932–34.

Blake, William. *The Complete Poetry and Prose of William Blake.* Edited by David Erdman. Rev. ed. Garden City, N.Y., 1982.

Brontë, Charlotte. *Jane Eyre.* Edited by Richard J. Dunn. Norton Critical Edition. New York, 1971.

Brontë, Emily. *Wuthering Heights.* Edited by William M. Sale. Norton Critical Edition. New York, 1963.

Browning, Robert. *The Poetical Works of Robert Browning.* Oxford Standard Authors. London, 1940.

Burke, Edmund. *The Works of the Right Honourable Edmund Burke.* 6 vols. London, 1906–1907.

Byron, George Gordon, Lord. *Byron's Poetry.* Edited by Frank D. McConnell. Norton Critical Edition. New York, 1978.

———. *The Complete Poetical Works.* Edited by Jerome J. McGann. 3 vols. to date. Oxford, U.K., 1980–81.

———. *Don Juan: A Variorum Edition.* Edited by Truman Guy Steffan and Willis W. Pratt. 4 vols. Austin, Tex., 1957.

———. *Byron's Letters and Journals.* Edited by Leslie A. Marchand. 12 vols. Cambridge, Mass., 1973–82.

Carlyle, Thomas. *The Works of Thomas Carlyle.* Centenary Edition. 31 vols. New York, 1897–1901.

Carroll, Lewis. *The Annotated Alice.* New York, 1960.

Clare, John. *Clare: Selected Poems and Prose.* Edited by Eric Robinson and Geoffrey Summerfield. London, 1966.

Coleridge, Samuel Taylor. *Biographia Literaria.* Edited by J. Shawcross. 2 vols. London, 1907.

———. *The Collected Works of Samuel Taylor Coleridge: No. 4; The Friend.* Edited by Barbara E. Rooke. 2 vols. Princeton, N.J., 1969.

———. *The Complete Poetical Works of Samuel Taylor Coleridge.* Edited by Ernest Hartley Coleridge. 2 vols. London, 1912.

———. *The Notebooks of Samuel Taylor Coleridge.* Edited by Kathleen Coburn. 3 vols. to date. New York, 1957, 1961; Princeton, N.J., 1973.

Davy, Humphrey. *Consolations in Travel; or, The Last Days of a Philosopher.* London, 1831.

Descartes, René. *Descartes' Philosophical Writings.* Selected and Translated by Norman Kemp Smith. London, 1952.

Dickens, Charles. *The Works of Charles Dickens.* Gadshill Edition. 32 vols. London, 1898.

Edgeworth, Maria. *Castle Rackrent.* New York, 1978.

Eliot, George. *The Writings of George Eliot.* 25 vols. Boston, 1907–1908; rpr. New York, 1970.

Fielding, Henry. *The History of Tom Jones: A Foundling.* Edited by Fredson Bowers. 2 vols. Oxford, U.K., 1975.

Fitzgerald, Edward. *The Variorum and Definitive Edition of the Poetical and Prose Writings of Edward Fitzgerald.* Collected and Arranged by George Bentham. 7 vols. New York, 1902; rpr. 1967.

Gay, John. *Poetry and Prose of John Gay.* Edited by Vinton A. Dearing, with Charles E. Beckwith. 2 vols. Oxford, U.K., 1974.

Godwin, William. *Caleb Williams.* Edited with an Introduction by David McCracken. London, 1970.

———. *The Enquirer.* London, 1797.

———. *Thoughts on Man: His Nature, Products and Discoveries.* London, 1831; rpr. New York, 1969.

Hawthorne, Nathaniel. *The Centenary Edition of the Works of Nathaniel Hawthorne.* Edited by William Charvat *et al.* 16 vols. Columbus, Ohio, 1962–85.

Hayley, William. *Poems and Plays.* 3 vols. London, 1788.

Hazlitt, William. *The Complete Works of William Hazlitt.* Edited by P. P. Howe. 21 vols. London, 1930–34.

Hogg, James. *The Private Memoirs and Confessions of a Justified Sinner.* New York, 1970.

Huxley, Thomas. *Methods and Results.* New York, 1898.

Keats, John. *The Letters of John Keats.* Edited by Hyder Edward Rollins. 2 vols. Cambridge, Mass., 1958.

———. *The Poems of John Keats.* Edited by Jack Stillinger. Cambridge, Mass., 1978.

Lamb, Charles. *The Works of Charles and Mary Lamb.* Edited by E. V. Lucas. Companionable Edition. 6 vols. London, 1912–13.

Paine, Thomas. *The Writings of Thomas Paine.* Collected and Edited by Moncure Daniel Conway, II. 4 vols. New York, 1902–1908; rpr. 1969.

Peacock, Thomas Love. *The Works of Thomas Love Peacock.* Edited by H. F. B. Brett-Smith and C. E. Jones. 10 vols. London, 1924–34.

The Romantics Reviewed: Contemporary Reviews of British Romantic Writers. Part A: The Lake Poets. Edited, with Introductions, by Donald H. Reiman. 2 vols. New York, 1972.

Ruskin, John. *The Works of John Ruskin.* Edited by E. T. Cook and Alexander Wedderburn. 39 vols. London, 1903–12.

Scott, Walter. *The Letters of Sir Walter Scott.* Edited by H. J. C. Grierson. 12 vols. London, 1932–37.

———. *The Waverley Novels.* Edited by Andrew Lang. Large Type Border Edition. 24 vols. London, 1898–99.

Shelley, Mary. *Frankenstein; or, The Modern Prometheus.* Edited by M. K. Joseph. London, 1969.

Shelley, Percy Bysshe. *The Complete Works of Percy Bysshe Shelley.* Edited by Roger Ingpen and Walter E. Peck. Julian Edition. 10 vols. London, 1926–30.

———. *The Letters of Percy Bysshe Shelley.* Edited by Frederick L. Jones. 2 vols. Oxford, U.K., 1964.

———. *Shelley's Poetry and Prose.* Edited by Donald H. Reiman and Sharon B. Powers. Norton Critical Edition. New York, 1977; 2nd printing, corrected, 1980.

Sterling, John. *Essays and Tales, by John Sterling.* Edited, with a memoir of His Life, by Julius Charles Hare. 2 vols. London, 1848.

Tennyson, Alfred, Lord. *Poetical Works: Including the Plays,* Oxford Standard Authors. London, 1953.

Thackeray, William. *The Works of William Makepeace Thackeray.* Biographical Edition. 13 vols. New York, 1898–99.

Trollope, Anthony. *Ayala's Angel.* World's Classics, No. 342. London, 1929.

———. *The Claverings.* World's Classics, No. 152. London, 1924.

———. *He Knew He Was Right.* World's Classics, No. 507. London, 1948.

———. *John Caldigate.* World's Classics, No. 502. London, 1946.

———. *Mr. Scarborough's Family.* World's Classics, No. 503. London, 1946; re-issued, with an Introduction by John Pope Hennessy, 1973.

———. *Orley Farm.* World's Classics, No. 423. London, 1951.

Wordsworth, William. *The Letters of William and Dorothy Wordsworth: The Early Years.* Edited by Ernest De Selincourt; 2nd ed. rev. by Chester L. Shaver. Oxford, U.K., 1967.

———. *The Letters of William and Dorothy Wordsworth: The Middle Years, 1806–1820.* Edited by Ernest De Selincourt; 2nd ed. rev. by Mary Moorman and Alan G. Hill. 2 vols. Oxford, U.K., 1969–70.

———. *Lyrical Ballads.* Edited by R. L. Brett and A. R. Jones. New York, 1963; rev. ed. 1965.

———. *The Poetical Works of William Wordsworth.* Edited by Ernest De Selincourt and Helen Darbishire. 5 vols. Oxford, U.K., 1940–49; 2nd ed. and corrected rpr. 1952–63.

———. *The Prelude, 1799, 1805, 1850.* Edited by Jonathan Wordsworth *et al.* Norton Critical Edition. New York, 1979.

———. *The Prose Works of William Wordsworth.* Edited by W. J. B. Owen and Jane Worthington Smyser. 3 vols. Oxford, U.K., 1974.

———. *The Salisbury Plain Poems of William Wordsworth.* Edited by Stephen Gill. Ithaca, 1975.

Secondary Materials

Abrams, M. H. "English Romanticism: The Spirit of the Age." In *Romanticism Reconsidered,* edited by Northrop Frye. New York, 1963.

———. *The Mirror and the Lamp: Romantic Theory and the Critical Tradition.* New York, 1953.

———. *Natural Supernaturalism: Tradition and Revolution in Romantic Literature.* New York, 1971.

Aers, David, Jonathan Cook, and David Punter. *Romanticism and Ideology: Studies in English Writing, 1765–1830.* London, 1981.

Altieri, Charles. "Wordsworth's 'Preface' as Literary Theory." *Criticism*, XVIII (1976), 122–46.

Arac, Jonathan. "Romanticism, the Self, and the City: *The Secret Agent* in Literary History." *Boundary 2: A Journal of Post-Modern Literature*, IX (1980), 75–90.

Auerbach, Nina. "Jane Austen and Romantic Imprisonment." In *Jane Austen in a Social Context*, edited by David Monaghan. Totawa, N.J., 1981.

Averill, James H. "Wordsworth and 'Natural Science': The Poetry of 1798." *Journal of English and Germanic Philology*, LXXVII (1978), 232–46.

———. *Wordsworth and the Poetry of Human Suffering*. Ithaca, 1980.

Baker, Jeffrey. *Time and Mind in Wordsworth's Poetry*. Detroit, 1980.

Ball, Patricia M. *The Heart's Events: The Victorian Poetry of Relationships*. London, 1976.

Bate, W. J. *The Burden of the Past and the English Poet*. Cambridge, Mass., 1970.

———. *From Classic to Romantic: Premises of Taste in Eighteenth-Century England*. Cambridge, Mass., 1946.

Beer, John. *Wordsworth and the Human Heart*. New York, 1978.

Bialostosky, Don H. *Making Tales: The Poetics of Wordsworth's Narrative Experiments*. Chicago, 1984.

Blake, Kathleen. *Play, Games, and Sport: The Literary Works of Lewis Carroll*. Ithaca, 1974.

Boulger, James D. "Imagination and Speculation in Coleridge's Conversation Poems." *Journal of English and Germanic Philology*, LXIV (1965), 691–711.

Bowra, C. M. *The Romantic Imagination*. Cambridge, Mass., 1949.

Brantley, Richard E. *Locke, Wesley, and the Method of English Romanticism*. Gainesville, Fla., 1984.

Brisman, Leslie. *Romantic Origins*. Ithaca, 1978.

Brown, Julia Prewitt. *Jane Austen's Novels: Social Change and Literary Form*. Cambridge, Mass., 1979.

Brown, Lloyd W. "The Business of Marrying and Mothering." In *Jane Austen's Achievement*, edited by Juliet McMaster. London, 1976.

Brown, Marshall. *The Shape of German Romanticism*. Ithaca, 1979.

Bruns, Gerald R. "The Formal Nature of Victorian Thinking." *Publications of the Modern Language Association of America*, XC (1975), 904–18.

Buckley, Jerome. *Season of Youth: The Bildungsroman from Dickens to Golding*. Cambridge, Mass., 1974.

———. *The Victorian Temper: A Study in Literary Culture*. Cambridge, Mass., 1951.

Butler, Marilyn. *Jane Austen and the War of Ideas.* Oxford, U.K., 1975.

———. *Peacock Displayed: A Satirist in His Context.* London, 1979.

———. *Romantics, Rebels, and Reactionaries.* Oxford, U.K., 1981.

Chernaik, Judith. *The Lyrics of Shelley.* Cleveland, 1972.

Clubbe, John, and Ernest J. Lovell, Jr. *English Romanticism: The Grounds of Belief.* De Kalb, Ill., 1983.

Cooke, Michael G. *Acts of Inclusion: Studies Bearing on an Elementary Theory of Romanticism.* New Haven, 1979.

———. *The Romantic Will.* New Haven, 1976.

Curran, Stuart. *Shelley's Annus Mirabilis: The Maturing of an Epic Vision.* San Marino, Calif., 1975.

Dekker, George. *Coleridge and the Literature of Sensibility.* New York, 1978.

Dickstein, Morris. *Keats and His Poetry: A Study in Development.* Chicago, 1971.

Donohue, Joseph W., Jr. *Dramatic Character in the English Romantic Age.* Princeton, N.J., 1970.

Duckworth, Alistair M. *The Improvement of the Estate.* Baltimore, 1971.

Durrant, Geoffrey. *Wordsworth and the Great System.* Cambridge, U.K., 1970.

Eichner, Hans. "The Rise of Modern Science and the Genesis of Romanticism." *Publications of the Modern Language Association of America,* XCVII (1982), 8–30.

Empson, William. *Seven Types of Ambiguity.* 3rd ed. rev. London, 1953.

Engell, James. *The Creative Imagination: Enlightenment to Romanticism.* Cambridge, Mass., 1981.

Farrell, John P. *Revolution as Tragedy: The Dilemma of the Moderate from Scott to Arnold.* Ithaca, 1980.

Ferguson, Frances. *Wordsworth: Language as Counter-Spirit.* New Haven, 1977.

Ferry, David. *The Limits of Mortality.* Middletown, Conn., 1959.

Fleishman, Avrom. *The English Historical Novel: Walter Scott to Virginia Woolf.* Baltimore, 1971.

Foakes, R. A. *The Romantic Assertion: A Study in the Language of Nineteenth-Century Poetry.* New Haven, 1958.

Forbes, Duncan. "The Rationalism of Sir Walter Scott." *Cambridge Journal,* VII (1953), 20–35.

Frye, Northrop. "Towards Defining an Age of Sensibility." *ELH: A Journal of English Literary History,* XXIII (1956), 144–52.

Gleckner, Robert. "Most Holy Forms of Thought: Some Observations on Blake and Language." *ELH: A Journal of English Literary History,* XLI (1974), 555–77.

———. "Romanticism and the Self-Annihilation of Language." *Criticism*, XVIII (1976), 173–89.

Griffin, Andrew L. "Wordsworth and the Problem of Imaginative Story: The Case of 'Simon Lee.'" *Publications of the Modern Language Association of America*, XCII (1977), 392–409.

Hart, Francis R. "Scott's Endings: The Fictions of Authority." *Nineteenth-Century Fiction*, XXXIII (1978), 48–68.

———. "The Spaces of Privacy: Jane Austen." *Nineteenth-Century Fiction*, XXX (1975), 305–33.

Hartman, Geoffrey. *Wordsworth's Poetry, 1787–1814*. 1964; rpr. New Haven, 1971.

Haven, Richard. *Patterns of Consciousness: An Essay on Coleridge*. Amherst, Mass., 1969.

Hirsch, E. D. *Wordsworth and Schelling: A Typological Study of Romanticism*. New Haven, 1960.

Houghton, Walter E. *The Victorian Frame of Mind*. New Haven, 1957.

Johnson, Edgar. *Sir Walter Scott: The Great Unknown*. 2 vols. London, 1970.

Jones, John. *The Egotistical Sublime: A History of Wordsworth's Imagination*. London, 1954.

Kiely, Robert. *The Romantic Novel in England*. Cambridge, Mass., 1972.

Kincaid, James R. *The Novels of Anthony Trollope*. Oxford, U.K., 1977.

Kroeber, Karl. "'Home at Grasmere': Ecological Holiness." *Publications of the Modern Language Association of America*, LXXXIX (1974), 132–41.

———. "Jane Austen, Romantic." *Wordsworth Circle*, VII (1976), 291–96.

———. *Romantic Narrative Art*. Madison, Wis., 1960.

Land, Stephen K. "The Silent Poet: An Aspect of Wordsworth's Semantic Theory." *University of Toronto Quarterly*, XLII (1973), 157–69.

Langbaum, Robert. *The Poetry of Experience: The Dramatic Monologue in Modern Literary Tradition*. New York, 1957.

Levine, George. "High and Low: Ruskin and the Novelists." In *Nature and the Victorian Imagination*, edited by U. C. Knoepflmacher and G. B. Tennyson. Berkeley, 1977.

———. *The Realistic Imagination: English Fiction from Frankenstein to Lady Chatterley*. Chicago, 1981.

———. "Sir Walter Scott: The End of Romance." *Wordsworth Circle*, X (1979), 147–60.

Lipking, Lawrence. *The Ordering of the Arts in Eighteenth-Century England*. Princeton, N.J., 1970.

Lukács, Georg. *The Historical Novel.* Translated by Hannah and Stanley Mitchell. London, 1962.

McCracken, David. "Wordsworth on Human Wishes and Poetic Borrowing." *Modern Philology,* XIX (1982), 386–99.

McFarland, Thomas. *Coleridge and the Pantheist Tradition.* Oxford, U.K., 1969.

———. *Romanticism and the Forms of Ruin: Wordsworth, Coleridge and the Modalities of Fragmentation.* Princeton, N.J., 1981.

McGann, Jerome J. "The Aim of Blake's Prophesies and the Uses of Blake Criticism." In *Blake's Sublime Allegory,* edited by Stuart Curran and Joseph Anthony Wittreich, Jr. Madison, Wis., 1973.

———. *"Don Juan" in Context.* Chicago, 1976.

———. *Fiery Dust: Byron's Poetic Development.* Chicago, 1968.

———. *The Romantic Ideology: A Critical Investigation.* Chicago, 1983.

———. "Romanticism and the Embarrassments of Critical Tradition." *Modern Philology,* LXX (1973), 243–57.

Manning, Peter J. "Wordsworth at St. Bees: Scandals, Sisterhoods, and Wordsworth's Later Poetry." *ELH: A Journal of English Literary History,* LII (1985), 33–58.

Mayo, Robert. "The Contemporaneity of the *Lyrical Ballads.*" *Publications of the Modern Language Association of America.* LXIX (1954), 486–522.

Mellor, Anne K. *English Romantic Irony.* Cambridge, Mass., 1980.

Morgan, Susan. *In the Meantime: Character and Perception in Jane Austen's Fiction.* Chicago, 1980.

Murray, Roger N. *Wordsworth's Style: Figures and Themes in the "Lyrical Ballads" of 1800.* Lincoln, Nebr., 1967.

Parrish, Stephen Maxfield. *The Art of the "Lyrical Ballads."* Cambridge, Mass. 1973.

Peckham, Morse. *Beyond the Tragic Vision: The Quest for Identity in the Nineteenth Century.* New York, 1962.

———. "On Romanticism: Introduction." *Studies in Romanticism,* IX (1970), 217–24.

———. "Toward a Theory of Romanticism." *Publications of the Modern Language Association of America,* LXVI (1951), 5–23.

———. "Toward a Theory of Romanticism: II. Reconsiderations." *Studies in Romanticism,* I (1961), 1–8.

———. *The Triumph of Romanticism.* Columbia, S.C., 1970.

Piper, H. W. *The Active Universe: Pantheism and the Concept of the Imagination in the English Romantic Poets.* London, 1962.

Pulos, C. E. *The Deep Truth: A Study of Shelley's Skepticism*. Lincoln, Nebr., 1954.

Rajan, Tilottama. *Dark Interpreter: The Discourse of Romanticism*. Ithaca, 1980.

Rauber, D. F. "The Fragment as Romantic Form." *Modern Language Quarterly*, XXX (1969), 212–21.

Reed, Mark L. *Wordsworth: The Chronology of the Early Years, 1770–1799*. Cambridge, Mass., 1967.

Reiman, Donald H. "Poetry of Familiarity: Wordsworth, Dorothy, and Mary Hutchinson." In *The Evidence of the Imagination*, edited by Donald H. Reiman *et al*. New York, 1978.

Sheats, Paul D. *The Making of Wordsworth's Poetry, 1785–1798*. Cambridge, Mass., 1973.

Sherry, Charles. *Wordsworth's Poetry of the Imagination*. Oxford, U.K., 1980.

Simpson, David. *Irony and Authority in Romantic Poetry*. Totowa, N.J., 1979.

Sperry, Stuart M. "Toward a Definition of Romantic Irony in English Literature." In *Romantic and Modern: Revaluations of Literary Tradition*, edited by George Bornstein. Pittsburgh, 1977.

Stallknecht, N. P. *Strange Seas of Thought*. Durham, N.C., 1945; 2nd ed. Bloomington, 1958.

Stillinger, Jack. "The Hoodwinking of Madeline: Scepticism in 'The Eve of St. Agnes.'" *Studies in Philology*, LVIII (1961), 533–55.

Swingle, L. J. "Frankenstein's Monster and Its Romantic Relatives: Problems of Knowledge in English Romanticism." *Texas Studies in Literature and Language: A Journal of the Humanities*, XV (1973), 51–65.

———. "Wordsworth's Contrarieties: A Prelude to Wordsworthian Complexity." *ELH: A Journal of English Literary History*, XLIV (1977), 337–54.

Timko, Michael. "The Victorianism of Victorian Literature." *New Literary History: A Journal of Theory and Interpretation*, VI (1975), 607–27.

Walling, William. "'On Fishing Up the Moon': In Search of Thomas Love Peacock." In *The Evidence of the Imagination*, edited by Donald H. Reiman *et al*. New York, 1978.

Wasserman, Earl R. "The English Romantics: The Grounds of Knowledge." *Studies in Romanticism*, IV (1964), 17–34.

———. *Shelley: A Critical Reading*. Baltimore, 1971.

———. *The Subtler Language*. Baltimore, 1959.

Watt, Ian. *The Rise of the Novel*. Berkeley, 1957.

Weiskel, Thomas. *The Romantic Sublime: Studies in the Structure and Psychology of Transcendence*. Baltimore, 1976.

Wilkie, Brian. "Wordsworth and the Tradition of the Avant-Garde." *Journal of English and Germanic Philology*, LXXII (1973), 194–222.

Woodring, Carl. "Nature and Art in the Nineteenth Century." *Publications of the Modern Language Association of America*, XCII (1977), 193–202.

Wordsworth, Jonathan. *The Music of Humanity: A Critical Study of Wordsworth's Ruined Cottage.* London, 1969.

Zwerdling, Alex. "The Mythographers and the Romantic Revival of Greek Myth." *Publications of the Modern Language Association of America*, LXXIX (1964), 447–56.

Index

Abrams, M. H., 18n, 110n, 164n
Abyss, 48, 73–77, 75n, 80, 82–83, 85, 88, 93, 178, 194
Akenside, Mark, 23
Arnold, Matthew: "Dover Beach," 169; "The Scholar-Gipsy," 169, 176–77; "Stanzas from the Grande Chartreuse," 168–69; mentioned, 164
Austen, Jane: *Emma*, 39, 122, 127–28, 129, 131, 154, 155–59, 180; *Mansfield Park*, 155, 159–60; *Persuasion*, 122, 125, 129–30, 131, 159, 161; *Pride and Prejudice*, 124, 154–55, 156–59, 160, 161; mentioned, 39, 117, 119, 153–61
Averill, James H., 108n

Bate, Walter Jackson, 15, 20, 30n
Beaumont, Lady, 103–105, 106
Beaumont, Sir George, 138
Bernstein, Gene M., 133n
Bialostosky, Don H., 99n
Blake, William: "The Chimney Sweeper" (*Songs of Experience*), 6; "A Dream," 140; "The Ecchoing Green," 140; *The [First] Book of Urizen*, 43–44, 67; "The Human Abstract (*Songs of Experience*), 71–72; Introduction to *Songs of Innocence*, 45, 140; *Jerusalem*, 52; "The Lamb," 45–46, 100; "The Little Boy Found," 140; "London," 6, 46, 75, 141; *The Marriage of Heaven and Hell*, 3, 18, 58, 60–62, 69, 75, 78, 104, 120, 124, 128, 134, 174, 178; "The Mental Traveller," 178; *Milton*, 4; "My Pretty Rose Tree," 119–20, 139–41; "Night," 140; "Nurse's Song" (*Songs of Innocence*), 140; "The Sick Rose," 48–49, 141; *Songs of Innocence and of Experience*, 45–46, 139–42, 188; "To S——d," 119; "The Tyger," 5–6, 62, 77, 140–41; mentioned, 7, 12, 17, 51, 64, 73, 78, 100, 125, 131, 141–42, 144
Bloom, Harold, 20
Boulger, James D., 56
Brantley, Richard, 30n
Brisman, Leslie, 20n
Brontë, Charlotte, 172
Brontë, Emily, 171–72
Brown, Julia Prewitt, 154n
Brown, Lloyd W., 129n

207